Chile
in
My Heart

Chile
in
My Heart

Kate Clark

First published in Great Britain in 2013 by

Bannister Publications Ltd
118 Saltergate
Chesterfield
Derbyshire S40 1NG

ISBN 978-1-909813-02-1

Typeset in Sabon by Escritor Design, Chesterfield, Derbyshire

Cover designed by Geoffrey Arias, London
www.geoffreyarias.com

Printed and bound in Great Britain by SRP Ltd, Exeter

To Ricardo

FOREWORD

By the Rt Hon Tony Benn

The story that Kate Clark tells in this book is indeed a remarkable one. Coming from an ILP family who had joined the Communist Party, she studied at Manchester University, went to Moscow, and fell in love with Ricardo from Chile.

They then went to Chile and both taught English, and this book is an account of that period during and after the election of the Allende government.

What happened then makes this book a powerful, moving, perceptive and personal account of her life and the people she met, whom she describes in a way that brings them to life and makes them real for the reader.

It was during that period that she saw the overthrow of the Allende Government by Pinochet and the hopes and fears that it released in her are brought out most beautifully, by someone who understands the ideological argument very clearly.

The story of Ricardo's imprisonment and how she was able to marry him in prison and in this way secure his release is even more dramatic and made it possible for them to come to Britain, after which their three children were born.

But the book also brings out very clearly one of the most famous examples of American determination to dominate Latin America, beginning with the Munroe Doctrine and carrying through to the attempt to overthrow Castro, the full support for Pinochet and even today the hint that the coup in Honduras may have been planned in Washington.

For these reasons to get this personal insight from someone who was a witness makes it a book of exceptional personal and political interest and readers will find the vivid description of events all the more interesting and influential.

Introduction

Over the years, many people have urged me to write the story which follows. For a long time I was reluctant, because it is a personal story, though one set against the backdrop of a fascinating and historic episode – that of Chile's Popular Unity Government 1970-73, led by President Salvador Allende.

On 11 September 1973 a cruel military coup put an end to that government, and to the happiness of many thousands of Chilean people. As an English-woman who lived through the entire period of that people's government in Chile, and who shared the hopes and dreams of so many who desired a better life for all Chile's working people, I suffered with them when that dream was so brutally shattered.

If my story can help in any small way to illuminate that particular historical episode, then I will be glad. There is a place for academic histories of events, but there is also a place for personal memoirs of those same events. By putting my story into the public domain, I hope that it will contribute to a better understanding of the Popular Unity process and complement more academic studies of the subject.

Acknowledgements

Beginning this memoir, at first I decided simply to try and set down my impressions and recollections of these interesting years before I forgot them. I felt I should put together in a more coherent way the many stories we have told our children over the years about our lives in Chile, so that they would have a more complete understanding of that period their parents lived through and which so marked their lives. So I have shown the book to a very few people, since I did not want my own personal memories to be influenced by other people's memories or opinions. This is my story, and no one else's.

I am grateful to Ricardo, my compañero, who shared his memories of the same events and was able to make many valid observations and suggestions. I much appreciate the encouragement given me by Tony Benn, who has kindly written the foreword. I am grateful to Chile's leading human rights lawyer, Eduardo Contreras, for finding the time to help recall certain events. My deepest thanks go to Dr Genia Browning, who made invaluable comments and detailed, helpful ideas for improving the text.

Emma Smith, whose writing I greatly admire, kindly read the book and gave me the benefit of her long experience as a writer with some fresh ideas as to structure. Emma was a great encouragement to me at the stage when I was still not wholly convinced I wanted to write the book. Wuzzy Fawdry helped with encouragement and in attempts to get the book published. I am grateful to Pedro Gajardo and Maria Cristina Valenzuela for their contribution concerning the deaths of Ricardo Lagos and family.

My thanks to Joe and Shirley Clark for welcoming our student, Carlos Lagos, into their home in 1972 and for their constant support and encouragement. Our son Victor, author of *Allende: Revolutionary Democrat,* Pluto Press, 2013, and daughters Liza and Martha have helped in unsuspected ways by always being willing to exchange opinions and discuss these events and their importance. And my thanks in a more general way go to our many relatives and friends with whom we have had endless discussions and exchanges of opinion over the years on the events and processes we witnessed during the turbulent life of the Popular Unity Government led by Dr Salvador Allende.

CHAPTER ONE

All the past we leave behind,
We take up the task eternal, and the burden and the lesson,
Conquering, holding, daring, venturing,
as we go the unknown ways,
Pioneers! Oh pioneers!

(from *Pioneers*, by Walt Whitman
– and my old school song)

I was 25 when I arrived in Chile. I had met a Chilean when I was abroad, fallen in love with him, and here I was, in 1969, arriving at Pudahuel airport with a Spanish grammar book under my arm and without knowing a word of the language.

In those days young people didn't travel much. It was uncommon for British young people to go anywhere outside Europe. Now it's totally different. My children have done lots of travelling and they're only in their thirties. But in my time it was unusual. I can remember my mother's reaction when I told her I had decided to follow my love. "To Chile? But that's the end of the world!"

My mother was an intelligent woman and the main thing she wanted for me was that I should be happy. So she never tried to dissuade me from this project, however crazy it might have seemed to her.

Pudahuel. I can still remember my first impressions. I arrived on 24 March 1969 dressed in a pale green striped summer dress with a white collar, looking for all the world like an innocent schoolgirl. I had my long flaming red hair loose, and it blew around my face as I walked down the steps from the aircraft. The airport looked like those little-used aerodromes that you can find in many parts of Britain, with a small airport building and very few aeroplanes parked on the tarmac. "My God," I remember thinking, "it really is like the end of the world!"

I felt both trepidation and excitement – I knew that in a few moments I'd be seeing the man I loved whom I had not seen for seven long months. When I caught sight of him I immediately knew that it was not a crazy thing to have done – to leave a secure job as a language teacher and my parents' home and my entire family, for an uncertain future in a country which was not only totally unknown to me but whose language I did not even speak – no, I knew immediately that I was where I wanted to be, forever – at his side, because wherever I was, as long as I was with him, it felt right and I was very happy.

The road from the airport to Santiago city centre looked very different from that from Heathrow to London. I was struck by how brown everything looked – the grass verges, the fields. Wherever you live in Britain, our countryside is so green – the trees, grass, the leaves of the flowers and bushes. Whereas here the predominant colour was brown, the colour of mud and dust. And the road had only one lane in each direction, like an A road, whereas the road from Heathrow to London, even in those years, was a motorway carrying lots of traffic.

I realised that all the Chileans I could see around me were dressed for the autumn. Clearly my first mistake! Ricardo had told me to expect a temperature of about 20 degrees centigrade – which seemed to me like the height of summer. Fortunately I had a cardigan with me, so I quickly put it on so that I didn't look so different from everybody else.

Those first days in Chile were full of emotions and impressions. I understood practically nothing of the language, but I could see that the friends of Ricardo's I met were attractive, lively people, with a good sense of humour, and it was clear to me right from the first moment that they all held Ricardo in great affection and esteem.

I had a contract as lecturer in English at the Ñuble campus of the University of Chile in Chillán, and Ricardo too, but as lecturer in English literature. But before we left Santiago for Chillán, we spent a few very happy and enjoyable days in Santiago, in the home of the writer Poli Délano and his wife at the time, Maruja.

One morning – I don't know if it was the first or second day after my arrival in Chile – Ricardo called up to me from downstairs. "*Gringuita!*"[1] he shouted. "Come down here!" I went down the stairs and saw Ricardo, Poli and Poli's father – the writer Luis Enrique Délano – who were having an animated conversation punctuated by laughter in the kitchen, whilst they were preparing something for lunch. Poli came towards me, holding a large shell open in his hand. "*Gringuita*," he said, "try this!" I took the shell from him, but then Poli said, "Oh, wait a moment, we've forgotten something…" and he reached for a half lemon and proceeded to squeeze the lemon over the shell in my hand. When I saw that what was in the shell began to contort visibly, I threw the shellfish across the room, shouting in English: "Aagh, it's alive… you barbarians!"

---

[1] *Gringuita,* the diminutive of *gringa* is an affectionate term for a fair-skinned person from Europe or the United States.

Everyone, of course, laughed at me, but they couldn't convince me that day to try raw clams! But I did try the shellfish juice mixed with chilli pepper and lemon that Poli made – what he called his cocktail – and found it delicious. It would be several months before I started to try and enjoy raw shellfish. In Britain hardly anyone, I thought, ate shellfish except the rich, who ate oysters as a delicacy. Of course in centuries past people did eat shellfish, but by the end of the nineteenth century our seas had become contaminated by industrial waste, which killed off many of the mussel and cockle beds.

On another occasion during those first few days of holiday in Santiago we were invited to the home of some friends of Ricardo's, all of them academics from the University of Chile. They were great fun, there were a lot of jokes and everybody was much interested in the two of us and our future together. All of a sudden I saw that a circle was being formed, people were all taking hands and they started chanting "*Arnal, Arnal, Arnal nuestro fiscal!*" I, of course, couldn't understand a thing, apart from the rhythmic chanting, but their laughter was infectious and I laughed anyway. Later I found out that that chant belonged to an anecdote that Poli was fond of telling, when one of their academic friends – whose surname was Arnal – had been up for election as a *fiscal*. Among the academics there was the Head of the English Department at the Pedagogical Institute of the University of Chile, Rodolfo Rojo, and another academic from that same Department, Pito Henríquez, so I could talk to them in English.

I didn't speak any Spanish. I remember that Poli's wife, Maruja Broughton, came up to the bedroom where I was and started talking to me in Spanish. I didn't understand a word, only that she was trying to help me, she didn't want me to feel left out. She started repeating a few words, which she pronounced with certain movements of her hands to indicate the meaning, and I repeated them after her. Maruja was very beautiful and as a teacher of mime and dance, she could make herself understood very well. She had beautiful long, thick eyelashes, an enchanting smile and a statuesque body.

A few days later we took the coach to Chillán, where we were both to start our contracts as lecturers at the University. My first impressions are still fresh in my mind. We arrived by Lit company coach at the bus station in the centre of Chillán at about two or three in the morning. We got off the coach and I saw a group of little kids sitting and squatting above a metal grille on the pavement outside the cafe where you could have a cup of coffee or tea whilst you waited for your coach. The cafe's kitchen was in the basement, so the heat from the kitchen filtered up through the grille, giving warmth to the scruffy-faced children, who looked anything from eight to twelve years old. They were the first street kids I had ever seen in my life.

Chillán seemed to me to be a real one-horse town, a provincial backwater, if ever there was one. My heart sank the morning after our arrival, when we went out for a walk round the centre. I had been living in London and Moscow before that, and Chillán just seemed so provincial. It had one attractive central square, with beautiful trees and benches and pathways crisscrossing the square, and all the other streets were in blocks, squares of the same length, all straight, all square, not at all like English streets.

The modern cathedral dominated the central square, and the shops along the central streets looked old-fashioned and a bit dowdy to my eyes. The market was colourful and folkloric, but there were frequent reminders of the poverty of people's lives – drunks in stinking clothes, unshaven and unsteady on their feet, who begged for money at every corner. Worst of all, for me, was the frequent sight of children begging, their little old-before-their-time faces with tough, red-brown skin and ragged clothes like something I imagined from a Dickens novel. Some of them worked during the day as shoeshine boys in the central square or on the street corners, then begged in the evenings, late into the night. I didn't like myself for ignoring them, and I didn't like myself when I gave them paltry amounts either. It just made me suffer to see them, and I often think that that was one of the main reinforcements to my already pretty firm conviction that there had to be a better society than this, a fairer scheme of things, where there wouldn't be poor people like these.

I was already a socialist when I arrived in Chile. My parents had joined the old Independent Labour Party when they were in their twenties, and then they joined the Communist Party during the Spanish Civil War, when they, like many progressive British people, supported the Republican government and saw Franco's aggression as a precursor to the out-and-out fascism of the Second World War. For a time it was possible to be members of both the ILP and the CP, and this was what my parents did, until the ILP disaffiliated from the Labour Party in 1931 and joint ILP/Communist Party members were forced out. My parents were actually expelled from the Labour Party for refusing to give an undertaking to cease supporting the Daily Worker.

Whenever we would listen to the news whilst having dinner with our parents, my brother and I would hear our father regaling the BBC and giving his caustic comments on whatever were the issues of the day. It wasn't so much a discussion as a diatribe against what he saw as bias by the BBC against working people and the progressive movement. One of his particular bugbears was the typical BBC use at that time of the word "idle" to describe workers on strike. "Idle?" he would snarl, "they're not idle, they're on strike, fighting for a decent wage!"

I had a pretty ordinary childhood. My parents were good people, my father very hard-working, determined and focused, my mother a warm, generous and affectionate human being who had many friends and was very well-respected in the community. They were both committed Communists, though my mother was much more active than my father during the years I was growing up, since my father was trying to build up a business from scratch and therefore had very little free time. My mother, who had always wanted to go out to work, but had agreed to stay at home because that was what my father saw as the proper role of a married woman and mother, dedicated herself to being an unpaid Party activist, and there was often a duplicator on the table and hundreds of leaflets being produced when I came home for lunch from school, instead of a meal on the table! But she was a wonderful mother: she loved my brother Joe and me unconditionally, and spent a lot of time with us, helping us to learn homework tasks and taking us walks in the countryside with picnics. When we got tired towards the end of those walks, she would get us to sing: "This old man went hippety-hop, hippety-hop, hippety-hop, this old man went hippety-hop, all the way home!" and we would limp exaggeratedly in time with the word "hippety". We also sang songs like "I'm the man, the very fat man, who waters the workers' beer!" and "Hallelujah, I'm a bum":

> Oh, why don't you work like other folks do?
> How the hell can I work when there's no work to do?
>
> *Refrain*
>
> Hallelujah, I'm a bum,
> Hallelujah, bum again,
> Hallelujah, give us a handout
> To revive us again.
>
> Oh, why don't you save all the money you earn?
> If I didn't eat, I'd have money to burn.
>
> Oh, I like my boss, he's a good friend of mine,
> That's why I am starving out on the bread line.

My brother and I went to local junior schools and both passed the 11-Plus exam that existed in the early Fifties. Joe went to a mixed Grammar School and I went to a rather select Grammar School, called St Helena School for Girls, an establishment which had taken private students until the year that I went up in 1953. It was a rather strict school which prided itself on its academic standing and had little time for pupils who did not show much academic prowess. The Head was a Classics graduate, the wife of an Anglican vicar, who cut an imperious figure as she swept along the corridors in a flowing black gown and sometimes even wore a mortar-board at assemblies.

As a convinced atheist (though she had been brought up a Christian), my mother did not want me to attend the religious assemblies held every morning before lessons. These were held in the main school hall, which was a lovely room with huge windows all down one side, and with a bigger-than-life-size plaster cast of Venus de Milo in one corner. So my mother went up to school to see the Head about withdrawing me from the morning assembly. She was told that I could be excused on conscience grounds, and could spend the time together with the Jehovah's Witness girls, who did not attend either. I think my mother must have decided in the end that the normal assemblies would be better than sitting outside in the company of budding Jehovah's Witnesses, and I was not withdrawn.

One spring morning at one of these religious assemblies, with the sun streaming through the floor-to-ceiling windows, the headmistress, Mrs Miller, suddenly interrupted the proceedings and proclaimed in a dramatic voice to the few hundred children and staff in the big hall, "Oh Kathleen! Your hair shines like burnished gold!" My auburn hair had, it seemed, caught the sun's rays and caused this dramatic exclamation which resulted in the entire school turning round to look in my direction, muffled giggles coming from dozens of mouths. Humiliating wasn't the word. I can still remember wanting the floor to open and swallow me up.

You might have thought from this that I was some sort of teacher's pet. Far from it. I was considered naughty during the first few years there, and insolent and cheeky during the middle years.

I think I must always have been pretty independent-minded: one of my earliest memories is of toddling off by myself up to the top of the lane where we lived, on the outskirts of Chesterfield, and my mother finding me later, quite happily sitting in a dimly-lit shack chatting to the man who lived, or perhaps just worked, there. He was giving me a really fatty bacon sandwich, my Mum recalled later, and I was relishing it. I seem to remember that we did call there at this old man's workshop a few times, and my Mum would chat to him. I must have been three or four at the time, I think. Of course no one in Britain now would allow their child as much freedom as we had in those days. These were the days when my mother would leave the back door unlocked, and tramps would come and sit on a chair my Mum provided for them at the back door, while she gave them a cup of tea and a biscuit or two.

In those days people would come round occasionally and perform the local song "The Derby Ram" at the back door. I can remember one of them would have a sack over his head and perform on all fours; presumably he was the ram! It's a long yarn, and they would recite it in its full length while we watched from the kitchen. Then my Mum would pay them and they would go off to the next house, where I suspect they might not have got such a good reception.

My brother Joe and I roamed the countryside on our own from an early age. We would go down to the canal, and look for insects and water creatures in the murky water, scraping the dark green slime from the sides on to our hands and arms (my brother said it was like soap), then get on our bikes and cycle madly off along the country roads.

I would play with my school-friend, Veronica, and we also played with a gaggle of kids from the butcher's shop at the top of the lane who went to a different, nearer school than we did. We would organize plays in our back yard, which we would write and rehearse ourselves, and then perform, usually in front of my mother alone, since no other parents ever came to the house, and my father would always be at work.

We had a row of tall poplar trees which bordered the garden on one side, alongside the perimeter wall. We used to tie a rope from one of the trees, climb up on to the high wall, clutching the rope with a big knot tied at the end of it between our legs, and swing like Tarzan between the trees. We also built little "houses" with blankets and cardboard between the trees, which were about two metres apart. There we would crouch or sit at the makeshift house's doorway, having drinks and sandwiches, acting out our adult lives ahead.

From my earliest years I remember being a tomboy. I climbed and ran and scratched my knees, just like any boy. I even used to wear grey school shorts like those my brother wore. I don't know why, but girly things never interested me in the slightest. I would have preferred to be a boy, my role models being the adventurous girls of "Swallows and Amazons" and other Arthur Ransome books, which my brother and I loved reading as children.

My mother was not at all a typical mother of that time. It's true that she was a housewife, but housework or having a beautiful home never interested her. Her interests were outside the home – the Cooperative Women's Guild (she was secretary of the Whittington Moor branch), the Communist Party, and the peace movement. She was one of the founder members of a precursor to the Campaign for Nuclear Disarmament (CND), which was called the Chesterfield Council for the Abolition of Nuclear Weapons. This later merged with national CND, once that was formed.

I can remember one evening pleading with my Mum not to go out, as she was getting ready to leave for one of these meetings. She patiently explained to me that her working for peace was important precisely for our future, since nuclear weapons threatened us all and the very future of the world. You couldn't argue with that, even if you'd preferred her to be around of an evening!

Sometimes she would take me along to some of these meetings. I learnt my first lessons in how to chair meetings, how to take minutes, how to give a vote of thanks and much else besides, from these meetings, at which my mother was a prime mover. She was not one to seek the limelight particularly though, she was simply more capable than most of the other people there, it seemed to me.

I must have used this knowledge when I formed a secret society later, at secondary school. It was called the Six Black Bombers. It was my idea, and I attracted five other girls to my side in this endeavour. The posh, very traditional and conservative St Helena School for Girls had never seen the likes of a group like ours. We knew that down at the bottom level of the three tiers of netball pitches and tennis courts at the back of the school there were some air-raid shelters left over from the Second World War. We found a way in to one of them, creeping through a tiny space the ill-fitting metal door allowed, and jumping down into a long, dank and musty passageway reaching far under the netball pitch of the terrace above. We took candles and matches to school, elected a Chairman and Secretary, and held our meetings of the secret society there by candle-light during the lunch-hour.

We were fourteen at the time. I apparently wrote the Six Black Bombers song, to the strains of which, after we'd lit the candles, we'd form a circle and sing, jumping up and down for the choruses. Years later one of the six members reminded me what the words were:

> We're the six black bombers
> and a jolly six are we.
>
> ......
>
> Fighting for our own way,
> until we get our own say.
> We mean to get our justice.
> Boom, boom. Boom, boom.
>
> We'll always hate Miss ...*
> and stupid ...* too.
> Fighting for our own way,
> until we get our own say.
> We mean to get our justice.
> Boom, boom. Boom, boom.

> *names of teachers we disliked

One day we were discovered by a senior prefect who was prowling round the grounds and must have heard our song, for we were caught in full flow, as we sang. We were sent in disgrace to the Headmistress, who gave us a good telling-off, but nothing more than that. We never told anyone else about our adventure, and the air-raid shelters were put strictly out-of-bounds, and later removed entirely.

Another time I was hauled over the coals by the Head for having the temerity to ask the members of a panel who had just interviewed me for a scholarship to university whether they enjoyed doing that work. I had taken seriously their routine question at the end of the interview: "Have you any question you would like to put to us?" The Headmistress found my action incredibly cheeky and rude. For the life of me, I still can't see what was so terrible about it.

It was a horrible feeling to be standing in splendid isolation in the corridor outside the Head's office, waiting to be ushered in and knowing you were in for it. I can still remember how nervous I was, those times outside Mrs Miller's office in the corridor.

I was quite political and took part in all the political debates run at the school. I became known as a Red, which was even more apt due to my flaming auburn hair. Academically, I was not very good during the first three or four years, but then when I was fifteen, I had a lovely friendly French teacher called Miss John and began to work harder because I liked her and wanted to please her by doing well. From being in the bottom division for languages, I moved up to the second, then the top division, all due to this one teacher's benign influence. It made me realize why so many children fail at school: if you're not motivated, you don't do well, whereas when you're motivated, the sky's the limit.

I got good results at 'A' level, and applied to Manchester University to study Russian. Our school did not do Russian, so the only languages I had studied were French, German and Latin. But I thought that with détente and increasing trade relations between Britain and the USSR, there would be more jobs open to me if I studied Russian. I was accepted, on the understanding that I would have to undertake a Beginners' course in Russian during my first year, and only if I did well enough in the end-of-year exams would I be allowed to transfer to the Russian Honours course.

I worked hard and was able to transfer to the B.A. Honours in Russian Studies course at the end of my first year. I enjoyed my university years, working quite hard and being very active in the university's CommSoc (Communist Society). I was in love, too, during those years, with a fellow young Communist from Stockton-on-Tees, Peter Atkinson, who was studying mechanical engineering, and whom I had met at a YCL (Young Communist League) camp at Glossop the summer before we went up to university.

Though Peter and I were in love, as the years went by, I began to feel that the traditional path of marriage and a family after University was not for me.

I wanted to experience more than the provincial life of Chesterfield and Manchester, which, although a big city, was not cosmopolitan at all at that time. I admired my Professor of Russian, D.P. Costello, who was a New Zealander and often told us students tales of his travels and residence in other countries. My fellow students of Russian were a mixed bunch, one Yugoslav, one New Zealander, a Jewish girl who'd lived in Israel, another a descendant of the Armenian composer, Aram Khachaturian.

And because my level of spoken Russian was poor compared with most of these other students – since I had only studied it for a year before joining the Honours course – I resolved to go to the Soviet Union to improve my fluency. At that time there were no bilateral agreements with the USSR to enable Honours students to spend a year abroad, as part of the degree course, as there are nowadays.

So at the end of my third year, I arranged to go on a trip to the Soviet Union to attend a month-long International Seminar of Youth and Students, through the auspices of the British-Soviet Friendship Society, to which my parents belonged. It was a wonderful trip. It was my first venture abroad on my own, by train through Europe to Moscow.

It was while at that seminar that I first saw the Chilean *cueca* danced. There was a small group of Chileans at the Seminar, two of whom performed the Chilean national dance at the final social event, when all three of the Seminar's sections, which had been to different parts of the Soviet Union to look at different aspects – the nationalities question, agriculture, industrial development – came together for the last few days. I remember being enthralled by the music of the *cueca*, the rhythmic clapping by the dancers and other Latin Americans and found them very attractive. It was my first introduction to Latin America.

My section of the Seminar had travelled to Baku, the capital of Azerbaijan, to study the Nationalities question. I had always been fascinated by the complexity of the Soviet Union's ethnic and linguistic make-up, and so chose to be part of that section. Baku was my first visit to an eastern city, with its middle-eastern-like music and dance, its people who spoke a language very like Turkish. I loved Baku, finding it exotic and appealing, despite the evidence everywhere of the oil industry. We visited the famous Nyeftyaniye Kamni, an oilfield out at sea off the coast of Baku with miles of roads built on stilts on the sea bed, and had a hair-raising trip in the back of a lorry as it hurtled along these wooden roads – like a massive network of piers – as we were shown round these unique oil installations.

Years later, as Moscow correspondent for the Morning Star, I was to visit Baku again, staying in the same central hotel. This time it was to hear of how "disastrous" the Nationalities policy of the USSR had been, and to witness

the effusive welcome given to Turkish journalists and Government representatives at a press conference at the time of the break-up of the Soviet Union in
1990. It was more than a little ironic.

After that first visit to the Soviet Union, in 1963, I went again a few years
later, in 1967. This time it was to stay for a year, having won a scholarship
to study Russian at Moscow State University. It was during this year that I
met Ricardo, the love of my life.

After that year in Moscow, while still in Europe, Ricardo and I discussed
the possibility of our making our lives together in Chile. And so it was that,
seven months later, early in 1969, I came to be living with Ricardo in Chile.

Ricardo requested, and was granted, a transfer from the Temuco branch
of the University of Chile, where he had worked for the previous few years,
to Chillán, which was where he had managed to arrange a contract for me.

When I first saw the building of the University where I was to work, in
Chillán, I was horrified. By our standards, it was hardly a university at all. It
was very small, both in its buildings and in the number of students it catered
for. This regional branch of the University of Chile had been set up three years
earlier, and before that the main building had belonged to the Arts Centre of
Chillán. It was only three storeys high and the University occupied rooms
along just two of the floors. Next door was a building which was to remain
unfinished all the five years I lived and worked there, which was to have been
a municipal theatre. However, the University did have a Department of
Languages which was 100 metres away, just across the road from the *pensión*
where we lived, in fact – a longish, low building, which had a few classrooms,
a staff-room and a biggish room which I was later to turn into a Language
Laboratory.

It was obvious that this provincial branch (*sede*) of the University of Chile
did not receive nearly enough funding from the State, and it was not surprising
to find out on later visits to Concepción – a bigger city than Chillán – that,
in contrast, that city's private University had a beautiful big campus, with
attractive new buildings.

In our *sede*, however, the staff had to do all their own typing and
duplicating (no photocopiers or computers in those days!) and I even learned
that if a visiting lecturer came to Chillán on university business, it was
customary for the staff to have a whip-round to take him or her out to lunch!

The Head of the English Department was Hugo Pizarro, a tall, rather thin
man who had very good English and was clearly glad of the opportunity to
use it with me, since he knew that I had come straight from Britain and that
I did not speak Spanish. It was Hugo who had been instrumental in getting
the University to give me a contract, and we were very glad to see that he was
a nice person who ran an efficient department. We were invited to dinner with

him and his wife, who was a dentist and had a small practice in Chillán, and had a very pleasant evening with them.

As a colleague, Hugo was pleasant and helpful and we got on with him very well. But because he was a born language teacher, he could not resist telling me every mistake I was making when I was trying to speak Spanish, which was more than a little off-putting.

Before I could become an official member of staff at the University – even though I had a contract – I had to obtain an Identity Card (something all Chileans have to have), a Health Certificate and official translations of my academic degrees, certificates etc. I had to go to the Identification Bureau and stand in a queue for ages, after which I was sent to an office where I was asked a lot of questions about myself and why I was in Chile, and had my passport examined minutely by each official we came to in turn. Finally I got to the room where the Identity cards are actually issued, and there I was told to go and wash my hands. Then all my ten fingers had to be pressed into a sticky black dye to give all ten fingerprints. It took me ages to get the horrible black ink off afterwards! After that I had to go and have my photograph taken. Well, I thought to myself, since this will be in my Identity Card, I'd better run a comb through my hair at least. Spruced up, I duly sat before the camera, but, to my amazement, a sort of wooden, T-shaped thing with a long number written on it was thrust into my hands and I was told to hold it up against my neck. So all my attempts to look presentable came to nought. To my eyes, I looked more like a convict in the resulting photo.

This was just one of the many bureaucratic procedures I was to go through in my adopted country, and I can still remember how I used to seethe at the time you had to waste at all such offices.

Ricardo and I booked into a *pensión* on Libertad (Freedom) Street, a couple of blocks from Chillán station, and opposite the University's Department of Languages, which is where we would both work. We had a smallish room, with a double bed, a wardrobe, a small table and very little else, and had meals with the other boarders, who all worked at the University too. Two, Raquel and Isabel, were librarians and the other, Iris Campos, was a lecturer in Biology. They were all youngish – probably in their early thirties – and though at the time I found it hard-going to spend mealtimes with others all chatting in Spanish – which I didn't understand – it was actually very good for me. They were all very nice, and Iris was a lovely jolly person. She had big, light brown eyes which twinkled when she laughed, which was often. I soon found myself learning more and more Spanish as the days and weeks went by.

The *pensión* was interesting, and I found it very different from any digs I had lived in before. *Don* Exequiel, the owner, was a sickly widower who shared the house with his daughter Sonia and the housekeeper-cum-maid, Iris, an attractive and very capable young woman who had a baby girl. The baby was at that time just starting to walk in one of those contraptions with little wheels, and she used to whizz herself round at considerable speed on the parquet floor in her baby-walker, to the consternation of the elderly *Don Exequiel*.

Lunches were excellent at this *pensión*, and consisted of at least three courses. The only problem was that I had classes some days at 2 p.m. After a heavy lunch like that, teaching a class of similarly soporific students was the last thing I felt like doing, especially in summer, when the temperature would often be as high as 35 degrees centigrade.

Everyone at the *pensión* and elsewhere in Chillán treated us with extreme politeness, which I found quite surprising. I was to discover as I spent more time in Chile that this was a characteristic to be found everywhere, in offices, banks, shops, schools and universities; everyone you had to deal with in a formal or official capacity was always extremely polite, with what seemed to me genuine old-fashioned courtesy. Much later, when I visited Spain for the first time in 1993, I was to see that much of that courtesy was inherited from Spain, the 'mother country'.

My first winter in Chile (May-July) was cold and wet, with torrential rain that pelted the pavements with a ferocity I had never seen before in Britain. Thousands of poor Chilean families in the southern regions of that long country built their shacks near the banks of rivers, since that was the only land they could occupy without having to pay rent, so during rainy winters, they were the first to suffer, their flimsy shacks swept away in the floods. Local news reports that winter showed hundreds of flood victims who had lost their homes in our region of Ñuble.

There were so many impressions during those first few months of living in Chile, most of them positive and all of them interesting. I have always been interested in other peoples, other cultures and languages, and it was a rich experience to find myself in a new culture and observe the differences.

One thing which was immediately different and new to me was the custom between colleagues, friends and even new acquaintances of kissing when you met. Kissing is now much more common here in Britain than it was in the sixties, so perhaps this wouldn't seem so different to a modern English traveller. I found it quite an ordeal at first, until I got used to it, especially since I was never sure which side of the face was the one to be kissed, so I had quite a few nose clashes before I worked things out.

I had never seen so many dirt roads before. In Chillán the main central streets were all paved, but as soon as you left the town you saw that most of the side roads going off to smaller towns and villages were just dirt roads or tracks, and any passing vehicle would kick up huge clouds of dust.

Local buses were also something to be seen to be believed. Leaving from near the market-place, they were usually crammed with people and their bags – big round bundles wrapped in white linen, live hens held by their feet, babies in arms among all the bags and ancient suitcases. New, pungent smells invaded your nose – garlic on people's breath, the smell of all-pervading dust on clothes and feet, bodily sweat from so many people struggling to get on the bus with all their bags. And you realised what hard lives so many people live.

The *ferias* might have been crammed, but in other places it was surprising to see so few people around, for instance at the seaside. You could spend a whole day at the loveliest beaches and only see a few dozen people, even in summer. Chile at that time had a population of just over ten million, and even Santiago did not seem crowded, compared with London or Manchester. It never failed to amaze me, when Ricardo and I were in Santiago on a visit, that he would invariably meet someone he knew, by chance, on the street. It is then that you realise that it is very different to live in a country with a population of ten million, compared with the fifty or so million Britain had at that time.

I found Chileans very attractive, physically. Their wide cheekbones and olive skin, their dark, sometimes jet-black thick hair and dark eyes looked exotic and beautiful to me. Some of my female students were indeed very beautiful, and would have graced the cover page of any fashion magazine anywhere. Most young people were very smartly dressed, and always in clean, freshly-ironed shirts and blouses, even if they were obviously not new. In general Chilean people took a lot of care over their appearance, it seemed to me.

In my life, I have usually found that my first impressions tend to be confirmed. And so it was with my first impressions of Chile, my new country. Though I still didn't speak the language well, my first impressions of Chileans as warm, friendly and kind people, have been confirmed over the years. Though I was to see that in certain circumstances my colleagues could get quite heated and even angry, yet on a personal level they were always polite and friendly.

In over a year of living at the *pensión* with *Don* Exequiel, his daughter Sonia and Iris, their maid and her little daughter, as well as the other *pensionistas*, I never heard a cross word or saw any trace of temper or irritability.

As the months went by, and my Spanish improved, I began to get more and more out of the rich experience that is living in a different country than one's own. But I don't think I realised when I arrived in March 1969 quite how volatile the situation was in the country as a whole, or how fast things would begin to change.

CHAPTER TWO

Chile, fertile and renowned
in the famous Antarctic region
respected by remote nations
as strong, foremost and powerful;
the people she produces are so remarkable,
so proud, gallant and martial,
that they have never by king been ruled
nor to foreign dominion submitted.

(from the epic poem "La Araucana"
by Alonso de Ercilla,
16th century Spanish poet)

In 1969 there was a Christian Democratic government in Chile, headed by President Eduardo Frei. There was a strong left opposition, and the future Socialist Party President of Chile, Dr Salvador Allende, had already stood against his Christian Democratic rival several times, the last time in 1964 when he gained an appreciable percentage of the vote, 38.6%. There was a loose alliance between the two left parties, the Socialists and the Communists, both old-established parties that considered themselves Marxist.

"Of all the countries in the hemisphere, Chile was chosen to become the showcase for the new Alliance for Progress. Chile had the extensive bureaucratic infrastructure to plan and administer a national development program; moreover, its history of popular support for Socialist, Communist and other leftist parties was perceived in Washington as flirtation with communism. In the years between 1962 and 1969, Chile received well over a billion dollars in direct, overt United States aid, loans and grants both included. Chile received more aid per capita than any country in the hemisphere. Between 1964 and 1970, $200 to $300 million in short-term lines of credit was continuously available to Chile from private American banks." (US Dept of State report, Covert Action in Chile)

15

Eduardo Frei's Christian Democratic government had been elected in 1964 with a big majority – 56%[2] – and he had promised a *"Revolución en Libertad"* (Revolution in Liberty). The ideas of revolution had become increasingly popular in Chile, especially since the Cuban Revolution in 1959. It was what many saw as an answer to the grinding poverty of the peasantry and the underdevelopment forced on the country by the foreign companies that owned Chile's main natural resource, copper. Instead of nationalising the copper industry, Frei envisaged a more timid version, which he called "chileanisation", under which scheme the state would own fifty-one percent of the copper industry. But this did not affect the American companies in a major way, and they had continued to make big profits from Chilean copper.

Frei's strategy for the country's development sounded progressive, but lacked real teeth. He talked of "communitarianism", i.e. the state would fund social welfare, with no need for class struggle. Frei himself declared: "We do not propose for the country either a socialist road or a capitalist road, but one that emerges from our national reality and our national being, in which the state predominates as the administrator of the common good." And although much was made of the Christian Democrats' land reform, this had been more talk than action. By 1970, after six years of Christian Democratic government, the situation on the land was little changed.

Thus in 1969, when I arrived in Chile, dissatisfaction with the Christian Democratic Government was rife and police battles with homeless squatter families and street demonstrations were frequent.

As I travelled outside Chillán and to Valparaíso and the outskirts of Santiago, I soon saw evidence of the poverty in which many Chileans lived. The "mushroom" shanty-towns (*poblaciones callampas*) were so called because they sprang up here and there, unplanned by the authorities, as a result of *"tomas"*, seizures of land organised by groups of squatters. The houses these squatters built were like shacks, with roofs of corrugated iron, and walls made of anything from cardboard to planks of wood. Some of these *poblaciones* managed eventually to get electricity and water laid on, after long battles with the authorities.

A reform was underway in the University of Chile, which, despite its lack of funding – in the provincial *sedes* at least – was still the oldest and most prestigious university in the country. The University Reform, demanded by staff and students alike, was intended to democratise what was formerly a totally hierarchical and autocratic structure. It aimed to introduce deep changes in that structure – the government of the university, the courses and all university activity. It aimed to modernise, and to ensure that all staff and

---

2 The United States poured $20 million into Frei's election campaign, to ensure his victory over the socialist Dr Salvador Allende.

students – even administrative staff – had a say in the University's affairs. It was intended to bring the University closer to the people and make it more responsible towards society as a whole. The reform process had started in Santiago the previous year, 1968, but its progress in the provincial branches of the University was patchy or non-existent.

In a letter to my brother, I explained the ideas of the University Reform like this:

> "The Reform is not just something of academic interest, concerning only the University. It aims to strengthen the links between the University population and the rest of the people – workers, peasants, etc. – to alter the situation where the University is a select and privileged body far removed from the lives and interests of the majority of the country's population." (Letter of 22.5.69)

One of the first things Ricardo did on our arriving in Chillán was to look up other Communists and any Socialist Party members there might be at the *sede*. It turned out that he would be the only full-time member of staff who was a Communist, though there were one or two part-timers, and that there were at most two or three identifiable Socialists. It seemed that Chillán was one of the more sleepy *sedes* - in terms of the Reform – and its Director Agustín Quevedo had done little to introduce any of the democratising aims of the Reform. Ricardo took me along to meet Mr Quevedo, asking him outright what had been done so far. Quevedo's answers were equivocal and he looked distinctly uneasy as he blustered his way through the meeting.

Ricardo had done his postgraduate work in Santiago two years earlier and was already more than familiar with what the Reform entailed. And he was not to be fobbed off by high-sounding plans and intentions. He organised a local meeting of the University's national staff trades union, ADIEX, Association of Lecturers, Researchers and Extra-mural staff. The hall was packed and the excitement palpable as Ricardo took to the floor and called for Chillán academics to join forces to push for implementation of the Reform. Lecturers spoke heatedly, testifying that so far the Reform had been in words only, and that the Director had done nothing but pay lip-service to it.

I didn't understand much of what was going on, because of my lack of Spanish, but I could see that Ricardo was the galvanising force at that heated meeting. He spoke forcefully and had everyone there spellbound. You could have heard a pin drop when he spoke. Here was a "new boy" who had really come to shake things up here, you could see people thinking.

In his first few weeks at his new University *sede* Ricardo had found an atmosphere of generalised dissatisfaction among the staff, both academic and administrative. Plenty of people were complaining but nobody was doing anything about it or putting forward any constructive ideas. So at this first meeting, Ricardo argued that dissatisfaction had to be turned into a more responsible form of protest if there really were so many causes for the overall discontent. It was unanimously agreed to begin a "University Reform Evaluation" process to look into what had been done since the Reform had begun at national level the previous year. Ricardo was elected president of the university staff professional body, ADIEX, and as such had to chair most of the Reform Evaluation sessions.

And so there began days of meetings and discussions, in which staff, administrative personnel and students took part. It was a strange introduction to my new life in Chile, a crazy mixture of impressions and experiences. And all the time I was trying my utmost, at these Reform Evaluation meetings, to pick up as much Spanish as I could so that I could actually understand what was going on. It was so frustrating not being able to follow what my colleagues were protesting and arguing about.

The University Reform process started in earnest, and meetings were held with what seemed to me to be great frequency, in the *Sala Shaeffer* (Shaeffer Hall) of the University building, opposite Chillán's main square. I would sit there, listening intently to members of staff getting up to their feet, obviously denouncing this or that, or arguing forcefully for something, but I wasn't at all sure what. Ricardo was often to be seen on the platform at these meetings, as he was clearly seen as a natural leader, ever since that first meeting at the start of term. In the evenings I would pore over Chilean newspapers, asking Ricardo what words meant, and found I could make out a fair bit, especially since I could guess a certain amount from the roots of words, since I had studied both French and Latin at University. Ricardo was a very good teacher and he would often get me to repeat words and structures in Spanish as we walked along a street, for instance, and this also helped a lot.

There was a lot of humour at these Reform Evaluation meetings, most of which passed me by because I could not understand enough Spanish. There was one incident, for instance, where a young woman colleague, in a long, at times heated, speech, was arguing that she was not part of a group led by one prominent lecturer at the University: "It's a long time since I have had relations with him!" she declared. At that, the entire hall resounded with laughter at her unintentional *double entendre*.

My new job was to teach English (it was called Practice) and English Phonetics. I had studied Russian Phonetics as part of my degree course, but didn't know much about the Phonetics of English. But I had the necessary textbooks, and soon found that both subjects would be well within my capabilities. Moreover, being a native speaker gave me an enormous advantage, because the students had not had the opportunity before to hear English from a native speaker, and they seemed really appreciative of my being there. I worked hard, preparing my classes, running off exercises and comprehension pieces on an old mimeograph machine – this was the end of the Sixties, remember. I enjoyed my teaching, though the classes were quite big, 20-30 students in most of them. It was good that I didn't speak Spanish at first, because that way the students knew that I wouldn't understand if they tried to speak to me in Spanish, and therefore they had to try out their English.

The students were very polite and some had what can only be described as a deferential attitude towards me. One or two of them had been lucky enough to win exchange scholarships and had lived for a year in the USA, so spoke the language quite well and were confident. It was a bit of a problem to teach those students in the same class as other students, especially those who came from poorer backgrounds. The latter were timid and tended to speak inaudibly. Some of these students had teeth missing, even though they were young. In a country where medicine was privately-run, there wasn't money in poor households for non-essential dental work.

Dr Sheila Cassidy[3], in her book "Audacity to Believe" (Collins, 1977) remarked on this noticeable difference between the well-off and the poorer sections of society, when she lived in Chile in the seventies: "Chileans ... for generations had eaten so badly that they were shorter in stature and lower in intelligence than their richer brothers. It is ... well documented that the heights and weights of the children of the upper class residential areas of Santiago are the same, age for age, as those of children in North America. The heights and weights of children of corresponding ages in the peripheral areas of Santiago fall progressively away from the average as the areas become poorer. This, put in simple terms, means that children who are undernourished are shorter and weigh less than their luckier brothers and if this undernourishment is prolonged and severe they also grow up stupid."

One thing I soon realised as I started my work as a teacher of Phonetics was that I would have to change my accent. When I had first met Ricardo, I had teased him as "posh" because he spoke with an almost faultless RP (Received Pronunciation) accent. Now I realised that if I were to teach these students using the required set textbooks of the University of Chile's Phonetics course, I would have to modify my northern English accent to RP, otherwise the students might end up failing their course because of me.

The University of Chile's English degree course (*Pedagogía en Inglés*) was modelled on British University courses. The accent taught was RP, or Queen's

---

[3] An Englishwoman who in 1971 went to work as a doctor in Chile. In 1975, she was detained and tortured by the Chilean secret police, DINA, after she had agreed on compassionate grounds to treat a wounded resistance fighter, Nelson Gutierrez, of the MIR (Revolutionary Left Movement). On her return to Britain, after weeks of imprisonment in the most notorious of Santiago's detention centres, Dr Cassidy became a nun.

English, not – as elsewhere in other parts of Latin America – American English. Practically all the English teaching staff had English accents, even though many, like Ricardo himself, had never previously been to the UK. Ricardo's two great friends from his student days, Hernán Torres and Abel Vidal, both had excellent RP accents, and, like Ricardo, could recite whole chunks of Shakespeare at the drop of a hat! I found that most impressive. The University of Chile's English Department in Santiago prided itself on its ability to produce Chilean teachers with excellent British accents, and I was later to meet Mr Skewes and Mr Ewer, who were the two English native speakers that that Department boasted.

So I modified my accent, in line with the Phonetics textbooks, teaching the students "bus" and "mud" as in RP and not as they're pronounced in my native Derbyshire. Having always been good at languages, I didn't find it difficult to adopt the new accent, especially since there were no other English people around to hear me in Chillán!

In fact, I never heard of any other English native speakers there at all, apart from a couple of US Peace Corps young men who could sometimes be seen walking round the town, always together, always dressed in dark suits and ties, document case under their arms.

Among the Chilean people I met those first few months, there was quite strong hostility towards the US, and mistrust of the role of Peace Corps envoys. This ranged from stories about how they had meddled with the autochthonous traditions of the potters of nearby Quinchamalí, by getting the potters to make brightly striped pots alongside their traditional black clay with white designs, to stories that they were American agents disguised as do-gooders.

The fact that there were no other English speakers around was very good for me. I simply had to learn the language: it was sink or swim. Apart from anything else, among colleagues jokes and anecdotes were frequent, and I couldn't bear not to be able to understand them and join in the fun.

One of my best "teachers" was the owner of a little café on the ground floor of our *pensión*, whom everybody called "*El Viejo Torres*" – old man Torres. As the University Reform process became ever more heated and meetings held with great frequency, Ricardo and I quite often ended up missing our evening meal at the *pensión*. So we would slip into the café downstairs, where there was always a hot meal on offer, cooked in the Chilean way, with chilli pepper sauces and garlic galore. *El Viejo Torres* grew very fond of me, calling me "*La Gringuíta*", and I in turn liked his friendliness, his welcoming smile and the relaxed and cosy atmosphere of the little café. He would take delight in asking me something, knowing I wouldn't understand, so I would say "Say it again, I didn't understand!" in my poor Spanish, and he would say the same thing but a different way, using the colourful language of sayings you find among the people in Chile. Of course everyone who was nearby would burst out laughing as he got me to repeat these words, not understanding what I was saying! He wouldn't use foul language, mind, just sayings – like we might say "you were hauled over the coals" instead of "you got a good scolding" or "I came a cropper" instead of "I failed miserably". It was all good clean fun, and I joined in because I could see that they weren't poking fun at me, they were just having a laugh.

What with our frequent meals at *El Viejo's*, and lunch with our fellow-boarders at the *pensión*, and hearing one speech after another at interminable University meetings about the Reform, my Spanish improved by leaps and bounds, and in three months or so I was already speaking and understanding the language pretty well.

But learning a foreign language taxes your brain immensely, and when you're immersed in the language for hours on end, it can be extremely tiring until you reach that level in the language when you can say you're really bilingual. I remember one day, a few weeks after my arrival in Chile, one of the girls in the *pensión*, Iris, invited me to go with her to see her friend Raquél for the day while Ricardo was away in Temuco, seeing his children. I was still not at all fluent at that stage, and I can remember feeling pretty desperate by early afternoon, because I had become so tired with the constant effort of understanding and speaking Spanish with these new friends.

I was the object of much curiosity and fascination in that provincial town, as I later found out. Fortunately, since I didn't speak the language and had come from Britain, where separations and couples living together without being married were hardly uncommon by the Sixties, all such gossip passed over my head.

Perhaps that was as well. It wasn't easy, each time Ricardo went back to see his children, when I stayed behind in the *pensión*. I fully supported Ricardo's determination to continue to see his kids at least once a month – Chillán is about a six-hour journey from where they lived, in Temuco. But of course it was lonely when he was away, because I still didn't have any real friends – you can't really have good friends until you speak the language well.

But with time it got easier, and after a few months, Ricardo took me along and I met his former wife and children, and after a year or so, they were allowed to come and spend holidays with us in Chillán. Separations are never easy, and relations with your partner's children can be difficult and hurtful even, but I'm a firm believer that love conquers all, and Ricardo and I certainly loved each other from day one.

We had met in Moscow in 1967. We were on a course for intending or currently-practising teachers of Russian, at the prestigious Moscow State University, one of the seven "wedding-cake" architectural landmarks of the

21

city. I had a degree in Russian from the University of Manchester and had been teaching Russian the previous year at St. Albans College of Further Education, and living in London. Ricardo did not know any Russian, but as an active member of the Chilean-Soviet Cultural Institute and teacher of English at the University of Chile, he had been awarded a scholarship to go and study Russian with the idea that he would return to teach the language there, alongside his English teaching.

The previous year, 1966, I had applied to the British Council for one of their postgraduate scholarships to further my studies of Russian, since I was well aware of the inadequacies of my spoken Russian after four years of a degree course at the University of Manchester, which was much more focused on history and literature, Old Church Slavonic and Old Russian than on modern spoken Russian. I was invited to an interview at the British Council and remember entering the room where an interviewing panel of some six people were sitting behind a long table. I was asked all sorts of questions, one of them being the direct question: "Are you a member of the Communist Party of Great Britain?" At this point I realised that my chances of getting the scholarship were equal to nil, and I knew there was no point in not telling the truth – which would have been contrary to my nature, anyway, since I was brought up always to be truthful – so I smiled wryly and said yes, I was a member, and basically, so what? As I thought, I did not get that scholarship.

So the following year I applied for and won a scholarship from the Society for Cultural Relations with the USSR[4]. Thus I arrived in Moscow in September 1967 and found myself with some 60 or so people of many nationalities, all there to improve their knowledge of Russian, among whom was Ricardo from Chile, so in this way we both ended up on the same course. I was put in the top group, together with people of other nationalities who also had degrees in the language, whereas Ricardo was in the bottom group – three students who had no prior knowledge at all of Russian.

Ricardo had arrived a bit later than everybody else, and since he didn't speak any Russian, but did speak excellent English, he and I would talk in English and soon discovered that we had similar tastes in literature, music, politics and general outlook on life. I think both of us tried not to fall in love, since I knew from the beginning that he was married and had children in

---

[4] The SCR was founded in 1924 as the Society for Cultural Relations between the British Commonwealth and the USSR, following the United Kingdom's establishment of diplomatic relations with the new Soviet state. Its founding members were a group of key British and Soviet artists and intellectuals of the day, including EM Forster, Julian Huxley, Maynard Keynes, Bertrand Russell, Sybil Thorndyke, Alexei Tolstoy, Virginia Woolf, and Konstantin Yuon. They sought to collect and diffuse information in both countries on developments in science, education, philosophy, art, literature, and social and economic life. The Society has continued its work uninterrupted until the present day. In 1992, following the break-up of the Soviet Union, the Society changed its name to Society for Co-operation in Russian and Soviet Studies - SCRSS

Chile. But we lived on the same corridor, we went to classes at the same building every day, we went on excursions to Leningrad, Volgograd, Suzdal and Vladimir together with the rest of the people on the course, and it just happened gradually that we were drawn more and more to each other. I loved his sincerity, his kindness, his loving nature. I loved discussing ideas and events with him, I loved his little student room at MGU (Moscow State University) where we would sometimes make tea together, I loved the courtesy and affection with which he treated the other students and staff, I loved hearing about Chile's political situation, history and prospects that he saw for the future. And I loved the way he looked, his kind, strong, dark-skinned features and athletic body, his complete lack of self-consciousness.

By the halfway point in the year's course, we were both much in love with each other. By the end of the year we decided that we would make our lives together, despite all the seeming impossibility of that becoming reality. We spent seven months apart before this all came together. During those seven months Ricardo wrote to me several times a week and I too wrote him just as frequently. It was enough time to see whether our love would last the separation and the confrontation with reality and former lives. It did, and we are still together forty or so years later.

In Chillán I soon saw during my first year there that the students were very politically active. The clamour for University reform echoed the nationwide clamour for policies which would bring Chile out of its underdevelopment and its dependence on the United States. In Chillán, the Town Hall was festooned with a huge banner which read "The Yanks are the Ruin of Latin America! This Municipality demands Authentic Nationalisation of Copper!" In August there were widespread disturbances in six of the main cities of Chile, including Santiago and Valparaíso. The police used a riot squad called the "Grupo Móvil" to break up the demonstrations; there were tear-gas casualties and even deaths.

In May 1969, there was a strike by the non-academic staff at the University of Chile, which lasted several weeks, demanding restoration of the provision for this sector of university workers to have a say in the Reform process, which the University Council in Santiago was trying to weaken. One of the aims of the University Reform was to strengthen the links between the university population and the Chilean people as a whole – to alter the situation whereby the University was a select and privileged body removed from the lives and interests of the majority of the country's population.

The students of the Girls' Technical School in Chillán were on strike demanding better buildings and equipment. The school was next door to the University, on one side of the city's Central Square. On the morning of 25 August 1969 the Grupo Móvil raided the building and started beating up students occupying the premises. Police threw tear-gas bombs into the foyer and lecture-halls of the neighbouring University buildings whilst lectures were in progress, which caused bedlam as staff and students tried to escape the suffocating tear-gas.

I had gone to the central University building after my classes that day to meet Ricardo and go home together. As we were there trying to decide what to do about the occupying school students next door and the *Grupo Móvil's* response, we heard the first tear gas bomb explode in the foyer and immediately felt its effects down the corridors as we ran. More tear gas was fired into the inner courtyard of the University, which was our only way out, since the police were blocking the front entrance. Ricardo grabbed my hand and ran through the interior courtyard, dragging me along as fast as he could. I really thought at one moment that I was going to die. I literally felt I couldn't breathe, and the pain in my chest was agonising. Ricardo pulled me along away from the worst area affected and out through a back door into the street. I seemed to have suffered a far worse reaction than other people, and once outside, collapsed onto the pavement to try and regain my breath. I felt weak and shaky for several hours afterwards.

Ricardo and I, together with a small group of lecturers who had been in classes and had therefore got caught up in this, set off to the *Intendencia*, the government representative body in charge of the police, to demand they order the police to stop their action to give a chance for the students to retreat. Then Ricardo went back to the University to talk to the police and get them to back off.

Ricardo at this time was president of the University staff professional body, ADIEX, so, after meeting with the province's *Intendente* in this capacity, he went up on the roof to tell the striking school students that the *Intendente* had agreed to order the police to withdraw. But he was too late. While he was up there trying to defuse the situation, he was struck on the leg by a tear-gas canister fired by the police from the roof of the half-built Municipal Theatre next door to the University. His leg was immediately very painful and swelled up impressively.

The angry open wound this caused was about three inches long and his leg turned deep red and purple, from mid-calf to his ankle. The wound later became seriously inflamed and had to be lanced, after which he had to spend two weeks in bed recovering.

A big protest meeting was organised in front of the *Intendencia*, where local political and trades union leaders spoke, together with the Senator for that parliamentary constituency, Jorge Montes, to denounce the actions of the *carabineros* against the striking students.

The University of Concepción, which was the nearest university to our branch of the University of Chile in Chillán, was a big, private institution of some prestige in Chile. There a university reform was also going on, and it was a hotbed of student unrest where the ultra-revolutionary group, MIR (Revolutionary Left Movement), was particularly active. One of the crazy things this group did at this time was to kidnap the Deputy Editor of the local, fairly right-wing newspaper, force him to strip, beat him about the head, then force him to appear naked with only feathers as a cover, in front of a large crowd emerging from a meeting of University academics.

Some might have considered this merely student high jinks, but the consequences were serious. The police raided the university campus and made some arrests, which set a precedent for infringing the autonomy of the University in the future. Up till then the principle of respect for university autonomy had been sacrosanct in Chile.

Our University staff union, ADIEX, immediately condemned the MIR's actions against the journalist, but also condemned the police action in raiding the University.

My first Chilean summer was full of new and fascinating experiences. One Sunday we took the early train at 6 a.m. from Chillán station to Dichato on Chile's Pacific coast, for a day-trip. It was quite cloudy, but warm. After we'd had breakfast there and been for a walk, we lay down for a rest near some rocks and fell asleep. Since it was overcast, we slept there fully clothed. I had on a trendy purple cotton trouser-suit, I remember, that I had bought in Swiss Cottage. We must have slept a couple of hours, I suppose, but enough for the damage to have been done – I got severe sunburn. When we got back to the *pensión* later that night, my face and feet were lobster-red and my lips and face horribly swollen. Ricardo was really worried and got a doctor to me as soon as he could next morning, who was able to give me some cream to protect my poor face. It was a lesson to me, that even when the sky is overcast, you can still get sunburnt in Chile! Ricardo, of course, with his dark skin, hadn't suffered at all.

One of our closest friends that first year in Chillán was Eduardo Contreras, who at that time was one of the city's Communist councillors, later to become Mayor of Chillán. We spent many evenings having dinner with Eduardo and Maruja, often together with Eduardo's parents, who were very nice people. As a student, Eduardo had been part of a movement inspired by the Radical Party, but he had soon gravitated to the left, becoming a Communist by his early twenties. Maruja was the daughter of a police colonel, and was a quiet, thoughtful, gentle soul, who didn't express political opinions, but whose sympathies were with the poor and needy, who were all around us. Eduardo was like a dynamo whose enthusiasm and hard work and natural organising

25

ability made him a real force to be reckoned with in the Council Chamber where he was a councillor, before being elected Mayor.

One time when we ate at Eduardo and Maruja's, we were served mud crayfish, dozens of them boiled and piled high on a huge dish in the centre of the table. What I especially loved was the way that we all spent ages picking at the meat from the tiny legs, sucking the flesh from them, as you do with crabs, and all the time discussing, chatting and joking while the mound of crayfish got slowly smaller. It's a good way to enjoy a long, leisurely conversation with friends, eating something that takes a long time to consume!

Eduardo, as a local councillor, was always very busy. The situation in the country was getting worse, there were increasingly frequent protests and squats by the homeless, there was police repression of protesters, and as a consequence, the Communist and Socialist parties were growing steadily, whilst the ruling Christian Democratic party was fast losing support among the poor workers in the towns and cities and peasants in the countryside, because despite election promises to improve their lot, people were not seeing their living standards improve. Wherever there were sit-ins or squats, Eduardo would be there, talking to the people, and trying to get things done at a local level. He was very well known, often featuring in the local newspaper *La Discusión* and interviewed by the local radio station. Yet somehow, he always had time to have dinner with friends, even if it was late in the evening by the time he managed to get free of his work.

One evening, in June 1969, Eduardo called at our *pensión* after we had been to see a Soviet dance ensemble, called "Jok", perform at the local city theatre. It must have been about 9.30 p.m. Eduardo insisted we had to go with him to the *peña*[5] to meet "the Russians", who had given the performance in Chillán and who couldn't talk to anybody or make themselves understood because they didn't have a translator with them. Most of the ensemble were not Russians, but Moldovans, though they did speak Russian as well as their own language, which is similar to Romanian.

We got to the *peña* about 10 p.m. and the Moldavian ensemble dancers were finishing their meal. They couldn't talk to any of their hosts because none of the dancers spoke Spanish and none of their hosts spoke Russian, let alone Moldovan! We were heralded upon our arrival as the great solution, since we both spoke Russian. The problem was that since I had only been in Chile a few months, my head was full of the Spanish I was trying so hard to learn, and Russian had been shoved somewhere into the recesses of my brain for the time being.

Little groups of the performers formed around me and Ricardo, everyone trying to converse and get to know each other. Soon it was evident that a

5 peña – a restaurant where artists sing and play folk music

group of the male performers had clustered around me, and a similar circle of female dancers were grouped around Ricardo. All of a sudden, Ricardo came over to my group and has often related since how he heard me emphatically saying "*Ahora, ahora*" amid a stream of Russian words, clearly not realising that the word "*ahora*" was Spanish, and obviously convinced that I was speaking Russian!

Our Councillor friend Eduardo introduced us to the then Mayor of Chillán, Ricardo Lagos, who was a member of the Socialist Party. The Mayoralty rotated between the different Councillors elected from the major parties and 1969 was Ricardo Lagos's turn. Eduardo became Mayor after him in 1970. It was Ricardo Lagos, through his business friends, who arranged a loan for Ricardo and me when we first arrived, since our salaries were held up for the first three months or so due to bureaucratic delays in Santiago. He was a quiet-spoken, unassuming sort of man, and we soon became friends with him and his wife Victoria, and their two sons, Ricardo and Carlos. Ricardo Jnr was away at University, and Carlos was a student of English at the University where we taught, and became a student of mine in his second year. Little did we realise when we first met Ricardo and Victoria that their lives would become so tragic.

I found the friendship and comradeship between Communists and Socialists very interesting and encouraging. The Socialist Party of Chile was founded in 1933, and was based on Marxist philosophy, so both parties considered themselves "Marxist". The Socialist Party did not, however, align itself with the Soviet Union, and did not consider itself Leninist. It was Latin Americanist in outlook, a strong supporter of Cuba, and many of its members were in favour of the armed struggle, as opposed to the peaceful road to socialism, which was the line the Communist Party of the Soviet Union and most Latin American Communist Parties espoused at that time. Both parties, as the two big left-wing parties in Chile, sensed their responsibility in trying to achieve the maximum possible unity, and in fact their programmes, certainly as far as domestic issues were concerned, were very similar.

What was most refreshing to me, coming from one of the hotbeds of the Cold War, where anti-Communism was rife, was that in Chile it was not an oddity to be left-wing, or to declare oneself a Socialist or a Communist, as it was at that time in Britain. I had felt anti-communism at close hand already by the time I met Ricardo when I was 25. The first time was as a student at Manchester University. I had been an active member of the Communist Society and was on the National Student Committee of the Communist Party. Like others in "CommSoc", I used to sell *The Daily Worker* on the steps of the University Union, and remember once being spat upon by one of British fascist

Oswald Mosley's entourage as he came up the steps and into the Student Union building where he had been invited to take part in a student debate.

The second time was towards the end of my final year as a student of Russian when I was applying for posts using the language. I had an interview for a job as a Translator and Administration Officer at Imperial Chemical Industries (ICI), the UK's biggest chemicals company at the time. I was given the post, and started work in September 1964. A few weeks into the job, I was called to see Dr. Duncan Davies, the Head of the company's central research laboratory, which is where I worked. He told me that the acting head of the Russian Department at Manchester University, whom I had given as a referee, had written in his reference that I was an active Communist. I was furious. An academic reference should only be about my academic capabilities, not my extra-curricular activities. Of course I did not see Dr. Dumbreck's reference myself, so I don't know what else he said about me, but fortunately for me, Dr Davies, who was a broad-minded and intelligent man, laughed it off and told me that as long as I didn't cause any problems at the lab, he was prepared to let me stay. And he didn't even sack me when, a bit later, I caused an uproar by demanding equal pay with a male Administration Officer colleague. In the Sixties, sex discrimination was commonplace everywhere, and there was no equal pay for work of equal value in private companies.

It has always amused me that if you're any sort of a leading Communist in Britain, you are immediately considered by some as extremely dangerous and subversive. Yet the Party's policies were published openly in its programme, *The British Road to Socialism*, which did not envisage any kind of violent takeover of power, and the Party was entirely open about its activities.

But whilst I was working at ICI, another thing happened that showed me once again that to be a Communist in Britain at that time was not only to be seen as an oddity, but to suffer in unexpected ways. One day I was sitting in the Library at ICI's Central Research Laboratory, using the library's diction-aries to translate a chemicals paper in Russian so that I could write an abstract of it for the chemists working at the lab. A young man I hadn't seen before sat opposite, and followed me out as I left for a break. We got chatting, and it turned out that he was the son of one of the top directors of ICI, was studying at Oxford, and just using the lab's library during his vacation. Over the next few days we chatted more, and he asked me out. We went for several drives out into the countryside, had drinks in pubs and argued about politics. I was a couple of years older than him, and on politics, I really knew what I was talking about. He was clearly fascinated by me, perhaps because I was different from the sort of girls he had met before. One day he invited me to dinner at the poshest hotel in Chester, and we had a long leisurely meal where we discussed politics, laughed about things and generally had an enjoyable time. Dropping me off at my flat late that night, he dared to kiss me on my cheek as he said good-night, and I realised that for his part, the friendship was not merely platonic.

The next thing I knew I was hauled up in front of the top boss, Dr Davies, again and this time told that the young man's father – a director of the company – was most concerned at his son's interest in me, and had forbidden his son to have anything more to do with me since I was a Communist. His son had been packed off on holiday sharpish, and that was to be the end of the matter.

I was flabbergasted. For one thing because the relationship was hardly even that, we had simply been out a few times together. But mainly because it seemed incredible to me that, simply because I had certain political views, I could be considered off-limits for his precious son.

So that was that. A fine friendship nipped in the bud by an overbearing and ambitious father. Not that he need have worried, since his son would no doubt never have suited me in the life I wanted to lead. But it was an early and object lesson in how strong anti-communism was in the UK in the early Sixties.

In Chile it was quite different. To be a Communist was to be normal, respected, even admired. The Communist Party had a strong and well-deserved reputation as consistently fighting for the interests of the working people of Chile, and had, like other parties, contested elections, gradually winning a bigger and bigger share of the vote. In other words, as a Communist you felt part of the mainstream of politics. However, it had not long been like this: Ricardo often told how, as a young teacher, he first became interested in finding out about communism after unexpectedly finding himself dismissed – "accused of being a communist" – from a private school where he had been teaching. That was because he had been defending the teachers' rights and entitlements, so the school's management decided he must be a communist. Yet at that stage in his life he had had nothing to do with left politics at all. In the Fifties, anti-communism was still very strong in Chile, but by the early Seventies, things had begun to change very rapidly.

The maid at the *pensión* where we lived that first year, Iris, was an attractive and lively girl with a very pleasant personality. I was struck by her good-naturedness, when it always seemed to me that she had a very hard life. Chilean tradition dictated that lunch was the main meal of the day, with three courses, and *Don* Exequiél was a stickler for tradition. So Iris spent all morning shopping and cooking. She would start early in the morning, and by ten she was already getting on with the day's lunch for the five *pensionistas*, *Don* Exequiel, his daughter Sonia and herself and the baby. She was an excellent cook, and the menu was very varied. We would have an *"entrada"*

– hors d'oeuvres – of salad with egg or shellfish, for instance, then a soup of some kind, usually a *cazuela* of beef, lamb or chicken, which was an entire meal in itself, I found, and then a hot dish of fish with potatoes, or beef, pork, lamb, chicken, goat, with rice or potatoes. Once we even had a cooked little bird, whose name I can't remember, and another time we had a frog, its arms and legs splayed outwards on the plate! One of my favourite dishes was a mashed potato roly-poly, with melted cheese inside the mashed potato, and icing sugar sprinkled on the top. It was delicious.

As you can imagine, it took a long time to cook all these separate dishes, plus a sweet of some kind, either fresh fruit or tinned fruit, or caramel. But it was always on time, always delicious, and always served with friendliness and cheerfulness. I wondered how she managed to be so cheerful, when her whole life seemed to consist of cooking and shopping and in between, managing to look after her little girl, whom the whole household adored. There was no husband around, and I soon learned that hers was a typical story of many country girls in Chile at that time. She came from a rural spot some 15 miles or so from Chillán, where her family worked on the land of one of the big *latifundistas* who owned the vast majority of the land in Chile. She had got pregnant, rumour had it by one of the sons of that *gran señor*, and so was shipped away quietly out of the village, nothing more being said about the matter.

Later I came across so many other examples of young girls from the countryside, who were single mothers by the time they were in their late teens. However, despite Chile being a Catholic country, I never got the impression that these girls were looked down upon or frowned upon. Perhaps that was because motherhood is considered so important and precious in Chile, so once there is a child, that becomes the main thing, and everybody pulls round to help the girl fulfil her role as mother.

I grew to love my students. They were such a nice crowd of young people. They all seemed friendly to me and to each other, and were keen to learn, if not very disciplined about doing their homework.

I can still remember them, their bright young faces looking at me, trying to understand me as I spoke in English. One was Cecilia, a small, very pretty girl in the fourth year, who walked on crutches as she had had polio as a child. She walked with great difficulty, but hardly ever missed a class, and was one of the most assiduous students. Another was Maruja, the wife of our friend Eduardo, who was one of the final year students. She was a quiet and reserved student, very hardworking, and with a keen interest in literature.

One of the third year students for Phonetics and Practice was called Laura. She stood out among the students because she was fair-haired and fair-skinned, unlike most, who were dark, like most Chileans. She and her boy-friend Ramón were inseparable, always coming to class together and working together.

One day several of the students came to class in tears. Laura had died the day before from a back-street abortion. Since I had only been teaching the group a few months, I hadn't realised that her growing size had been due to pregnancy. Ramón and her friends were distraught. Apart from anything else, Ramón feared he would be charged for having aided and abetted the abortion, since he had apparently found the back-street abortionist willing to perform it. A representative of the Christian Democratic students, who was in Laura's class, came to see Ricardo at home, accusing Ramón of being party to this "murder". And one of the administrative staff in the former Director's office urged Ricardo, who by that time had been elected Secretary-General of the *sede*, to take the matter up officially and seemed to want to make a scandal out of the tragedy.

We both felt that this was a tragedy, not a crime. It was two young people who loved each other but did not have the money or acceptance of parents to marry, and in a country where society did not accept young people having sexual relations before being married. As a result, back-street abortionists abounded, and Laura was the unfortunate victim of one of them.

I was heartbroken for Laura, but also felt sympathy for Ramón, who had loved her, and who now faced possible criminal charges to boot. Ricardo managed to defuse the situation, and in the end no criminal charges were brought against the young man.

One of the first actions the Popular Unity Government of Salvador Allende did was to introduce a draft abortion law reform bill, which envisaged permitting abortions on socio-economic grounds, with the consent of two doctors. Allende, being a doctor himself, knew well what back-street abortions meant, and pointed out that such illegal and insanitary abortions caused half of all female deaths in Chile at that time. The Popular Unity Government proposed other changes to the draft abortion law, including measures to protect the family by improving maternity benefits and child allowances. Whilst some progress was made in terms of such allowances, abortion did not become legalised, even under Allende, such was the opposition mounted by the Catholic Church and the right-wing parties.

In my letter home at the time, I wrote:

> "It was a horrible end-of-term. A terrible mad rush, with two or three teachers doing the work of seven because the other four chose to slope off with characteristic irresponsibility. And then last Saturday (February 1970), we were just leaving the U at the end of the morning and breathing huge sighs of relief because that was our last 'shift' of this term, when a student of ours came up to us and told us that a

31

fellow-student had died the night before. Later it turned out to be the most terrible thing and awfully upsetting. The girl died of a back-street abortion. She was 20 years old and our best student in the third year. Her boy-friend, in the same class, an extremely nice lad, was in a terrible state, of course, and came to our house and Ricardo spent hours talking to him and giving him help. You see, if the girl's parents took legal action, he and the abortionist would be held responsible for the girl's death, because he went with her to this abortionist's house, and it was he who found out about the abortionist and took the girl there in the first place.

"God, it's so tragic. You see, this being a Catholic country, it's difficult for young people to find out about contraceptive methods, and in this couple's case, they just used the 'rhythm' method, and of course eventually it failed. Apparently the girl went to the doctor but he refused an abortion because the pregnancy was too far advanced, and so what alternative did they have? No financial means to enable them to marry and have the baby, parental opposition on the part of the girl's parents, and so they decided to do the same as thousands of others in this bloody tragic country.

"It's the lad I feel most sorry for now, because can you imagine the feeling of guilt he has, aggravated by the attitude of people who will doubtless get to know about it and who will accuse him either openly or in a more masked way, of having 'murdered' the girl, (all the religious moralising types of whom there are many here) and aggravated still more by the very real fear of legal action, for if it were taken, he might well find himself in prison for a number of years.

"You can't blame individuals in this poor society in cases like these. Women are all the time dying from abortions carried out in the most primitive and unhygienic conditions, and this happens because of the social system. How can you tell a woman who has eight kids that it's wrong to have an abortion when her husband doesn't earn enough to look after even half that number of kids, let alone nine or more? How can you encourage them to use contraceptives, when the cost of these is so high that working-class people and peasants couldn't possibly afford them? How can you condemn couples going to a back-street abortionist, when there are no state services to perform abortions, because abortion is illegal, and the price charged by a private doctor is so high that only the rich can afford it?" (Letter of 6 February 1970)

For me personally, Laura's death in such tragic circumstances was a sobering brush with Chilean reality. I knew of such things happening, theoretically, but now I was confronted with the reality for the first time. It was difficult to get back to classes and the normal routine after that.

But life went on, of course, and my heavy workload ensured that I had to focus on my teaching and class preparation. Increasingly I found I really enjoyed my English Phonetics classes. I soon realised where I would need to put the emphasis on correcting common mispronunciations, which arose from the interference of the students' native Spanish. Most students found it hard to start an English word beginning with an 's', for instance, saying 'estreet' and 'esplendid' instead of 'street' and 'splendid'. I devised all sorts of exercises to work on with my classes, to help them distinguish between 'ship' and 'sheep', between 'chip' and 'cheap', 'chit' and 'cheat' – and, of course, how to pronounce 'sheet' with due care! We had a lot of laughs, and I dare say I fell into a few pitfalls by not knowing certain bad words in Chilean Spanish!

Not only the University was in turmoil while undergoing reform. The whole of Chilean society was in turmoil. There was widespread dissatisfaction with President Eduardo Frei's Christian Democratic Government, which had come to power promising a "REVOLUTION IN LIBERTY". There didn't appear to be revolution of any kind, libertarian or otherwise. After his election in 1964, Frei had enacted an agrarian reform and soon the peasants, who for decades had been passive and tied to their *latifundio* bosses, became politically active for the first time and started demanding rapid expropriation of land and its distribution to the peasants who actually worked the land. The homeless squatters were more and more organised and mass seizures of land by squatters became commonplace round the outskirts of Santiago and the bigger cities. The Christian Democratic Government, whose rhetoric before its election had been similar to that of the Left, in terms of the need to tackle poverty and social injustice, was not willing to hurt the interests of the big business and landowners, or foreign, mainly US, capital, and so did not have the means for redistribution of wealth. The answer of President Eduardo Frei's Christian Democratic Government to the increasing popular militancy was repression. People were up in arms over the riot police's handling of demonstrations, such as the one when slum dwellers had seized an area of unoccupied, but privately-owned, land outside the southern town of Puerto Montt. Early on the morning of 9 March 1969, police were sent in to dislodge the squatters. Songwriter Victor Jara, who was one of the most committed and well-known singers of the Popular Unity period, put the blame for this massacre fairly and squarely on the then Christian Democrat Minister of the Interior, Edmundo Pérez Zukovic, for the deaths of 11 men, women, and children during the Puerto Montt massacre. Zukovic had authorized 250 armed police to attack and open fire on the 91 homeless peasant families who had occupied that private wasteland. Tear gas grenades, dogs and machine gun fire were used to terrorize and evict the impoverished peasant squatters, many of whom were wounded in the armed raid. Victor's song goes:

Usted debe responder	You will have to answer
señor Pérez Zukovic	Mr Pérez Zukovic
porqué al pueblo indefenso,	why defenceless people
contestaron con fusil.	were met with guns.
Señor Pérez su conciencia	Mr Pérez your conscience
la enterró en un ataúd	is now buried in a coffin
y no limpiarán sus manos	and all the southern rains
ni toda las lluvias del sur.	won't clean your hands.

One of the strengths of the left was its folklore. There were several very popular folk-singers like Victor Jara, Angel and Isabel Parra, groups like Quilapayún and Inti-Illimani, who were identified with the Left and the campaign to get a Left candidate elected. From my very first days in Chile I loved Chilean folk-music, and one of my greatest pleasures was going to the local *peña*, where a variety of artists would perform while you ate a delicious meal with friends. I liked Argentinian music too, such as songs by Atahualpa Yupanqui and Jorge Cafrune: the rhythm of these songs was unlike any other folk-music I'd ever heard.

The *peña* in the countryside outside Chillán had a mixed clientele. There were professional people like us, who loved folk-music, and there were the young *latifundistas* of the area and their friends, who would arrive in their big Chevrolet pick-ups in large groups and take over one whole part of the restaurant. They often looked quite different from most Chileans, in that the women were usually fair-haired and fair-skinned, the men similarly European-looking, and with hair sleeked down so that not a hair was out of place. Some people in Chile even called men affecting this style *"paltas"*, because their smoothed-down and greased hair looked like the dark rounded skin of the avocado (*palta*)!

One of our students, Eliana Solís, was very knowledgeable about Chilean folk-music, and she would frequently come to visit, with armfuls of records of Violeta Parra, the legendary Chilean researcher and performer of authentic Chilean folk music, and LP's of Hector Pavez and others. She would tell me what the songs were about, since I still didn't speak Spanish well enough at the time to be able to make out the words, and explain the popular groundswell of enthusiasm for reclaiming Chilean folk-music from the rather twee folk-groups that had previously been popular, where the songs didn't reflect the common people's reality very much, but were simply about love, the beauty of nature etc. Now the new generation of folk-singers, Eliana explained, sang of the people's suffering, the injustices of society, and tragic events that had shaped Chile's political past.

One of these events, commemorated in a cantata sung by the group Quilapayún, called *Santa María de Iquique*, told of the tragic massacre by the army of over 2,000 striking workers and their families in the northern town of Iquique in December 1907. The nitrate miners were on strike, protesting against their miserable wages and desperately poor living conditions, and had occupied the Domingo Santa María school in the port of Iquique as a protest. Many of the people who had herded themselves into the Santa María School building were women and children, not just the miners who were on strike. The anger and hatred provoked by this bloody massacre of so many innocent people must have fed into the popular movement in the far north of Chile at that time, because it was in that same city of Iquique that only five years later, in 1912, the *Partido Obrero Socialista* (Socialist Workers' Party) was founded by Luís Emilio Recabarren. That party later became the Communist Party of Chile in 1922.

I loved all the music Eliana brought for me to listen to, and started to buy whatever records of Chilean and Argentinian folk-music I could.

Students throughout the country were becoming increasingly militant, and stand-offs with the police were commonplace. There was a general feeling in the country that the Christian Democrats had done very little of what they had promised, and were giving in to the *latifundistas* and big business. So the parties of the Left, principally the Communists and Socialists, were growing in membership and influence, and by 1969, the campaign to elect a candidate of the Left for forthcoming presidential elections in September 1970 was already well underway. Just as the University was a ferment of reform and protest against antiquated management and systems where neither staff nor students had any say in its running, so the country as a whole was hotting up.

The University Reform, after several weeks of debate at packed meetings, came to a head with the decision, in line with the recommendations of the national University Reform guidelines, to hold fresh elections to elect new authorities of the *sede* – a Vice-rector[6] and Secretary-General[7] – together with a new body called a *Consejo Normativo* (Normative Council), which would be responsible for drawing up policies. The elections were fixed for July 1969.

Under these guidelines, the weighting of the academic staff's vote would be 60%, that of the non-academic staff 15% and that of the students 25%. Ricardo was asked by his party to be the Communist Party's candidate for

---

[6] Equivalent to the position of Vice Chancellor at a British university.

[7] Deputy to the Vice Chancellor, or *Vice-rector*.

the post of Secretary-General. His running mate for Vice-rector was to be Julio Stuardo, a newcomer to the University, a Socialist and and a lawyer by profession. Other political parties ran their own candidates for the top posts, such as the Radical Party and the Christian Democratic Party. But the Christian Democrats were tainted by the general discontent with their Government, so didn't stand much of a chance.

There was quite a good campaign, with meetings, posters, leaflets and interviews on local radio. The local paper, *La Discusión* gave quite a lot of coverage to the election and the issues.

Ricardo and Stuardo ran together on one list, and both men were quite charismatic figures in different ways. Ricardo had won a lot of support from academic, non-academic staff and students from his role in being the first to bring up and popularise the ideas of the national University Reform, to democratise the university and make it more accessible to the poorer sectors of society. He was an excellent speaker and very well-respected as an academic, having postgraduate studies both in Chile and abroad, and having worked at the university for several years. Stuardo was a somewhat bombastic character, given to sharp decisions and sweeping statements, but who had experience of being in the public eye and who had considerable talent in "working the votes". He was also tall and European-looking, which was apparently a sure vote-winner among female voters. Personally, I didn't like him much: he seemed more interested in blowing his own trumpet than in working to improve things at the University – an impression which was to strengthen later, when not long after being elected Vice-rector, he left the University to take up a Popular Unity Government post in DIRINCO[8], and later a top job as *Intendente* (governor) of Santiago.

So after a few weeks campaigning, Ricardo and Julio Stuardo were duly elected, and a new Governing Council too, which would be the new authorities of the University. Ricardo now moved into a spacious office overlooking the main square, and had a secretary, *Doña* Marta, a middle-aged lady who had long worked at the *sede*. *Doña* Marta terrified everybody but certainly made sure that no one would pass the Secretary-General's threshold unless they had a legitimate reason for doing so.

One of the priorities Ricardo began to push for was to obtain suitable premises for our University in the province of Ñuble. The accommodation then rented by the University was woefully inadequate, and growing numbers of students meant that the situation was now at crisis point. Ricardo took it upon himself to do everything possible to solve this problem, and, as we shall see later, he was successful. What is now called Bío-Bío University has its own premises in an attractive campus not far outside Chillán, entirely due to

---

8 Dirección Nacional de Industria y Comercio (National Board for Industry and Commerce).

Ricardo's efforts over two to three years from 1970-73. What was immensely galling to both of us was when, on our first trip back to Chile together in 1998, after all the years of Pinochet's dictatorship, we were taken to see the new University campus in the company of fellow academic and writer, Juan Gabriel Araya, and saw the memorial stone at the entrance dedicated to the former owner of the land, Fernando May, yet no mention anywhere of Ricardo Figueroa, who was the only person who actually campaigned and fought for the premises. It was Ricardo who carried out all the detailed and difficult negotiations with Mr May, who was initially offering to sell the University his country house at an exorbitant price. Ricardo persuaded him to donate much more land than he had originally envisaged, on the basis that the University would also buy the house. Then Ricardo had to hold protracted negotiations with the University authorities at national level to obtain the funding for the new campus.

Of course, it was to be expected that the dictatorship would blot out all the pro-Popular Unity Government people who had worked at the University before September 1973. We all suddenly became non-people, sacked without redress and some of us killed or disappeared, but more on that later. Suffice it to say that one day I want to see a plaque on Bio-Bio University's entrance dedicated to Ricardo Figueroa.

During October 1969, my first autumn (but spring in Chile), we went up into the Andes for a day trip to see a ski championship which one of our students was skiing in. We drove up in our friend Eduardo's car, and other friends hired a bus, which took us up to a point where we had to leave the vehicles behind and walk.

We were ill-equipped for walking in the snow. I had ordinary winter boots on, and most people were wearing shoes, and it seemed a long way to get to where the ski championships were being held. After a couple of hours' stiff walk, we arrived, freezing cold, to see the very end of the skiing. But the party was only just beginning. In the bus which had taken us from Chillán up to the mountains as far as the road went, there had been a sheep, which I now realised was there to be slaughtered. We were going to have a Chilean *asado*, or open-air roast.

I've heard that some Chileans, after cutting the throat of the unfortunate animal, catch the blood in a bowl, mix it with chilli pepper, garlic, salt and pepper and then drink it. It is supposed to be extremely invigorating. Fortunately on this occasion no one did that, but the poor animal was butchered and an hour or so later, mutton ribs were slowly roasting on an open fire, the sun warm on our faces amid the purest white snow you ever saw.

Perhaps because I didn't actually see the sheep being killed, and because I was cold and exhausted from the long climb up, I tucked in to the meal and ate as heartily as the rest. And of course it was accompanied with copious amounts of *pipeño*, or new wine, of the region.

We were all enjoying the jokes and chatter when all of a sudden a swirl of mist came down and enveloped us. I have never seen anything so quick or so frightening. Where just a few moments before, we had all been sitting in a circle laughing and talking, now voices were muffled, you couldn't see a metre ahead of you and you didn't know where you were.

Eduardo, born organiser that he is, bellowed to everybody to keep close, and he and the skier friend who knew the mountains well led us all to safety to a nearby refuge, where we waited until the mist cleared and we were able to start the descent.

It was pretty scary, and I was well aware that the outcome could have been very different. After we got back to Chillán and to Eduardo's house, we were able to laugh it all off, but it had been quite a fright for his wife, Maruja, who had taken their six-year old boy, Toti, on the excursion, and Eduardo's father, who had also been with us. What would have happened if the mist hadn't cleared? None of us was equipped for the cold, if we had had to spend the night in that wooden refuge, which was little more than a hut.

It never failed to surprise me that the majority of people we met in Chillán never went up the Andes mountains, or, as they put it "to the snow", despite the fact that the mountains are clearly visible from the city. Apart from a few people – invariably, the rich – who went skiing, no one else ever seemed to go. Even though Chillán was famous, even then, for its *termas* (thermal waters), very few people we knew ever went there. It must be remembered that at that time only a minority of people owned a car, and tourism was not at all well developed. In the five years I lived in Chile, the occasion I describe above was the only time I saw the *termas*, passing them as we drove further up the mountains. I remember the strong sulphurous smell, the yellow-brown colour of the boulders and rocks and the clouds of steam all around. It was only much, much later, on a return visit to Chile in 2006 that we bathed for the first time in the thermal pools there, enjoying the delights of being immersed in the natural hot water in the open air, surrounded by the stunning scenery of the Andes mountains.

Everything was new and strange that first year in Chile. I discovered that the first of November, for instance, was the "Day of the Dead", or All Saints' Day, when people go to the local cemetery to honour the dead. Chillán has a large cemetery with lovely old yew and pine trees, and there are many high walls with niches in them, each bearing the inscription and, inside, the ashes, of the deceased.

Outside the cemetery there were a few skinny street children and women with thin babies in their arms, begging. There were flower-sellers too, offering visitors flowers to put in the niches or on the graves of those who had tombstones. I was surprised that it just seemed like a day out, with people dressed up in their best, whole families flocking there to visit their deceased relatives and friends.

One day my friend Eliana Solís and her sister Zita came to tell me that their mother had died. She had been suffering from cancer for some months. They invited me to the wake, which would last for several days. I had never been to a wake before, it not being part of English tradition, though I had read of wakes in Irish literature. I found it a very sad and mournful occasion. The coffin was open, placed on a table to one side of the room, and people were sitting all round the edges of the room looking solemn and not talking. I didn't know what one was supposed to do, approach the coffin, look at the deceased, or what. I simply sat down and observed the other people coming in. They went up to the open coffin, kissed the corpse and then crossed themselves before sitting down or going over to give condolences to the two daughters. They were very composed and brave, I thought. Perhaps their mother's illness had given them time to get used to the fact that she would not last out the year.

My first Christmas in Chile, December 1969, was quite a strange affair. It was boiling hot, the sun shone with its usual ferocity and Christmas trees with cotton wool on the branches looked somewhat incongruous. Ricardo felt he had to spend that first Christmas with his children in Temuco, and I agreed with him, of course, though I knew it would be hard for me. Luckily, a colleague from the University, Fernando Guajardo, invited me to spend Christmas Day and Boxing Day with him and his family who lived in the countryside in San Carlos, near Chillán. He had also invited another young couple who were recently arrived from the extreme north of Chile and had no family in Chillán, so it was quite a pleasant Christmas, but not at all Christmassy.

I couldn't help but notice, however, that the family's maid was working non-stop during the couple of days that we were there. I presume she would have had time off in lieu on another occasion, but while we were there she made us all breakfast, cooked three-course lunch, *onces* (afternoon tea) and a cooked evening meal, all pretty much on her own.

I found it difficult to accept that progressive, left-wing people could have maids and find that quite natural. Yet that was the case among all our University colleagues and friends, who all had maids. Most of them were girls from the countryside, with little education and from poor backgrounds. Most of them lived in the same house as their employers, in little rooms near the kitchen, often with their own toilet and shower. Sometimes, as in the case of Eduardo and Maruja, their maid nearly always ate with the family, went on holiday and on outings with them. In other cases the maid would serve the meals, take away the plates and then retire to her own room.

One of our friends explained to me that in a country where there is great poverty, especially in the countryside, and little employment, people like teachers, lawyers, doctors and University lecturers were actually doing a service to those young girls, because otherwise they would live in even worse poverty and not be able to help their parents or their own child, if they were single mothers.

It never seemed right to me, but I came to the conclusion that it was the system that was at fault, and that the agrarian reforms which were in the Popular Unity programme would start to make the situation better for Chile's rural poor. For it was obvious as you drove through the countryside that poverty and under-development were everywhere.

The Socialist Party and the Communist Party formed an alliance to back a united candidate in the 1970 presidential elections. Talks were held with other smaller parties with the idea of forming a broad alliance, which would be called Popular Unity, to form the next Government. There were realistic hopes of winning the forthcoming elections, since the Socialist Party's candidate, Salvador Allende, had obtained 38.6% in the 1964 elections, and this time the Christian Democrats, who in 1964 had won outright with 55.6%, would not have the advantage of being a fresh face with newly-coined slogans like "Revolution in Liberty". After six years, the people of Chile could see that there hadn't been, and wouldn't be under the Christian Democrats, any kind of revolution. The acute problems of poverty and under-development were the same as they were before, if not worse.

At first the different parties which had agreed to form the new electoral coalition each declared their own candidates for the Presidency, with the idea that out of these candidates would emerge the one who was best suited to be the united candidate to take on Frei and the Chilean Right, i.e. the National Party, under Jorge Alessandri.

So by the end of 1969 several Popular Unity presidential pre-candidates had already been declared. The Communist Party's pre-candidate was the famous poet Pablo Neruda, who would later be awarded the Nobel Prize for Literature. We all knew that he was not likely to come out as the coalition's preferred candidate. Salvador Allende had a headstart, having stood in the previous three elections (1952, 1958 and 1964), and being from the biggest party in the bloc. And though Neruda bore his duties as a candidate honourably enough, for the sake of the Party, we all knew that he would have been the last person to wish for the Presidency of the Republic. He was a poet, not a politician.

A poet friend of ours at the University, Sergio Hernández – himself born and bred in Chillán – was fond of relating how once during this campaign of the pre-candidates for President he had been to see Neruda after a packed public meeting. Dozens of people were thrusting forward towards the poet-candidate to ask for his autograph and Neruda, finding himself suddenly surrounded, pushed and shoved by masses of people, shouted over to our friend nearby, "Aaagh, *Flaco,* get me out of here in a helicopter, let's go and eat *centollas* (crabs)!" ("*Flaco*" – skinny – is a nickname for thin people in Chile).

Chileans love nicknames: all our friends and colleagues seemed to have their own names and a nickname by which they were more commonly called. Our poet friend was *El Flaco,* our Mayor friend was *El Gordo* (fatty) simply because he had a round full face, I was *la Gringa,* Ricardo, because of his dark skin, was *El Negro,* another colleague whose features were a little oriental was *El Chino,* and so on.

A lot of fair-haired or fair-skinned people were called "*gringo*" or "*gringa*". Someone explained to me that the term had originated with English sailors in Valparaiso heard singing "Green Grow the Rushes, O", where the words "Green grow" are repeated every chorus, and so the Chileans had cottoned on to that refrain to refer to the English. Sometimes the term was affectionate, as most of the nicknames I heard people use seemed to be, and I certainly felt people's affection when I was called *gringa,* or, more commonly *gringuita* – but the word was also used in a pejorative sense when Chileans referred to the Americans of the United States as *gringos*; that negative connotation was common in many countries of Latin America at that time, and still is today. *Los gringos del norte* is a term of abuse for the United States.

Only once did I suffer the term *gringa* as a term of abuse directed to me. I had been living in Chile over two years by that time and knew a fair bit about local prices and Chilean ways. I took a taxi home from the town centre because I was carrying a heavy tape-recorder, and when the taxi-driver, whose taxi had no meter of any kind, told me the price, I contested it, knowing it was way above the normal. He must have thought I was a tourist, not a long-term resident, I suppose. Having paid what I knew to be the right price, I heard the driver snarl "*gringa de mierda*" under his breath as I got out of the cab!

Because Ricardo was so involved with the University Reform and the elections, we would often miss our *pensión* evening meal, and so sometimes we would go straight from the University to a café in town and have what they called a "*pichanga*". This was a big plate set in the middle of the table, with square chunks of cold cooked pig's hock, boiled in the way the Germans do, and with cubes of cheese, and olives and pickles, together with bread and butter and, of course, good Chilean red wine. In the company of whatever friends we happened to be with, we would all pick at this *pichanga* until we'd had our fill. We had great fun, relaxing in this way with friends over a simple, late-night meal, after the tensions of the day, and in this way, my Spanish improved by leaps and bounds and I was soon able to hold my own with repartee and funny comments.

Life with Ricardo was fun. I had never been so happy as during those years. We were incredibly busy, both with academic work, the University Reform, me learning the language, Ricardo's family commitments, teaching Russian in our spare time, and following the political process going on around the time of Allende's election – but it was all invigorating, interesting and in the company of great friends, many of whom are still close friends today over 40 years later.

As I said earlier, Chile's great poet, Pablo Neruda, was the Communist Party's pre-candidate for the presidential elections in September, 1970, and all the other parties which comprised Popular Unity each declared candidates of their own, knowing that the coalition would later choose the most likely candidate to succeed as President out of them all. The Socialist Party's candidate was Salvador Allende, a doctor by profession and an experienced politician who had gained nearly 39% in the presidential election last time round in 1964. Allende was not an immediately charismatic character: he had none of the glamour of a Che Guevara, or the charisma or strength of personality of a Fidel. He was portly, bespectacled and ordinary-looking. But he was consistent, he had fought several elections, was a well-known Senator in the Congress and was a forceful and eloquent public speaker. Though not exactly prepossessing in looks, he was given to wearing natty polo-necked sweaters and suede jackets, which made him seem more modern and less hide-bound by tradition than the tie-and-suited Christian Democrats and members of the right-wing National Party. He had a huge following among the masses, reflecting both the strength of the Socialist Party itself and his personal following as someone who had consistently over three decades been on the side of the poor and dispossessed.

During the weeks when the different parties were campaigning on behalf of their individual candidates, Allende came to Chillán where a big fund-raising dinner was held for him. We sat close to him, at the front table, since Ricardo was by then Secretary-General of the University, and I was struck by his forceful, passionate even, speech outlining his vision for Chile's future, later encompassed in Popular Unity's Basic Programme, a programme "towards socialism" in Chile. He came over as an immensely capable, deeply committed man, and quite charming on a personal level. It was the only time

I ever met Allende in person, but he made a deep impression on me at that dinner. Less than four years later I was not surprised that he, as the legitimate President of Chile, remained in the Moneda Palace on that fateful day of 11 September 1973 during the treacherous coup d'etat that deposed him, preferring to die than to seek ignominious exile under any arrangement offered by the traitor Generals.

Neruda, the Communist Party's pre-candidate, was quite a contrast to Allende. Whereas Allende was grave, with a slight air of self-importance, Neruda was unconventional and refreshingly unpolitical, a poet whose commitment to Chile's working people was shown more in his poetry than in anything else he could do. He wasn't a bad speaker, but it was clear from our friends who knew him that he would rather have been anywhere else than giving a speech to a packed hall. But you couldn't help but admire his commitment, shouldering the task his Party had requested of him.

I had long been a great admirer of Pablo Neruda. I had first heard his poetry long before I met Ricardo, when he came to London in July 1967 and gave a recital at the Queen Elizabeth Hall on the South Bank. I was living in London at the time and often went to events staged there, so my first acquaintance with Neruda's poetry was more or less fortuitous, since I did not speak Spanish or have any particular interest in Latin America at the time. But I recall being absolutely bowled over by his poetry, recited by Neruda himself[9]. I remember being especially moved by his "*España en el Corazon*". Since childhood I had heard a lot about the Spanish Civil War from my parents and had read the poetry of English poets like John Cornford, who had died in Spain fighting as part of the International Brigade in 1936:

> Heart of the heartless world,
> Dear heart, the thought of you
>   Is the pain at my side,
> The shadow that chills my view.
>
> The wind that rises in the evening,
> Reminds that autumn is near
>   I am afraid to lose you,
>   I am afraid of my fear.
>
> On the last mile to Huesca,
> The last fence for our pride,
> Think so kindly, dear, that I
>   Sense you at my side.

---

[9] In that Neruda recital, which was part of the South Bank's Poetry International 1967, translations were read by Ted Hughes and Patrick Wymark.

And if bad luck should lay my strength
   Into the shallow grave,
   Remember all the good you can;
   Don't forget my love.

(Huesca[10], by John Cornford)

Neruda's *España en el Corazon* moved me immensely. The outrage at the injustice of Franco's vicious onslaught against Spain's legitimate Republican Government is still keenly felt today. That sense of outrage at injustice - when the world's powerful classes repeatedly crush attempts by common peoples struggling for a better life - has stayed with me all my life.

Later when I had learned Spanish and was able to read and understand Neruda in the original it was a double pleasure. I had always admired the subject-matter, but now I could appreciate the wonderful humanism and poeticism of his great works such as *Canto General* and *Residencia en la Tierra*.

Man was earth, a vessel, the eyelid
Of the quivering clay, a shape of potter's earth,
Carib spout, Chibcha stone,
Imperial cup or Araucanian silica:
He was gentle and bloody, but on the hilt
Of his wetted glass weapon
The earth's initials were
Written.
     No one
Could later recall them: the wind
Forgot, the water's idiom
Was buried, the code was lost
Or inundated by silence or blood.

(from *Canto General*)

So when, three or so years later, I found myself in Chile, I followed Neruda's campaign with great interest. It was an impressive sight to see thousands of people standing silently in the street listening to Neruda reciting his poetry at the end of his rallies, most of them poor people, in *ponchos* and sandals made out of rubber from old tyres. I have heard friends say they didn't like the way Neruda recited in that sing-song way of his, but I have always loved it. Ricardo had several LP's of him reading his poetry, and I used to listen to them for hours on end, drinking in the musicality of the verse.

---

[10] During the Spanish Civil War (1936-39) the "Huesca Front" was the scene of some of the worst fighting between the Republicans and Franco's army.

In February 1970, during the first long summer holidays since his separation, Ricardo took his children camping by Todos los Santos lake in the south of Chile where his parents lived, whilst I went to Concepción to stay with Luís and Nidia Bocaz. Luís was a lecturer in French literature at the prestigious University of Concepción and Nidia was a psychologist, though at the time she didn't work. They had been to see us a couple of times during the previous months and I had got on very well with them. The three of us enjoyed talking and discussing politics, and it was a good opportunity to see something of a big city after being in Chillán for so long.

When Ricardo returned, we spent a few days together with Luís and Nidia, then he and I went north to the popular coastal resort of Viña del Mar for a few days. I didn't particularly like Viña, much preferring the wild, unspoilt beaches and resorts of the coastal area to the west of Chillán, such as Dichato, Penco or Lirquén. These places were completely uncommercialised, and yet you could easily find a simple restaurant serving the most wonderful fresh seafood, both shellfish and fish. They were uncrowded and beautiful, with cliffs, rocks and big expanses of golden or grey sand over which the giant white-topped waves of the Pacific would come crashing in.

On 22 January 1970 the six parties which would make up the Popular Unity coalition chose the single candidate who would run for President of Chile in the September 1970 elections, and that was, as expected, Dr. Salvador Allende. The coalition was formed by the two big parties of the Left, namely, Allende's own Socialist Party and the Communist Party, plus the Radical Party, which was an old centrist or left-of-centre party and one which was largely secular, having many freemasons in its ranks. Then there were three newer, much smaller parties, the MAPU (Movement of United Popular Action), which was a left-wing breakaway from the governing Christian Democrats, the Social-Democratic Party and another called Independent Popular Action.

The objective of all the six parties comprising the Popular Unity, as expressed in its Basic Programme, was a socialist society:

> "The united forces of the people seek as the main objective of their policy to replace the present economic structure by putting an end to the power of national and foreign monopoly capital and the *latifundio*, in order to begin the building of socialism."

The Programme promised to "transform Chile's institutions to establish a new State where the workers and the people really exercise power."

> "In Chile the "reformist" and "development" recipes put forward by the Alliance for Progress and adopted by the government of Frei have not managed to change anything important. In the main it was a new

45

government of the bourgeoisie at the service of national and foreign capitalism, whose weak attempts at social change floundered ignominiously amidst economic stagnation, high cost of living and violent repression of the people. With this it has once again been demonstrated that *reformism is incapable of solving the people's problems.*" (My emphasis) (From the Programme of the Popular Unity Government)

Once Allende was declared as Popular Unity's candidate, the campaign really started to move into top gear. There was a palpable fervour throughout the country, with mass meetings, huge demonstrations and big, colourful murals appearing overnight on walls up and down the country. These murals, painted by the *Ramona Parra* brigades (named after a young communist killed on a demonstration in 1946) depicted the struggle of the working people for a better life. They included political slogans, they were colourful, cheerful and quite artistic and did much to brighten up the shanty-towns and run-down parts of cities. Later, incidentally, in exile in Italy after the coup d'etat, muralists from the Ramona Parra Brigades were invited by the town council of Bologna to paint murals in various locations thereabouts.

Our closest friend at this time – 1969 and 1970 – was Eduardo Contreras, the only Communist councillor on Chillán's Council. Young and dynamic, Eduardo was never happier than when he had a hundred things to do at the same time. He would call for us in his little white Fiat 600 (which had a sticker in the back: "Virginity causes cancer – get vaccinated!") and together with his wife Maruja we would go off to have dinner at a local *peña* in the surrounding countryside. But before we would get there, Eduardo would call in at X or Y's house – he just *had* to sort something out, or tie up a loose end here or there, or arrange a meeting, or see to it that somebody was doing whatever they had promised. Sometimes we would sit there in the car for 15 or 20 minutes while he did his bits of business, then he would appear, happy and cheerful, get in the driving seat and drive off as if it was the most normal thing in the world.

He talked at an alarming (for me, as someone still learning the language) rate – he still is the fastest talker I have ever met – but he was great fun to be with, always full of amusing stories and anecdotes from the local political life of the city. He knew everybody, and everybody knew him, and he was held in great esteem, certainly by people on the Left, but also by many others too, as a true-born *chillanejo* (person born and bred in Chillán) and as an excellent lawyer with a well-established law firm in the city. *Chillanejos* are very proud of their city, and often like to claim that most of Chile's famous people come from Chillán: it was the birthplace of Bernardo O'Higgins, founding father of modern Chile after independence from Spain in 1818, and of the world-famous opera singer Ramón Vinay, the renowned classical pianist Claudio

Arrau and well-known Chilean sculptor Marta Colvin; some claim famous folk-singer Violeta Parra as a *chillaneja*, though she was actually born in nearby San Carlos, and some even claim Pablo Neruda, because he hailed from nearby Parral!

One time Eduardo and Maruja had called for us in their car, and on the way out of the city, Eduardo stopped to call in on a friend, a man who was a *chillanejo* born and bred. Eduardo wanted to introduce us to him, so we all got out of the car. We were immediately invited in, and ushered into the dining room, where a large number of guests were seated around a long dining-table. Our host would not hear of us not joining them for a meal, as they were just beginning their dinner. I protested, in the polite English way, that we had not long since eaten, and no, we couldn't possibly stay. It was true that we had had dinner, but it was clear that whatever we had said would not have made the slightest difference: chairs were brought in, everybody squeezed up a little, and the four of us found ourselves being served a full-course Chilean dinner.

I discovered that this sort of hospitality was very common in Chile. Chileans pride themselves on it, and always seem to make more food than what is needed just in case someone drops in unexpectedly. That evening, as we got talking to these new friends, I discovered that the man of the house belonged to Chillán's Tennis Club, so I arranged there and then to play tennis with him. Tennis was not at all a popular sport in Chile at that time, no one else I met knew how to play, and tennis clubs seemed to be exclusively for the rich or upper middle class people. I was not particularly good at tennis (at school I had been in the rounders team) but at least I knew how to play, and could give him a proper game.

When Eduardo became Mayor, one of the initiatives he had was to invite Chile's leading muralist painter, Julio Escámez, to paint a mural on the vast wall of the Town Hall's entrance hall. Julio normally lived in Santiago but now for months on end he camped out in Chillán's Town Hall where he worked day and night on his mural. Escámez was a painter in the great muralist tradition of Mexican muralists Diego Rivera and David Siquieros. In fact one of Chillán's schools, the *Escuela México*, has a huge mural painted by Siquieros in 1941. We would often go and see Julio and marvel at his mural, titled *"Principio y Fin"* (Beginning and End) as it was taking shape. It was full of both realistic and somewhat grotesque figures, intertwining shapes and motifs from Chile's history and present struggles.

Julio was a great character. He was a skilled raconteur, telling the most incredible stories at great length, with many humorous episodes and usually an unforeseen climax. I remember one such story he told about a couple of lovers who had gone to the cinema and found themselves trapped there by the great earthquake of Chillán in 1939. The young man, leading his lover by

47

the hand, goes through all sorts of incredible feats to get out of the destroyed cinema, rubble and bodies all around, and eventually makes it to the outside, turns round to his lover whom he has been leading by the hand all this time, only to discover that it is nothing but a bodiless hand that he has been clasping. Gruesome, but told in such a way that Julio would always have us holding our sides laughing.

One day Ricardo and I went with Julio and a University colleague of ours, Olivia Concha, to Coliumo, a coastal village in the area Julio was originally from, near Concepción. The idea was to spend a day at the beach and then have a meal of shellfish prepared by the local fishermen. We got there, and Julio went off to find a fisherman who could prepare the shellfish for us. When we came back from a walk along the beach, we came back to the little house where we were going to eat, only to discover that the fisherman had turned up with a huge sack of only one type of shellfish called *piure*, a red mollusc tasting of iodine. Though *piures* are reputed to be excellent aphrodisiacs (something none of us, as healthy young people, were in particular need of) what we had really been looking forward to was a variety of shellfish such as you can get in all the markets of Chile, which are delicious washed down with cool local *pipeño* white wine. Julio didn't have the heart to refuse the fisherman, who had caught them specially for us, so we all four of us set to in the attempt to consume this vast quantity of *piures* piled high on an enormous dish in the centre of the modest table. If you've ever tried to eat pure iodine it must taste like these *piures*. After manfully downing six or seven of these strong molluscs, I gave in and confessed I could not manage more. One by one we all succumbed, and were forced to leave the fisherman with most of his sack still untouched. None of us could face a *piure* for months after that.

Julio, who was single, though very attractive to women, took us to see a mural which he had painted in the Maluje Pharmacy in Concepcion, which was called "Homage to Medicine". It depicted butchered animals and a fair quantity of blood, as I remember. It was clear that Julio had a somewhat macabre side to his personality, at least in his artistic visions. Later that same day, he took us to see his parental home, now empty since the death of his mother, and I was surprised to find that her room had been left untouched since the day of her death. All her clothes and shoes were still in the wardrobes, the bed made. I found it deeply sad, but perhaps for Julio it was his way of holding on to someone who had clearly been very dear to him – his mother.

Just as Rivera's great mural painted in New York's Rockefeller Foundation Centre provoked the ire of American big business and was destroyed in 1934[11],

---

11 Mexican muralist Diego Rivera, inspired by Communist ideals and his cultural heritage, painted murals in several municipal buildings of Mexico City. His talent attracted wealthy patrons, including Abby Aldrich

so Julio's wonderful mural, which took him more than a year to complete, was destroyed on the orders of General Augusto Pinochet, after the military coup of 11 September 1973. Like the Mexican muralists David Siquieros and Diego Rivera before him, Julio Escámez too was forced to flee into exile after the coup, living and working for many years in Costa Rica.

After spending a year in the *pensión*, Ricardo and I set about finding a place of our own to rent. We found a little bungalow some four or five blocks from the centre of Chillán and moved there in June 1970. It was lovely to have the freedom to have more space and cook our own meals and spend time together, just the two of us, after having lived in the company of others for over a year. The owner was a middle-aged single woman, who had bought the house for herself, but who had to care for her elderly mother in a rather decrepit old house near the market, and had therefore decided to let it until such time as she were able to live in it herself.

It had four equally-sized small rooms in a square: a living room, a bedroom, a study, a kitchen and a tiny bathroom. It had a back garden, also small, with a little wooden shack along one side of the garden, to serve as a maid's living quarters. This room had an outside toilet and shower, as I was to find out much later. But at the time when we moved in, in the winter of 1970, the landlady kept that shack locked, so we never knew what was inside it.

The white-painted house was on the corner of two streets, Independence Street and Bulnes Street, and about four blocks from the cathedral and the central square of the city. It had parquet floors, which were a real bind to keep clean and polished. Wealthier people had electric machines to polish them, but most people scrubbed them with wire wool, swept off the dirt, then waxed them with wax polish and a cloth. I found the whole thing a waste of time, so we only did the floors when they became so dirty that we couldn't stand to look at them. Since Ricardo and I were both increasingly busy, cleaning floors was not one of our priorities.

Our study was our favourite room. We had a huge desk which was for two people to sit at, facing each other, and ten or so drawers on each side. Ricardo had come across that desk once in some abandoned outbuildings and had bought it for a song. He had then asked his brother Camilo, who was a

---

Rockefeller, who in 1932 convinced her husband, John D. Rockefeller, Jr., to commission a Rivera mural for the lobby of the soon-to-be-completed Rockefeller Center in New York City. Rivera proposed a 63-foot-long portrait of workers facing symbolic crossroads of industry, science, socialism, and capitalism. The fact that in the mural Lenin appeared in a section portraying a May Day parade proved too much for Rockefeller, and the Centre's managers ordered Rivera to remove the offending image. When Rivera refused, offering to balance the work with a portrait of Abraham Lincoln on the opposing side, the managers paid his full fee, barred him from the site, and hid the mural behind a massive drape. Despite negotiations to transfer the work to the Museum of Modern Art and demonstrations by Rivera supporters, near midnight, on February 10th, 1934, Rockefeller Center workmen, carrying axes, demolished the mural. Later, Rivera recreated the frescoes in the Palace of Fine Arts in Mexico City.

furniture restorer, to renovate it, and he had made a lovely job of it. Ricardo had his old English typewriter, and we had another one with a Cyrillic keyboard, which we had brought back from the USSR. We asked an odd-job man from the University to knock us up some bookshelves, and we had one wall entirely of bookshelves, floor to ceiling. We spent most of our time at home in that room and were very happy there among our books and music.

Winters are very cold in Chillán, and at that time people did not have central heating. It was mid-winter when we moved into the house, so we did as most Chileans did at that time, and bought a gas cylinder heater for the living room and a portable black paraffin stove which could be put wherever we needed it. When the gas cylinder ran out, you had to go and buy a new cylinder, exchanging the empty one for a full one. Our first gas cylinder had just run out, so Ricardo had gone out to buy a new one.

When he came back I was in the living room with the paraffin stove on. It was quite smelly and if you had either of these stoves on without an open window you started to get a headache after a while, since they consumed the oxygen in the room and there were no chimneys or flues to take the gases out. Ricardo came into the living room with the new cylinder, and proceeded to exchange the old one, still attached to the gas heater, for the new one. It was the first time either of us had ever done it. All of a sudden, before he could attach the new cylinder, a fierce jet of gas whooshed out and spun the cylinder around the room like a whipping top. I immediately grabbed the paraffin stove and took it out of the room to turn it out. Ricardo meanwhile, desperately trying to master the whizzing cylinder, finally got hold of it with one hand and with the other yanked the window lever to open the window to throw the cylinder out. Instead of opening the window, the entire window and its frame came out in his hand and crashed down on to the living room floor. Ricardo threw the errant cylinder out, its top still spewing out its furious jet of gas, now thankfully in the back garden. I meanwhile went out on to the street to warn any passer-by who might have been smoking, to put out their cigarette to avoid an explosion. Fortunately no one was about.

After the wretched cylinder had exhausted its energy and the danger had passed, we sat down, exhausted and shaking and looked at the shattered window and frame on our living room floor. Suddenly we saw the funny side of it and began to laugh hilariously, giggling anew every time we thought our laughter had subsided. It was just so ridiculous, yet we knew that it could have been so dangerous if there had been a naked flame nearby. Ricardo's face was still pallid with the fright of it and the exhaustion of trying to plug the cylinder top which had burst open and then catch hold of the spinning cylinder. After a while, still feeling shaky with the near escape we knew we'd had, we walked down to a late-night bar some four blocks away and ordered ourselves two stiff drinks, which we drank between renewed bouts of uncontrollable laughter.

By August 1969 the political situation in the country was heating up with every day that passed. One of the big issues was the demand for Chile's huge copper industry to be nationalised. Copper is Chile's main natural resource, it being the world's fourth biggest producer of the mineral, but at the time it was owned by several American companies, among them Anaconda. Its profits from Chilean copper for the two years 1967-68 were $188 million. In the 1964 presidential election, the only parties to have demanded nationalisation of the copper industry had been the Socialist and Communist Parties. The Christian Democrats, who won that election, offered their own version of nationalisation, which they called "chileanisation". But chileanisation did not mean Chilean ownership of the natural resource, a fact revealed in the following statement by the chairman of the Kennecott Corporation, another of the American companies exploiting Chilean copper, which showed clearly where the profits from the industry were going:

> "The profits of Kennecott, in the second quarter of 1967, have been the most sensational in the history of the company, reaching the record sum of $60,232,122, coming mainly from Chilean copper."

One Chilean newspaper quoted an editorial in the New York Times of 29 May 1969 which spoke approvingly of Chile's Christian Democratic President Eduardo Frei, comparing his "chileanisation" with the then Peruvian Junta's outright nationalisation:

> "...the participation of the Government in the basic companies, especially in those on which the economy of a country largely depends, seems to be turning into a familiar formula for Latin America following the precedent of "chileanisation". In spite of all its disadvantages, this formula is much more preferable than the outright expropriation carried out by the Peruvian Junta, and could be the only alternative in a continent of emergent nationalism." (my translation from the Spanish)

By now even the Christian Democratic Party had come out in favour of nationalisation, urged on by its rank-and-file. The weighty Confederation of Copper Workers also came out in support of the demand. The Christian Democrats' slogan in the 1964 election, when they won 55.6% of the vote, was "Everything in Chile must change!" But not enough had changed, and by 1969, with the 1970 elections looming, working people were tired of waiting for an improvement in their lives. Life expectancy was 59, compared with 71 for neighbouring Uruguay. In 1968 infant mortality in the first year of life stood at 86.6 per thousand. One calculation published at the time said that every 36 minutes a child died of hunger in Chile.

Chile's national debt – it was estimated at the time that every Chilean was born "owing" $300 – meant that the cost of living was constantly rising, yet wages and salaries were not keeping pace with inflation, so every waged person and their families felt their standard of living was going down all the time, not up. The dissatisfaction with the Christian Democrats, who had come to power six years earlier promising so much, was tangible, and strikes and sit-ins, *tomas* or seizures of land for squatting, and protest meetings and demonstrations were being held up and down the country.

Living in Chile you couldn't help but see what under-development and third world status meant for the ordinary people. I was horrified when a colleague who taught Chemistry at the University showed me round the science laboratories. As I wrote home at the time:

> "They have got nothing. They are worse equipped than the majority of our secondary school labs, I should say. The Chemistry lecturer told me that very often they have to teach the students the theory of what happens when you carry out a certain experiment, without the students having the chance to find out for themselves, because they simply haven't got the equipment to enable them to carry out any but the most simple experiments."

Added to this, the home situation of our students was far from adequate in terms of study conditions. Most of our students lived in boarding-houses where they slept four or five to a room and often did not even have a table to work at. The University carried out a survey into students' study facilities, which revealed that 75% of them had no proper facilities for study at all. Our University library, by the standards of British university libraries, was woefully inadequate. No wonder some of them failed to do their homework.

Many of our students worked to help finance their studies. One of my students, Gloria Veas, invited me to sit in on her English class at the local girls' secondary school. There were broken windows in the classroom. About 45 girls in the class sat at old-fashioned desks, sometimes three girls sitting at two-seater desks. They had to share textbooks, which were old and tatty. Yet the students were well-behaved and seemed keen to learn.

Thus it was not surprising to me that so many students were increasingly militant and identified with Salvador Allende's presidential election campaign. Once all the six parties that made up the Popular Unity coalition had agreed that Allende should be their sole candidate, all on the Left who wanted a progressive alternative to the ruling Christian Democrats started campaigning throughout the country to get him elected.

There were meetings, outdoor rallies, demonstrations, radio and TV programmes and articles in the press. Often the police used heavy-handed techniques in dealing with the unrest, raiding universities in Santiago and the big cities, bringing out the *Grupo Móvil* (riot police) on any pretext. People were wounded and one man died in such clashes that winter.

Chile celebrates her National Day on 18 September, commemorating Chile's independence from Spain in 1818. For three or four days after the 18th, Chileans organise folkloric *ramadas* with roofs made of fresh green leaves and earthen or wooden floors, typical Chilean *ponchos* and rugs festooning the makeshift walls, and musicians belting out *cumbias*, salsas and, of course, the national dance, the *cueca*.

There is drink aplenty, and people go from one *ramada* to another, dancing and drinking and chatting with friends. Some of the *ramadas* are quite well-built, even though they are temporary structures, dismantled each year as soon as the festivities are over. Typical Chilean pasties, called *empanadas*[12], are served.

I have always loved the *cueca*, ever since I first saw Chileans dance it that time in Moscow in 1963, and then later heard the music, on an old LP record that Ricardo had given as a present to my parents before I went to Chile. It is a dance where the man, often wearing a short striped *poncho* of the Chilean *huaso*, (rural horseman), and heeled boots with spurs, imitates the cock wooing the hen in a courtship dance. The girl wears a flowery summer dress with full skirt and white petticoats showing beneath, and both dancers wave a *pañuelo* (kerchief) above their heads as they dance, enticing each other. It can be a very seductive and erotic affair, though aficionados tell me that it's often not danced as it should be these days.

My most embarrassing moment was in 1969 during the 18th September festivities, when a Chilean acquaintance invited me to dance the *cueca* and simply would not take no for an answer. He dragged me on to the *ramada* floor, and I had to make a stab at doing the dance, which is difficult enough even for most Chileans, let alone an Englishwoman. I felt such a fool, and never forgave him his fun at my expense.

Though lots of people did have a good time at the 18th September *ramadas*, I always found them quite sad affairs, at least in Chillán, because there were always a lot of poor people, many of them drunk and getting into brawls.

Once Ricardo's father came to visit during the Independence celebrations of September 18th. Chillán, where we lived, was half way between where he lived, Puerto Varas in the south, and Santiago, where two of his sons lived,

---

12 *Empanadas* look a bit like a Cornish pasty, but they are filled with finely chopped-up meat in its own sauce, onion, hard-boiled egg, raisins and olives. President Allende once commented that Chile's revolution was "as Chilean as our wine and as tasty as our 18 September *empanadas*."

so he would stay the night with us, before catching the bus the following day to continue his journey to the capital. He was horrified to see, on the eve of the national holiday, that we had no Chilean flag flying from the wall of our bungalow, so he set off early the next morning to buy a flag and flagpole and he made sure that it was up and flapping in the breeze before he left for the next stage of his journey! A retired policeman, for him it was an affront not to have the national flag flying on Independence Day.

A month later, on 21 October 1969, there was an attempted coup d'etat in Chile, led by a General Viaux. His regiment, the Tacna regiment, planned to overthrow the Constitution and install military rule. He took advantage of the discontent in the ranks due to stagnant wages and the climate of fear which had been whipped up in the preceding months by the National Party and the Right in Chile. These right-wing sectors were called the "*momios*" (mummies) by those on the Left, and at demonstrations you would often hear the chant "*El que no salta es momio!*" ("If you don't jump you're a mummy!") accompanied by everyone starting to jump up and down repeatedly for minutes on end.

At the news of General Viaux's attempted coup, the Chilean trade unions, organised in the *Central Unica de Trabajadores* (CUT, something like the British TUC, but considerably more militant) called a national strike and there were spontaneous demonstrations on the streets against the coup attempt. The Christian Democratic Government interpreted the people's coming out on to the streets in defence of democracy and the occupation of factories as the people showing support for their Government. Whatever it in fact demonstrated, the fact is that the coup failed, and General Viaux was forced into retirement.

A year later, though, the same General Viaux was involved in another coup attempt, this time in an attempt to prevent the newly elected President, Salvador Allende, from being ratified by Congress. On this occasion, on 22 October 1970, Viaux's coup-plotters ambushed the constitutionalist Army Commander-in-chief General René Schneider, who was adamantly opposed to any coup, and shot him point-blank several times. He died three days later. General Viaux was later convicted of complicity in the plot and imprisoned. Several years later, Ricardo found out that one of his former students at the German Sankt Thomas Morus Deutsche Schule had been involved in this coup attempt.

As recently-elected Secretary-General of the University in Chillán, the second highest authority after Vice-rector, Ricardo was extremely busy dealing with most of the day-to-day problems of the University. And there were many problems. The main one was that the university did not have a campus of its

Sixth-former at
St. Helena School
for Girls, Chesterfield

The banner I painted
to carry on
Aldermaston march

The ICI Central Research Laboratory in Runcorn, where I had
my first job after graduating

Ricardo (extreme left) next to our vet friend, Chepo Sepúlveda, with
dancers from the Jok Moldovan dance ensemble, Chillán, 1969

Just before leaving for Chile, March 1969

Ricardo and Kate in 1968

Our first home together in Chillán, June 1970

Kate with our first car, a Fiat 600, in 1971

Picnic with our friends Edith Miranda (middle) and Juan Gabriel Araya and his wife Maruja (on right of picture)

On a day trip to Dichato, on the coast, in summer 1969

In Constitución, on holiday with our friends Eduardo and Maruja Contreras and their son Toti, January 1971

Ricardo with our friends, Chillán's Mayor, Ricardo Lagos (left) and wife, Victoria, and others

EN EL GRABADO: Salvador Allende cuando visitó la sede regional de la Universidad de Chile en Chillán, en plena campaña presidencial. Además aparecen de izquierda a derecha, Alejandro Witker V., Director del Servicio Central de Extensión y Acción Social; Eduardo Osorio, Presidente de FECH; Julio Stuardo G., Vice-Rector; Ricardo Figueroa F., Secretario General y Mario Mora A., Jefe Administrativo.

Newspaper photo of the Socialist Party's presidential candidate, Salvador Allende, on a campaign visit to our University in late 1969. Ricardo is on Allende's right, next to Vice-rector, Julio Stuardo

Our University main entrance, festooned with the campaign banners for Ricardo Figueroa as Secretary-General and Julio Stuardo as Vice-rector. The banner reads: "For a New University!"

Our University choir singing at Concepción stadium, on the occasion of Fidel Castro's 1971 visit. Choir conductor, Olivia Concha, on extreme right of picture

President Salvador Allende with Cuban President Fidel Castro, on his visit to Chile in November 1971

Packed Concepción stadium listening to Fidel's speech, November 1971

Ricardo (extreme right) at a 1971 Literary Festival organised by the University, with (from right to left) poets Omar Lara, Jorge Tellier (standing) and Sergio Hernández. Hispanic Studies colleagues Francisco Torres and Juan Gabriel Araya, with his wife Maruja, are standing (from left to right)

Ricardo at the coast, 1970

Above: Ricardo and Kate on a day trip to coastal village of Penco, 1970

Poli Délano, Chilean writer and friend of many years

Right-Left: Ricardo with our friends – mathematician and chess champion, Roberto Aravire, and painter/muralist Julio Escámez. Julio's great mural in Chillán's Town Hall was destroyed by order of the military Junta in September 1973

Quinchamalí pottery

Chillán Socialists on a demonstration in 1971. Mayor Ricardo Lagos, later murdered after the coup, second from right of picture, next to fellow councillor Dr Isidoro Tohá (extreme right of picture), brother of Allende's Interior Minister, José Tohá, who died as a result of torture in March 1974

A *guitarrera*, typical of the folk pottery of Quinchamalí near Chillán

Typical *cazuela* – a hearty soup made with chicken, lamb or beef

Some of the many low-priced books of Chilean and international literature published by the Quimantú state publishing house

Demonstration in support of Salvador Allende

1972 Popular Unity demonstration, Santiago

The mural *Principio y Fin* (Beginning and End) by Julio Escámez, on the main wall of Chillán Town Hall, at its inauguration in August 1972. Speaking: President Salvador Allende, with Mayor Ricardo Lagos on his right and councillor Eduardo Contreras to his left, next to fellow councillor Isidoro Tohá own, and that the halls of residence for students from outside Chillán were inadequate.

Despite all the problems, classes were held according to timetable, students did their work, exams were held and marked in the normal way, and students got their degrees. It was something of a miracle, considering the circumstances. As one of the most conscientious lecturers, I was put in charge of organising a Language Laboratory for the Department of Languages. I did some research and got the University to buy a Language Lab, consisting of some ten machines, from Akai, a Japanese firm. We had soundproofed booths built round the individual machines, and students were able to go to the Lab both as part of their classes and during their free time to listen to tapes with repetition exercises I had made. It was a great advance on anything they had had before, and was much appreciated by students and staff alike.

I chose one of my fourth year students, María Inés Sandoval, as Language Laboratory assistant. She was a very hard-working student, quiet and unassuming but with a good level of English. Ricardo used to joke that the only reason I had selected María Inés was that she was even smaller than me! It's true that she was tiny, even less than my five feet.

María Inés was a devout Catholic. She once invited me to tea at her *pensión* and had invited her priest to come along and meet me. It was a very old-fashioned room, with lots of lace and frills, dark and gloomy. We had a very polite and formal conversation over tea poured from the best china teapot, and delicate little sandwiches and biscuits. It was like stepping back into the previous century for a couple of hours.

Perhaps because of my success in getting the Language Laboratory up and running, I was later elected Head of the Department of Languages by the other members of staff. The person who had been departmental head when we first arrived, Hugo Pizarro, had left the *sede* to return to Santiago by this time. I did not really relish such a job, since it meant more hours working for no extra pay or rewards, but I took it on as a commitment to the students, since I knew that a more efficient running of the entire Department would benefit them.

Though there was little time, since Ricardo was extremely busy in his new post and my workload was much increased too, now that I was speaking the language fluently and could play as active a part as the other members of staff, we still managed to have some wonderful times together at weekends.

By 1970, the political situation in Chile was quite tense. Dissatisfaction with the Christian Democratic government of President Eduardo Frei was widespread, there were demonstrations and squats, police putting down demonstrators with riot gear and tear-gas, and everyone was preparing for the forthcoming battle for the Presidential elections due to take place on 4 September 1970.

University and school students were becoming increasingly militant, as this extract from my letter home of 3 July 1970 shows:

"On Monday there were incidents again at the University, similar to those of last year when Ricardo got his leg hit with a tear-gas bomb. Last Friday, during a peaceful demonstration of students in Santiago supporting a strike of workers and employees of the Ministry of Education, the Police used tear-gas and guns, with the result that one student was killed, shot in the chest with a bullet, which all the witnesses say was certainly from a policeman's gun, but which the Christian Democrats are trying to prove came from a gun which was not carried by a policeman...

"The (protest demonstration) in Chillán was peaceful, and quite successful until the very end of the demo, when a small group of secondary school students split off from the main columns and started collecting stones and throwing them at the police who were standing in the Square opposite the University building. This same group dragged the metal seats which adorn the Square on to the road which runs along the University, and built a barricade at one end. All this was open provocation, quite unnecessary, and harmful, of course, to the main purpose of the demonstration. So, of course, as expected, the police "opened fire" with tear-gas, throwing the first bomb in the direction of the students who were throwing stones from the entrance to the University...

"Ricardo meanwhile was telephoning the *Intendente* (provincial governor) to try and get him to order his men to stop the bombardment of the University and withdraw the policemen from the Square, on the grounds that, if they withdrew, there would be no one for the students to be throwing stones at, and therefore there would be peace again...

"The teachers decided to form a group and go and see the *Intendente*, whose offices are on one side of the Square, since it was impossible to do anything by phone. So we decided to go out by a back entrance of the University, to get to which you have to pass through a sort of open yard. So we ran down to the ground floor, and from then on I honestly can't tell you where we went, because I couldn't see a thing, blinded as I was by the gas-saturated atmosphere. It was terrible, really. Ricardo dragged me along as quickly as possible – he seemed able to resist the stuff much better than I was – but when we came to this open yard, it was really unbreathable. Everybody was coughing and spluttering and trying to get their breath. I felt desperate because I couldn't seem to breathe, and all your skin feels as if it's on fire, and your eyes too seem to burn, so that you can't open them..."

It was my second experience of tear-gas, and was no easier to bear than the first time. I suppose students everywhere tend to be more militant than adults, but sometimes their militancy seemed directed at the very University authorities who were trying to improve the lot of the students, instead of at the Christian Democratic Government, which was responsible for university and schools funding.

As I've said earlier, the Left's presidential candidate for the forthcoming September 1970 presidential elections was Dr Salvador Allende. The presidential candidate of the Right was Jorge Alessandri. He was the son of a former President of Chile, Arturo Alessandri, and had himself been the country's president from 1958 to 1964. During that presidency Chile suffered a big earthquake in 1960, which killed nearly 350 people in the Concepción area, and coalminers of that region went on strike demanding new homes and a wage increase, as they had suffered greatly due to the earthquake. Alessandri refused to discuss the miners' demands, and their strike lasted several months until they finally won the battle.

The miners of the Lota-Schwager company were the most militant in Chile. I went to see how they lived and was shocked at what I saw there. Lota is on the coast, and the mines are deep under the Pacific. We first went to the beautiful Isidora Cousiño park high up on the cliffs above the sea, walking among the many exotic species of plants and trees there and admiring the stunning views of the azure ocean from the cliff-tops. Then we made our way down to the town where the miners and their families live, which was like entering a different world. Blocks of shoddy flats and squalid terraced rows of tiny houses lined the streets close to the pithead. The bigger houses of the managerial and white-collar staff were further away and had neat little gardens.

Lota was a Communist Party stronghold, and given the history of Alessandri's refusal to meet their demands during their long strike after the 1960 earthquake, there was little or no support among the miners for Alessandri's candidature in the September 1970 presidential elections. He was met there by huge demonstrations. The miners and their families wouldn't let him speak, fights broke out and tear-gas was used as the police arrested some of the demonstrators.

Salvador Allende's presidential campaign, in contrast, was going very well in all working-class areas. When Allende came to Chillán, for instance, on his campaign tour, about 20,000 people went to hear him speak in front of the

Town Hall. From the third floor of the University building close by you could see people in whichever direction you looked, and traffic had to be diverted from all the central streets.

In the presidential election of 4 September 1970, I didn't have a vote, being a foreigner. Ricardo went off to Temuco where he was still registered to vote, and I stayed in Chillán, with a terrible cold that quickly developed into flu. We had no phone, and I felt so ill, and knew I was running a high temperature, that I took the desperate measure (since we had no telephone) of calling from our front door to a passer-by and asking him to take a message for me to Eliana Solís, my friend who lived a couple of blocks away, in which I asked her to call a doctor for me. A doctor duly came, gave me something to bring my temperature down and before leaving asked for his payment! I still remember the shock of discovering what it is like to live in a system where there is no National Health Service, and where you pay the doctor for each visit, unless you are on some scheme or other through your place of work. I didn't have enough money in the house to pay the doctor, but fortunately, he took me on trust and we agreed I would settle up once Ricardo got back.

While I was sweating out the flu, the country was for the first time ever voting in a socialist President. With 36.6%, Allende was the clear winner, against 28.1% for the Christian Democratic candidate, Radomiro Tomic, and 35.27% for the right-wing National Party's candidate, Jorge Alessandri.

Candidate	Party/Coalition	Votes	% of Total
Salvador Allende Gossens	Popular Unity (UP)	1,070,334	36.6%
Jorge Alessandri Rodríguez	National Party	1,031,159	35.3%
Radomiro Tomic	Christian Democratic Party	821,801	28.1%
Total valid votes		2,923,294	

But, since Allende had not won an outright majority, he still had to pass the hurdle of being ratified by the Chilean Congress, which gave the Right and the American CIA a little more space for manoeuvre:

> "Since no candidate had received a majority of the popular vote, the Chilean Constitution required that a joint session of its Congress decide between the first- and second-place finishers. The date set for the congressional session was October 24, 1970.

The reaction in Washington to Allende's plurality victory was immediate. The 40 Committee met on September 8 and September 14 to discuss what action should be taken prior to the October 24 congressional vote. On September 15, President Nixon informed CIA Director Richard Helms that an Allende regime in Chile would not be acceptable to the United States and instructed the CIA to play a direct role in organizing a military coup d'etat in Chile to prevent Allende's accession to the Presidency.

Following the September 14 meeting of the 40 Committee and President Nixon's September 15 instruction to the CIA, U.S. Government efforts to prevent Allende from assuming office proceeded on two tracks. Track I comprised all covert activities approved by the 40 Committee, including political, economic and propaganda activities. These activities were designed to induce Allende's opponents in Chile to prevent his assumption of power, either through political or military means. Track II activities in Chile were undertaken in response to President Nixon's September 15 order and were directed toward actively promoting and encouraging the Chilean military to move against Allende." (US Dept. of State FOIA (Freedom of Information Act) Franck Church Report, Covert Action in Chile)

Ricardo came back from Temuco after voting, and we celebrated Allende's victory with friends. It really felt like a historic moment. By this time I had been in Chile for about 18 months. Suddenly this little-known country (in Britain, I mean) leapt on to the world stage, and progressive and left-leaning people all over the world were immediately fascinated by Chile, holding Salvador Allende's Popular Unity coalition up as an example of how to win an election and begin a process of revolutionary transformation by constitutional means.

From London I was bombarded by requests for articles, and soon, the request to write a book, which I did, over the next year and a half. Published early in 1972, it was called *Chile: Reality and Prospects of Popular Unity* (Lawrence & Wishart, London).

"Between the September 4th election and the Congress ratification 2 months later, big efforts were being made both within Chile and in the US to prevent Allende being ratified as President by Congress. One of the big firms that was instrumental in those efforts, and to bring down Allende's Government later, was the ITT. That company's Chairman told another director, John McCone, that he was "prepared to put as much as a million dollars in support of any plan adopted by the government for the purpose of bringing about a coalition of the opposition to Allende so that ... this coalition would be united and deprive Allende of his position." (From "Allende's Chile, an Inside View" by Edward Boorstein,New York,1977)

We know from US State Dept and CIA documents that on 15 September, ten days after Allende's election, American President Nixon met Richard Helms, the Director of Central Intelligence, Assistant to the President for National Security Affairs Henry Kissinger and Attorney General John Mitchell. At this meeting Helms was instructed to prevent Allende from taking power.

"It quickly became apparent to both White House and CIA officials that a military coup was the only way to prevent Allende's accession to power. To achieve that end, the CIA established contact with several groups of military plotters and eventually passed three weapons and tear gas to one group. The weapons were subsequently returned, apparently unused. The CIA knew that the plans of all groups of plotters began with the abduction of the constitutionalist Chief of Staff of the Chilean Army, General Rene Schneider. The Committee has received conflicting testimony about the extent of CIA/White House communication and of White House officials' awareness of specific coup plans, but there is no doubt that the U.S. government sought a military coup in Chile.

"On October 22, one group of plotters attempted to kidnap Schneider. Schneider resisted, was shot, and subsequently died. The CIA had been in touch with that group of plotters but a week earlier had withdrawn its support for the group's specific plans.

The coup plotting collapsed and Allende was inaugurated President." (Op.Cit. Covert Action in Chile)

The assassination of General Schneider in October 1970, less than two months after Allende's election win, was a huge shock in Chile. Chileans were fond of telling you that they were "the English of South America" and that their history was different from most Latin American countries in the sense that they did not have a history of military coups and dictatorships as neighbouring Argentina, Peru or Brazil, for instance. They were proud of their constitutionalism, their political and civic system, their electoral system. Political assassination was something unheard-of, and deeply unsettling.

Chief of Staff Rene Schneider had declared in May 1970 that the Chilean Army "is a guarantee of a normal election, that whoever is elected by the people assumes the Presidency ... I insist that our doctrine and mission is one of backing and respect for the Political Constitution of the State ... our mission is to see that the decision of Congress is respected."

His firm backing for the Constitution, which meant in this situation that the newly-elected Allende must be ratified as President, as guaranteed under the Constitution, became known as the "Schneider doctrine". This doctrine of armed forces obedience to the Chilean Constitution cost General Schneider his life. It was the reason behind his sinister assassination, which was clearly designed to spark off a military coup to prevent Allende from taking power. It was an omen of the kind of lengths to which the Chilean Right, and their American backers, were prepared to go to prevent socialism from getting a foothold in Latin America, America's "backyard".

Despite CIA machinations, Salvador Allende's election as President was ratified by the Chilean Congress, and the difficult work of governing began. It was particularly difficult because in Chile's political system, the Presidency represents only one part of the power. The Congress (parliament), consisting of two houses, the Chamber of Deputies and the Senate, represented another part, and these chambers were not elected at the same time as the Presidency. So, whilst the Popular Unity coalition may have won the Presidency, it did not have a majority in the Chamber of Deputies or the Senate, which made the passing of legislation very difficult for the new President.

Though Allende's majority was slender, there were a lot of people among the Christian Democrats who had voted for their candidate, Radomiro Tomic, precisely because his platform was actually quite similar to the programme Popular Unity had put forward, and who, on the night of the victory of 4 September, came out on to the streets of Santiago to celebrate together with the forces of the Left. In fact, Tomic himself recognised the day after the election that the Popular Unity programme was the closest to himself and his own programme. (*Chile: Reality and Prospects of Popular Unity*, P. 59)

Certainly, if you put together all the forces of the Left and the part of the Christian Democratic Party that supported the Tomic programme, they represented a big majority among Chile's population. Tomic was more to the left than outgoing President Eduardo Frei, because the six years of that Government had shown many people that a government of the Frei kind was incapable of effecting major changes to Chile's economy and society, which the poorer sectors of society yearned for. If all those forces had been able to work together from 1970, they would surely have ensured the success of the Popular Unity experiment. Alas, that was not to be.

One weekend when we were in Santiago our writer friend Poli and his partner Maruja took us to the coast to his parents' house at Cartagena. The house had been built by Poli's father, the writer Luís Enrique Délano, in the shape of a boat, with its prow pointing out to sea, which could easily be reached on foot just below the house. We went down to the beach, had a lazy swim, then sunbathed a little amid the rocks. When we returned after walking up the path back to the house, Poli's mother, Lola, and Luís Enrique were busy cooking a meal for us. The dining-room was tiny, just like a ship's galley, with a big mast from floor to ceiling. The windows were portholes and everything was made of wood, the walls, ceiling, fittings, floor and table. We all crowded round the galley table and had a wonderful meal of cooked shellfish and fish.

On a later visit to Santiago three months after Allende's election, staying at Poli's house, we found ourselves at the leaving meal for his father, Luís Enrique Délano, who had been designated Chile's Ambassador to Sweden and his mother, Lola Falcón, who was a photographer. Luís Enrique and Lola were to leave at the beginning of 1971 to take up his new post. Luís Enrique had been Chile's Consul in Mexico from 1940-46, and in the US from 1946-49, and had twice in the past lived in exile during repressive (though civilian and constitutionally elected) governments in Chile. Poli's childhood was therefore spent partly in Mexico and the US, episodes of which he narrates delightfully in his book "When I was a Boy Neruda called me Policarpo"[13], which is the story, written through the eyes of a child, of his relationship with his parents' great friend, the poet Pablo Neruda, with whom they lived for a time in exile.

I never saw a full exhibition of Lola Falcón's work, but her large black and white photographs of Maruja, which adorned Poli's study in Santiago, were striking. I remember one in particular, which was of Maruja's head in profile, showing up her lovely long, sweeping eyelashes – stunning.

One day I received a telegram from England. It was to tell me that my first nephew, Daniel, had been born. My brother Joe and his wife, Shirley, who had married a few years before, had had their first child. I was delighted, and suddenly felt that I was now an aunt, not just a sister! It was a new feeling, and over the next few years I delighted in receiving their news in frequent letters from them.

My mother, too, was a very frequent correspondent. She would write at least once a week, and sometimes more. She would often enclose a tea bag (because I complained that Chilean tea wasn't up to much) or a Pontefract cake or two (you couldn't get liquorice in Chile!) and they always seemed to arrive through the post without any problems. Her letters were full of all her many activities – mainly CND and the peace movement – and she would tell me about my little nephew Daniel, whom she often looked after, and about the books she was reading at the time, as she was a great reader.

---

13 In English, translated by Sean Higgins, Groundwood Books, House of Anansi Press, Toronto Berkeley.

Her letters and those of Joe and Shirley helped me to feel that I still had a close family, and although I missed them, especially my mother, it was not unbearable, as I had such a full and happy life in Chile with Ricardo. I was also confident that she was happy that I was happy, and she wasn't the sort of person who would ever put her own wishes above those of either of her offspring. So she never urged me to come home or said anything about missing me; I never received any emotional pressure of any kind from any of my family, something which I took for granted, knowing what kind of people they were.

One time when I was in Santiago on my own (because Ricardo was tied up with his work in Chillán) and was staying with Poli and Maruja, I went with them to visit Delia del Carril, an Argentinian artist who had been Pablo Neruda's second wife. She was 87 when I met her, and though she was quite frail-looking, her mind was sharp and she was still painting and leading an active life. She lived in an old, somewhat decrepit house on *Calle Lynch* (Lynch Road) in Santiago, and we sat on her back porch talking amid the exuberant foliage of her large back garden, which sheltered from view any other houses nearby. She was rather European-looking, with fine features and kindly eyes, which readily showed interest and amusement.

Delia del Carril was from a rather privileged background and as a child had had tutors and governesses. Her father had given her a horse, and so began a lifelong fascination with horses and love for them, and indeed horses figure in many of her paintings, some of which can be seen in Neruda's house-museum *La Sebastiana*, in Valparaíso. Her father was a member of the Argentinian parliament, and after moving to Buenos Aires, Delia del Carril was educated at a school run by Italian nuns. When she was only fifteen, her father committed suicide, after which her mother decided to leave for Paris with her thirteen children. There Delia studied art, one of her teachers being Fernand Léger. It was in Paris that Delia joined the French Communist Party. Later, when she was already 50, she met Pablo Neruda, who was only 30. She was lively, intelligent and very attractive, and they fell in love, despite their age difference – a love which lasted twenty years.

La Hormiguíta (little ant), as she was affectionately known in Chile, where she had returned to live permanently in 1959, was a friend of Poli's, whose whole family knew Neruda very well. She was a friend to many struggling artists and intellectuals, and worked incessantly on their behalf, which was what earned her the pet name of *hormiguíta*. I have always loved painting. I was pretty good at art at school and I studied history of art as a subsidiary subject at university, so I was thrilled to meet Delia del Carril. She talked about the artistic scene in Chile and invited me to see some of her paintings hanging in rather dark rooms of the old-fashioned, unconventional house she had once shared with Neruda.

Whenever Ricardo and I went to Santiago for a few days, we would be invited to Poli's house, where there would always be writers, musicians and artists who were part of their circle. Or we would go out and have a drink at a well-known bohemian bar called El Bosco in the centre of the city. Once Poli Délano and another common friend, Luís Bocaz, started to sing tangos and boleros in El Bosco, ending in a sort of impromptu competition between the two of them as to who could remember and sing most tangos. Both had good voices and soon many drinkers in the famous bar were joining in.

Back in Chillán, after Allende's election our lives went on much the same as before. We had a great circle of friends, and I loved the Chilean sense of humour, which often consists of telling funny anecdotes about common friends and acquaintances. Food was always a great part of our socialising, and I found that even picnics were an elaborate affair, with tablecloths and whole cooked chickens and prepared and dressed salads, with the inevitable *garrafa* (5-litre carafe) of red wine. Whereas in Britain, a picnic is more something just to "keep the wolf from the door" until you return home to have a meal or find a suitable pub, and the main idea of the outing is to have a walk, or cycle in beautiful scenery, there I found that people on a picnic would find a scenic spot, settle down, spread everything out, and not move from the place until it was time to go home! Of course, that's partly, I'm sure, because our weather in Britain doesn't usually permit staying seated in one place outdoors for long.

In Britain we sometimes forget what we owe to those early ramblers who trespassed over Kinder Scout, in the Peak District, to protest at the lack of rights to roam freely over the countryside. As a result of their actions 70 or so years ago, the right to roam is firmly fixed in our country and ramblers can use thousands of footpaths throughout the country, even when they go through privately-owned land[14].

But in Chile the situation was very different. Most land was privately-owned and there were few public footpaths. It would have been dangerous for Chileans to try and walk across some *latifundista's* land – they could have been shot and they would certainly have been chased off.

One evening we were invited to dinner by a veterinary surgeon, *Chepo*, and his wife Gladys, who was an art teacher at the University. We were served

---

14 The mass trespass of Kinder Scout on 24 April 1932 was organised to highlight weaknesses in English law of the time. This denied walkers in England or Wales access to areas of open country, and to public footpaths which, in previous ages (and today), formed public rights of way. The trespass resulted in violent scuffles with gamekeepers on the mountain, resulting in a handful of arrests. The mass trespass forced changes in the law to allow all citizens access to public footpaths (and bridleways and byways), regardless of whether they crossed private land. This culminated in the Countryside and Rights of Way Act 2000, which sets down in law citizens' rights to walk on mapped access land. When I was a student at Manchester University, we would often walk in the Peak District, around the Snake Pass, and would sing Ewan MacColl's song 'The Manchester Rambler', which celebrates the Kinder mass trespass.

hors d'oeuvres of oysters, in their shells, which were totally fresh and delicious. Then Gladys brought out another dish, with a couple of smallish round brown things that looked a bit like meat balls, in splendid isolation in the middle of the plate. It turned out that they were a different sort of balls, *criadillas*, which *Chepo*, as a vet, came by, so to speak, in the course of his work as a rural vet.

Chepo had been in the Communist Party for many years, and had previously lived in Santiago. He once told us an anecdote which goes some way to illustrating how the Party had its roots very much in the working class and the poor. He had been doing a Party task which entailed going to one of the shanty-towns on the outskirts of the capital. It was late at night and he was trying to find the bus stop to catch a bus back to where he lived. All of a sudden he was grabbed by a couple of scruffy-looking youths, who demanded he give them his money. As he was struggling to free himself from the muggers, a third accomplice ran up and shouted to his mates: "Hey no, let him go! He's one of us!" He had obviously recognised him as a fellow Party member! It seems the Party had members and sympathisers among all sorts – the destitute and thieves among them.

During my years in Chile, I came to see that poverty and underdevelopment are often to blame for petty crime and delinquency. Poor nutrition as babies often results in low intelligence, which in turn makes it hard for such people to find work and hold down jobs.

That summer we went on a trip up to a plateau in the Andes organised by the communists in Chillán. We played football, walked around among the stunning scenery, ate an *asado* and drank copious amounts of local *pipeño*. On our way back to Chillán we called at a little roadside cafe which also served alcoholic drink. A group of short, skinny men were propping up the bar, ragged and barefoot, or wearing makeshift sandals from car tyres, drunk or at least tipsy, their eyes seeming to express defeat or resignation to their lot. As I got to know the countryside around Chillán over the months and years, I saw that this was the typical picture, and it always saddened me.

The countryside everywhere we went was so beautiful, yet most of the people who lived there and worked the land lived in abysmal poverty. A 1960 United States Department of Commerce report "Investment in Chile" concluded,

> "There is a very great concentration of agricultural land in the hands
> of a very few owners in Chile while an excessive number of agricul-
> tural properties are too small for economic exploitation ..."

In 1955, 2.8% of the population owned 41% of the arable land, whilst 64% of all land ownership was in the hands of a mere 12%. Moreover, the same report cites Chilean Ministry of Agriculture's information that, "on properties of 1000 hectares and over, i.e., the so-called *latifun-dium*, land is only partially used, mechanization and modern tech-niques are insufficiently utilized, and irrigated lands are frequently kept in natural pasture ..."

In an attempt to tackle childhood poverty and the stunted growth of many rural children, one of the very first measures the new Popular Unity Govern-ment introduced was a free daily half-litre of milk per child, distributed at schools throughout the country. Rural poverty and backwardness were everywhere to be seen. Frequently, people lived in little wooden shacks and had to cook on outside braziers, since there was no electricity. Water was obtained from wells or had to be brought from springs and streams. Clearly, full-scale land reform was sorely needed. But it was fiercely resisted by the *latifundistas* and only weeks into the new presidency, three peasants were killed in clashes over land reform in the southern province of Cautín, which had some very big *latifundios* and the largest concentration of indigenous people in Chile, the *Mapuche* people. As I wrote home at the time:

"The *Mapuches* live in even more backward and even more poverty-stricken conditions than the other Chilean peasants. In this province the owners of the land are trying to "war" the *Mapuche* peasants off against the (non-*Mapuche*) Chilean peasants – the old principle of "divide and rule" (Letter to parents, 21 January 1971)

We were very busy, I teaching and helping my students, Ricardo with his new post of Secretary-General of the *sede*. Our friend Eduardo, the Mayor of Chillán, was equally busy, and we didn't see as much of him and Maruja as we had done. But we went on holiday with them and their son Toti, who was six at the time, to the beautiful resort of Constitución, for a week in January 1971. Ricardo's 14-year-old son, Ricky, also joined us, and we had a wonderful time walking, exploring, swimming and sunbathing. We stayed in a lovely old boarding-house in the Spanish style which the Chileans call "*estílo colonial*", with an interior courtyard and fountain in the middle, and the rooms positioned in a square around the central courtyard. As always with friends, there were lots of jokes, anecdotes and laughter, and good fresh seafood with cold white wine.

Constitución is a very attractive resort, with dark grey sandy beaches and massive rocks rising up high out of the water in sculptural formations. Like the other coastal resorts I had already visited further south, this one was also unspoilt and uncrowded. We took a boat on the river, swam and sunbathed and walked up the steep rocky cliffs overlooking the deep blue Pacific.

We knew that once the long summer holidays were over, it would be back to work for the new term, and back to political activity too, for the municipal elections were looming in April 1971, and these would be the first test of Allende's popularity since the presidential election in September.

The campaign for the local municipal elections was brief but hotly contested. On the radio – we had just bought ourselves a set for the first time – you could hear adverts for the different political parties. The Socialist Party's ad was "Let's Build Socialism with the Socialists!" The Communist Party's was "Forward with the Communists!" And the Radical Party's was "For a Chile both Socialist and Democratic!"

We had a young Englishman staying with us for a few days before the municipal elections. He had been given our contact details by an old friend of mine, Stan Levenson, who was Sports Editor of the *Morning Star* and later wrote for the *Sunday Times*. This young man had come to Chile at this time, he told us, because he wanted to witness the elections, with a view to writing a book on his return. I never knew whether he did actually write a book, but remember feeling somewhat perplexed that someone could think they knew enough to write a book after a few days of observation in a country where he did not even speak the language.

The newspapers of the Right, meanwhile, were having a field-day with the left-wing film director Costa Gavras's film "The Confession". Earlier in Santiago Ricardo and I had seen and been much impressed by Gavras's anti-fascist film "Z". Gavras realised that the Right would use the anti-Stalinist message of "The Confession" against the parties of the Left – by telling the public that the interrogation scenes shown in the film, for instance, represented life under socialism. So Costa Gavras had apparently asked Warner Bros to put off screening the film in Chile until after the April municipal elections. But the Right made great play of this, that Chileans weren't being allowed to see a film that was on general release – *censorship!*

Municipal Election Day itself was quite exciting. I was an *apoderado* (representative) of the Communist Party on the table at which foreigners voted: foreigners in Chile could vote in municipal elections but not in parliamentary or presidential ones. It was interesting to discuss with the representatives of other parties any dubious votes afterwards – I had never done that before. On the whole, the foreigners' ballots were correctly marked, so there wasn't much room for discrepancies. The election process as a whole seemed very sober and serious, and I could see why Chileans were so proud of their electoral traditions.

The results were very good for Allende's Popular Unity Government (50.4%), though of course coming only five months or so after Salvador Allende's ratification as President in November 1970, they cannot really be considered as a solid verdict on his Government. They do, however, show that Allende's popularity was growing, not shrinking.

By 1971 Ricardo and his former wife, with the help of our lawyer friend, Eduardo, had begun the process of divorce. Since divorce, as such, did not exist in Chile at that time, a farcical procedure called 'annulment' had to be used, which in legal terms meant that the marriage had not happened. Ricardo, like most people on the left, did not like it, since it was a sham. But since divorce was not possible, due to the strong influence of the Catholic Church, it was the only way couples could effect a legal separation. Neither Ricardo nor I were bothered about being married, but Ricardo felt strongly that it was necessary to legalise his separation and had begun the process a year or so before.

Ricardo's children came to visit most holidays and occasional weekends, and we also travelled to Temuco, where they lived, some weekends. I won't pretend my relationship with them was easy, but over the years it gradually improved as we all got to know each other better.

In May 1971 Ricardo had to go to Santiago to have an operation on his ear. When I first met him in 1967, he was already slightly deaf, and we had seen a Soviet ear specialist together in 1968, who had made the same diagnosis as his Chilean doctor before then – otosclerosis. Gradually Ricardo's hearing had got worse and the Santiago specialist offered a stapedectomy operation in which the excess bone in the middle ear is cut away and a prosthesis inserted. We travelled to Santiago, Ricardo had the operation and afterwards we went to stay with Ricardo's older brother, Camilo, a widower who had a small house in Santiago. Ricardo had to lie still for a couple of weeks to give the operation the best chance of success.

Ricardo had the operation under a local anaesthetic, since the two surgeons had to keep asking him if everything was all right, as they sawed and drilled away. Ricardo said it felt and sounded as if his head was being drilled into, though he did not feel actual pain during the op. Being conscious throughout, he felt more than a little nervous as the two young surgeons chatted inconsequentially during the three hours the operation took, since he couldn't help but be acutely aware that a slight slip of the drill could be catastrophic. During his operation Ricardo learnt various aspects of their lives and secrets that day.

A friend, Ramón, drove us in his car from the hospital to Camilo's house, as Camilo did not have a car. Being a bit of a joker, Ramón's first greeting to Ricardo, on seeing him after the operation, was mouthed, without sound – to make Ricardo think that he couldn't hear at all now! That is typical of Chilean black humour, but thankfully we both found it very funny.

Ramón was an architect and lived with Sonia, his partner, who was a cellist in the Chilean Symphony orchestra, in a wonderful house he had designed himself. The lounge had a mezzanine floor all along the length of it taking up about a third of the width of the room, and the children had a great time playing up there while their parents entertained below. However, Ramón, as an enthusiastic cook, mainly liked to entertain over the big wooden table in their spacious kitchen, talking to their guests as he cooked or put the finishing touches to the meal to come. Once we had stuffed chilli peppers, the tiny green *puta madre* type of chillis which make your eyes water just to look at them. I have quite sensitive skin, and once I'd eaten the first one, my whole mouth was on fire, and when I inadvertently brushed against my eyes with a finger that had touched the chillis, my eyes burned and watered as if I was weeping. I tried to alleviate the effects by drinking water, but to no avail. Ramón advised me to rub butter on my mouth, which I did, but it was too late. The allergic reaction had set in, and no amount of washing my face and administering creams would work for several hours at least. *What a stupid idea, anyway, stuffed chilli peppers*, I thought. *These Chileans are mad.*

Sonia, Ramón's wife and mother of their little girl, Paloma (dove) would sometimes invite us to her symphonic rehearsals at the Municipal Theatre. I have always loved music: though we never went to concerts when I was a child (there weren't any live orchestral concerts in Chesterfield), when I was home on vacation from university, my mother would put different gramophone records on at full volume when it got to about ten in the morning, to wake me up in a nice way, Rimsky-Korsakov's Sheherazade, for instance, Grieg's Peer Gynt or Joan Sutherland singing some aria or other. She also liked Handel's Messiah, mainly because, as she often told us proudly, her older sister Ethel had had a beautiful contralto voice and had sung as a soloist in the Messiah in Mansfield where she lived. When I was a student in Manchester I started buying classical music LPs and later, when I was working in Runcorn, Cheshire, I had a monthly season ticket for the Liverpool Philharmonic and added to my classical music collection.

After his ear operation, Ricardo was to convalesce at his older brother Camilo's house. It was a very modest bungalow on a new estate. The roads were dried mud and there were no pavements. The houses on the estate consisted of one living room and one bedroom, but space was left for homeowners to add another room or two at the side, as and when they could afford to do so. Since Camilo was a self-employed upholsterer and restorer of antique furniture as well as being an unpaid Communist Party functionary, with six children, five of whom were still in school, he had not had the means to extend the house. There were no curtains at the windows, no carpets or parquet floors. It was very bare and unhomely. I went out and bought some lengths of white lace and made curtains on his wife's old sewing-machine to put up at the windows, in an effort to make the house look more like a home.

Camilo's wife had died of cancer in 1968 and the children were living partly with him and partly with various relatives.

Camilo had had a hard life. He was a half-brother of Ricardo's and had not grown up with the rest of the family. Ricardo only found out that he had a half-brother as he was leaving his native southern town of Puerto Montt to go to University in Santiago, when his father told him of Camilo's existence and gave him an address. Once in the capital, Ricardo had gone to the address his father had given him, but was told there that no one of that name lived there. It was the days of the Gabriel Gonzalez Videla dictatorship, and Camilo had gone underground to continue his political work. Ricardo was 28 when he first met his half-brother.

Camilo, six years older than Ricardo, had been brought up by his mother, who made a precarious living selling cakes and buns to train passengers at San Fernando station, for which they had to get up at four in the morning to be there when the long-distance train passed through. Camilo had to load and help carry the cakes which his mother had made the previous evening, and sell them from the platform. When Camilo was eleven, his teacher at school went to see his mother to urge her to let him stay on at school, because he was very bright and keen, but his mother wouldn't let him, saying she needed him to work so as to make a living. So he left school at that young age and worked from then right up to three months before he died, in April 2008, at the age of 84. But he was one of the most knowledgeable people you could meet, having educated himself through reading and through his political work in the Communist Party, which he joined as a teenager.

Ricardo convalesced at Camilo's, lying as still as he could, as the surgeon had recommended, and I went back to work in Chillán, returning to Santiago at weekends. After three weeks, Ricardo was permitted to travel back to Chillán and start work. Unfortunately, after a few months, we realised that the operation had not had the desired effect. The improvement in hearing was minimal, if indeed there was any. The surgeon had warned Ricardo before the operation that the metal prosthesis might be rejected by the patient's body. If this happened, he had told us, he would recommend re-operating and inserting a plastic prosthesis. In the event, Ricardo was so busy and the political situation in Chile increasingly tense, so that there never seemed to be time to go back and have the operation done again. So his hearing continued to deteriorate slowly, until later in 1976, when we were living in Edinburgh, Ricardo was able to have the operation again, and this time it was successful, giving him much improved hearing for about the next twenty years.

In June 1971 we put the down payment on a new car, a little Fiat 600. Ricardo was convinced that having a car would enable him to see more of his children and make our lives easier. Neither of us had ever driven before, so we had to learn fast. Ricardo's policeman brother, Sergio, taught Ricardo, on a big piece of waste ground in Santiago, and then out on the frighteningly busy streets of the capital, over the space of a couple of weeks, after which short time Ricardo took the driving test.

In Chile at that time the driving test seemed designed to test the driver's skill more than driving knowledge or understanding of what makes a safe driver. If you let your engine stall, for instance, you would definitely fail, even if you showed you were a careful and considerate driver. To my surprise, since he had had so little practice, Ricardo passed. We set off back to Chillán, driving at a slow pace, since the engine had to be run in, and arrived there, fortunately, in one piece. It must be added that there was very little traffic on the main north-south highway in those days, so it was not as daunting as you might think. But over the months that followed, before we got to be proficient drivers, we had a few scary moments driving our new Fiat 600.

I took my test later in Chillan. It was a bit of a farce, to put it mildly. All I had to do was drive round the block once, draw up at the kerb and then undergo a psychometric test. I passed, but by no stretch of the imagination was I a proficient or safe driver.

There was a considerable interest back home in what was going on in Chile. Since I had sent a few articles about the situation in Chile to the Morning Star and had them published, Jack Woddis, who was International Secretary of the Communist Party of Great Britain (as it was at that time, before the split in the Party) asked me if I would write a book about the Popular Unity process. I was 28 at the time and had never written a book before, but I immediately agreed, since I knew there was a lot of interest in Britain and Europe as a whole in this process, because of the fact that Chile was trying to effect radical change, not through revolution, but via elections and the constitutional road towards socialism. It seemed to many people on the left a beacon of hope. It was an example of what socialists in Europe could envisage for their own countries, with their long-established constitutional and parliamentary structures and traditions.

It was an uphill task for me to write the book. Firstly, because I had a full-time job, and moreover, I was by that time Head of the Department of Languages, which meant more responsibility and more of my time. And secondly, because Ricardo was in such a high-powered job, he had very little free time, so the house and household chores fell to me in the main. And thirdly, because the situation in the country was changing so fast that no sooner had I written one chapter than I felt it had to be updated, because of what that had happened in the meantime. I tried to write in the evening and at weekends, but it was hard-going.

Some time at the end of 1971 I was in the middle of a particularly difficult part of the book, where I was attempting to deal with the question of power, in an attempt to explain for my readers why it was that President Allende was unable to bring about many of the measures that were spelled out in the Popular Unity Programme, due to the structures existing in Chile, whereby a president can be elected, yet have both parliamentary chambers against him. Not to mention the armed forces, and the judiciary.

I was attempting to meet one of the many deadlines set me by the publishers, when Ricardo's younger brother decided to come and stay for a week or so during his vacations. Jaime, who is eighteen years younger than Ricardo, was a Maths student at the prestigious University of Concepción at the time. At the time he was much attracted to the ideas of the MIR – Revolutionary Left Movement – which was outside the Popular Unity alliance and frequently attacked the Allende Government for not going far enough fast enough. This was a distraction I didn't need, pressed as I was for time to meet my deadlines. But family obligations are sacrosanct in Chile, so if a family member lands on you, unannounced, you have to put aside whatever you are doing and see to them.

So I had to shop and cook and be part of all the discussions and conversations, as it would have been rude not to, since we didn't see him very often. Jaime, as most young men at the time, had been brought up to expect that all household chores are done by the woman of the house – and that, in our case, was me. But it was good to spend time listening to Jaime's rather hothead views on the current situation, typical of many of his fellow students in Concepción, and to hear Ricardo's more measured responses and explanations. And it was lovely to see the fond relationship of the two brothers, so far apart in age and upbringing.

Writing a book is no easy matter, as I soon realised. There is so much reading to do relating to the subject and painstaking research before and while you are writing. And all the time, the publisher was pressing me for another chapter, another, another... Looking back, I know that I did my best and couldn't have done more, under my particular circumstances. But I also know that I could have done a better job if I had been able to dedicate all my time to it, and thus have more time to absorb more of the books I read on the history of Chile and her political institutions. Another factor was that at the time when I started to write the book in 1971, I had been in Chile less than two years, and I had learned Spanish from scratch on arriving. So reading books, journals and newspapers for my research, most of which were in Spanish, was still not as easy as reading in English would have been. I did finally manage to send the typescript, a bit later than originally promised, and the book was published in 1972. Even by the time I received my first copy of the book, I knew parts of it were already out-of-date, due to the rapid pace of change in Chile during this period.

Despite our being so busy, we still managed to have a good time, and most weekends were spent in the company of friends. One weekend in winter we were at our friends' place about to have dinner. Roberto and Edith were young lecturers in Maths who were from the north of Chile, Roberto from Iquique and Edith from Antofagasta. We had become quite friendly with them, as they, like us, had no family in Chillán, and were about my age and without children. On this occasion, I was laying the table as we were about to eat, at about 10 p.m., when I felt a queer sensation and suddenly felt dizzy. I grasped the back of a chair, as I felt the floor beneath my feet move quite suddenly. Ricardo and Roberto shouted that it was an earth tremor, and we all hurried unsteadily to the nearest doorway, which is apparently the safest part of a house to be in when an earthquake strikes. It lasted about a minute, but somehow it seems longer when you're in it, and it's a really strange sensation to feel the floor move under your feet.

Once the tremor was over, we all began to laugh and talk excitedly. Ricardo couldn't stop laughing, because at the moment it had struck, he was about to open a bottle of wine with a corkscrew, and he couldn't understand why he couldn't seem to get the corkscrew to approach the cork and had thought to himself, before he realised what it was: "Oh my God, I seem to be tipsy before I've even opened this bottle!"

What was a mere tremor in Chillán was an earthquake further to the north and some 60 people were killed at the epicentre, in the town of Illapel in the province of Coquimbo, a further 30 died in the surrounding areas, even as far south as Valparaíso, and 300 were injured. I wrote to my parents at the time:

> "Thousands of people are homeless. What with the floods of the last two months and now this, the Government has got its work cut out to cope with the situation, trying to get the people re-housed temporarily. In Chillán, where there was no damage due to the earthquake – because it was only a tremor here – the Teacher Training College and one of the secondary schools are being used to house the hundreds of people made homeless due to the floods of the last two months. These people are the poorest sector, who live in shacks on the banks of the two rivers which run through Chillán, to the north and east, and so when the rivers swell with the heavy rains, all the area where these people "live" gets flooded.
>
> "Well, this happens every year almost, unless by chance the rainfall is less than normal one winter. It's something inherited from previous

governments. Of course, Frei[15] did a fair amount towards solving the problem, but nothing like enough, because he couldn't count on the necessary economic resources, not being willing to go as far as nationalising the country's basic industries.

"The people affected are almost always the poorest people. Properly built houses, modern houses built of reinforced concrete, don't suffer very much in an earthquake, except for cracks appearing in the walls, etc. So people who live in this sort of houses are not likely to be injured in an earthquake. The people who get killed and injured are the poor inhabitants of old buildings made of a brick of dried mud and straw, called *adobe* in Spanish, because the walls of such buildings simply crumble and fall in an earthquake, and the people get killed and injured by the falling rubble." (My letter of 9th July 1971)

Our friends Roberto and Edith caused us many a laugh, as we got to know them more. Because they were from the far north and had never lived in central or southern Chile before – they had both studied at the University of Antofagasta – they had some very funny observations, especially Edith. One winter when we were driving through the countryside in Ñuble, she asked, on seeing the cows in the fields: "Where do they go at night?" Another time she asked what trees water-melons grow on! That still makes me laugh, after all these years, the thought of massive water-melons dropping off trees once they're ripe!

She was so transparent, so ingenuous, so innocent. One of the first times we got together, when we invited them for a meal at the bungalow we had just moved into, she asked Ricardo what he taught at the University. When he told her that he was a lecturer in English Literature, she could not conceal her surprise and blurted out: "You an English teacher? Oh, I thought you'd be a Spanish teacher or something like that!" Ricardo found that hilarious. It will not seem funny or significant to most English people, I know, and it was something Ricardo had to explain to me. In Chile, most of the students who went in for English at the University at that time were from well-off families and tended to be lighter-skinned, more European-looking. Ricardo is dark-skinned, with jet-black hair, so Edith apparently couldn't imagine that he'd be an English lecturer!

Roberto was less prone to gaffes of this kind than Edith. They were a sweet couple, young and in love, on their first adventure away from home together.

What I liked about my life in Chile as a University lecturer was the wonderful circle of friends we had among colleagues, and what I found to be

---

15 Eduardo Frei was the Christian Democrat President of Chile before Salvador Allende became President in 1970.

the absence of any feeling of the rat race that I had encountered in my working life in England. When I taught at St Albans College of Further Education, for instance, there was a detectable attitude of superiority among those on higher grades to anyone on a lower grade, which I always resented and hated. Funnily enough, I didn't feel that at ICI Ltd when I had worked there, but that was probably because I had gone in at the highest grade possible for a recent graduate. We in Britain probably don't even realise the effects of our highly competitive and individualistic society on people trying to do a good job at their places of work. But what I found in Chile, at least at the University where we worked, was that nobody was competing against anybody else, either for promotion or favours, but simply working in a collaborative way, as colleagues on an equal footing. It made for a very happy working environment, and I feel I personally achieved a great deal in my work teaching English and Phonetics there.

I have already mentioned that I got the University to buy and install a Language Laboratory, and to give funds for a lab assistant for me. I spent hours and hours preparing exercises and readings from literature on tapes for the students to be able to use in their spare time, outside classes. I wouldn't say that the Lab was used to maximum efficiency, but it certainly helped the keenest students to improve their pronunciation and command of English. Between my assistants and me, we kept the Lab open all day until early evening so that anyone could use it whenever they wanted. Funds had not stretched to really good soundproofing for the booths housing each tape-machine, so that was a bit of a problem, but with the headphones on, it was perfectly possible to listen and repeat without too much interference from other students in adjoining booths.

Early in 1971 I was even filmed by the local TV at work in my Language Laboratory, as part of a film about the University in Chillán. Unfortunately we never saw the programme, since neither we nor most of our friends owned a TV. At that time the demand for TV's was so high, due to people's increased purchasing power, that they tended to sell out as soon as they came into the shops. It seems incredible now to think that in those days all we had was a radio and a record-player (for LPs). We didn't even have a telephone, since it was very difficult to get one installed, due to the shortage of telephone lines.

Because there was a shortage of suitable textbooks and teaching materials, I had to spend a lot of time writing my own. I wrote one new textbook for use with fourth-year students. It was based on Doris Lessing's short story "Through the Tunnel". A young boy, on holiday with his mother, sees a group of local lads dive in the sea and come up, minutes later, on the other side of a big rock. He acquires goggles, dives down and discovers a tunnel through the rock. He is determined to do what he had seen the other lads do, and starts to train, holding his breath under the water for longer and longer spells, suffering subsequent nose-bleeds. He finally manages the feat and feels a huge sense of achievement. The story is gripping, so I was sure it would keep the students' attention. I wrote all kinds of exercises using the text, exercises in comprehension, grammar, composition and pronunciation. I duplicated the book and stapled it together in sufficient quantities for my students. There was neither the time nor any particular interest on my part at that time in trying to get the textbook published, but it was, I think, a good effort and certainly made for some decent work by my students.

It was good to feel appreciated by students and staff alike, and was more than enough reward for all the hard work I put in, preparing classes and materials (the University never had enough money to buy much in the way of textbooks and teaching materials), marking students' work and holding one-to-one tutorials. Then there were meetings with other English-teaching colleagues and all other staff of the Department of Languages, which I had the job of running. It all took up a lot of time and energy, but I was much appreciated and held in high esteem, so it was worth it.

One evening in October 1971 our friend Eduardo, by then Mayor, called to ask us to go to dinner with an "English writer" to the local *peña* outside Chillán in the countryside. "He's here in Chile on a visit and wants to know about the Popular Unity process, with the aim of writing a book about it later!" Eduardo said. It turned out to be none other than Graham Greene. We drove out to the *peña* and Graham Greene was already there at the table, together with an elegantly-dressed Chilean woman of about 40 who was accompanying Greene on his travels in Chile. He didn't speak Spanish, and she was acting as his translator and companion. I had been a fan of Graham Greene since my University days and had read most of his novels, so it was a great pleasure for me to meet and talk to him. He was a tall man in his late sixties, with a slight stoop, as he stood to greet us. He sat at the head of the table and I was seated next to him to his right, with his translator companion to his left, and Eduardo and Ricardo next to us. I found him a most charming man, with a gentle but witty, self-deprecatory sense of humour, and with a lively interest in what was going on in Chile under President Allende and the Popular Unity Government. He told us about his trip to Panama where he had been to find material for a novel about the Omar Torrijos leftist dictatorship, which was later published under the title of "Getting to know the General". We chatted about the possibilities of the Left being able to succeed in Latin America, with so many dictatorships in surrounding countries. He wanted to know our impressions of what Allende and the Popular Unity Government were trying to do in Chile; we talked about his views on the Catholic church, his views on Czechoslovakia and the Soviet intervention there in 1968 and the recent writers' trials in the USSR. He was very companionable, and I loved that gentle, slightly cynical, sense of humour of his, which had always appealed to me in his novels. It was a very interesting evening, with Eduardo giving political explanations at his usual breakneck speed and Greene's Chilean companion and I attempting to give him adequate translations, with plenty of laughs in between.

Unfortunately Graham Greene was leaving for the south the following morning, so I wasn't to see or hear of him again until years later when he came to Moscow while we were living there during the Gorbachov years. But I have the wonderful memories of that evening - of him feeling that he was in the company of comrades and friends, and that he very much hoped our political venture would succeed.

I know many consider Greene to have been an agent for the British secret services, and perhaps he was, in the sense that he came from the upper class and had many friends and contacts with the Cambridge spies like Kim Philby and Anthony Blunt, being of their generation and class. Whether he was or wasn't working for MI6, his novels like *The Quiet American, Our Man in Havana, The Power and the Glory* and others show a definite sympathy for the cause of the Left and antipathy towards imperialism. It's of coincidental interest that, as I write these lines, I am living near Ashover, Derbyshire, where Graham Greene lived for a period after graduation from Oxford in 1925 when working as a sub-editor on the Nottingham Journal.

The fact is that Graham Greene had worked on the UK's Special Intelligence Service's Iberian desk before the famous Soviet spy Kim Philby, and clearly knew Philby quite well. In his book, *Philby KGB Master Spy*, Phillip Knightley writes: "The one person Philby might have been able to engage with on a reasonably frank basis would have been Graham Greene – as their many meetings later in Moscow testify, they had a lot in common, even at that time. As Philby recalled, "When Graham first came to work in my department we had a long talk. Of course, I couldn't talk to him as a Communist, but I did talk to him as a man of left-wing views and he was a Catholic. But at once there was human contact between us." The two began to lunch together frequently and their friendship grew. But Philby went down in Greene's estimation over what Greene later described as "a piece of [Philby's] office jobbery", over which he resigned. "I attributed it then to a personal drive for power, the only characteristic in Philby which I thought disagreeable," Greene wrote in the introduction to Philby's book. "I am glad now that I was wrong. He was serving a cause and not himself, and so my old liking for him comes back." (Philby, *My Silent War*).

We were lucky in having friends who were writers, artists and musicians. Often when we went to Santiago we would stay at Poli's house, which was a lovely old building with interior arches and a tranquil garden bordered by enormous trees. Poli was a great host and loved having guests. Expansive, loyal friend, lover of anecdotes, Poli's humour was complemented by his wife Maruja's expressiveness and beauty when she joined in the tale. As a dancer and mime artist, she knew how to illustrate a story with facial and hand gestures. One story Poli told was how once Maruja was teaching modern dance to one of her young (male) students in the room above the dining-room and Poli jokingly related how he became increasingly disturbed by the noises emanating from above. "Was it really dance they were engaged in?" he joked, assuming the role of jealous lover. "What could I do, challenge him to a duel?" Maruja would just laugh at him fondly.

Once, though, Poli had challenged a fellow writer to a fight. Ricardo himself was witness to it. It happened at a British Council cocktail party; the rector of the University of Chile was there and several lecturers, among them Ricardo and Poli. The two writers had both had a bit too much to drink, and literary jealousies got the better of them. Poli laid down the gauntlet, Hemingway-style, and the two of them went off to a room alone to "have it out". Ricardo tells how after a while thumps and thuds began to be heard from that room, like bodies crashing to the floor. Poli's wife, Maruja, was concerned and asked Ricardo to go and see what was going on. It turned out that the noise had been made by Poli dragging the furniture to one side to make room for the fight, but they had not come to blows. And nor did they, as tempers cooled. The writer Poli had challenged was the playwright Antonio Skarmeta, author of *Ardiente Paciencia* (Ardent Patience), the play on which the 1994 award-winning film about Pablo Neruda in exile, *Il Postino* (The Postman), was loosely based.

Poli was a great admirer of Hemingway, and perhaps his literary style in his short stories reflects Hemingway's influence. Certainly as a man, Poli loved to appear as a bit of a tough guy, hard-drinking and manly, though underneath the façade one always felt that there was a tender, gentle man being suppressed.

It was great fun to spend time with Poli and friends, and to discuss with them the fast-moving political situation in the country. It was a time of great hope and optimism. In Chillán the University hosted the *tren de la cultura*, which was an initiative by President Allende to take artists of theatre, music, dance and the visual arts by train to parts of the country where little or no cultural activity ever took place. The "culture train" travelled round different parts of Chile for a month during the summer of 1971, backed by the railway workers.

Everything seemed possible during those heady days. The Government was popular, new and exciting ventures were being launched, the University was being reformed and made more democratic, and the people of Chile were beginning to take an active part in all sorts of ways in shaping their future. It seemed like true democracy in action, and I was thrilled to have a part in it.

CHAPTER THREE

*"I don't see why we need to stand by and watch a country go
communist due to the irresponsibility of its people."*

Henry Kissinger (United States Foreign Policy Adviser
and Secretary of State, 1973-1977).

The situation in the country was far from tranquil. Popular Unity's aim,
as stated in its programme, was "to replace the present economic
structure, and do away with the power of foreign and national monopoly
capital and the *latifundia* in order to begin the building of socialism." And
those sectors of the economy which knew they would be threatened by this
began to organise.

We started to notice some scarcities of basic goods. Cooking oil began to
disappear, and people had to queue for it when it arrived at the shops. Beef
and pork became scarce, then all sorts of goods, from sheets and towels to
fridges and washing machines, started disappearing from the shops. The
Government suspected it was partly deliberate sabotage – and there is ample
proof that this was going on, as the *latifundistas*, copper-mine owners and
other powerful big business colluded with CIA advisers to bring about a
situation of economic chaos intended to bring the new government down.

Another reason for the shortages was that the Popular Unity Government
had raised wages and held inflation down, so obviously people had more
money to spend. People's spending power rapidly increased from 1971 and
they started buying TV's, radios, kitchen appliances and other household
goods that they could never afford before.

The Government brought in a big programme of new house-building, run
by the national Housing Corporation, CORVI (*Corporación de Vivienda*).
Housing was for the first time considered as a public right. As the Popular
Unity Programme says: "The objective of the Popular Government's housing
policy is for every family to become home-owners ... Neither monthly
mortgage payments nor rents should exceed 10% of the family income."

To counteract the problems caused by the shortages, the Popular Unity
Government encouraged the formation of neighbourhood committees, the

JAP (*Juntas de Abastecimiento y Control de Precios*[16]). The aim was to normalise supplies, look out for and report artificial shortages and prevent hoarding and price speculation. Everybody who lived within the area covered by a JAP would be able to get goods on production of a ration card. It was not ideal, but it did at least mean that people got all the basic foodstuffs they needed.

In some areas it must have been worse than others. We didn't really have much of a problem with supplies. If there wasn't any meat at the supermarket one day, we would buy fish, or eat lentils or beans, and fresh fruit and vegetables were always in full supply at the big market. The *feria* in Chillán is famous throughout Chile for its rich display of fruit and vegetables, brought in from the countryside by rural people selling their own home-grown produce, and for its wonderful stalls selling a huge range of bright and colourful textiles, *ponchos* and throws, Quinchamalí pottery, basketwork of all kinds, weird wickerwork animals and fish, and cane furniture. Since Ricardo and I were setting up home for the first time, we bought most of our wicker chairs there, and a cane table and chairs for the dining area. They were cheap and attractive, and I loved them.

The political situation in the country continued to be tense. The right-wing forces seemed determined to do all they could to prevent the Popular Unity Government from governing. Chile's main natural resource, copper, was dominated by US firms, but since the mineral accounted for over 70% of Chile's export earnings, it was essential to ensure that the revenue from these exports went to the government, not to private US companies. The issue of copper nationalisation had by this time become so widely accepted as necessary that, in July 1971, the government was able to get it passed unanimously in Congress. So the US-owned copper mines were taken over by the Government, without compensation being paid. In response, the US cut off all credit to the Government and pressed the World Bank to do the same. And the main US mining corporations, Kennecott and Anaconda, began legal proceedings against the Government.

The World Bank made no new loans to Chile between 1970 and 1973 and loans from the Inter-American Development Bank almost ceased. The USA's Director of Central Intelligence, Richard Helms, at a September 1970 meeting with President Richard Nixon recorded that his instructions included "Make the economy scream." Soon the US Ambassador Edward Korry was telling Frei that "not a nut or a bolt would be allowed to reach Chile under Allende" (from "A Model Operation – Covert Action in Chile 1963-1973", by Ralph McGehee).

---

16 Supply and Price Control committees.

82

Korry's successor as US Ambassador to Chile, Nathaniel Davis, subsequently explained to his British equivalent, Reginald Secondé, that the US government were concerned "not only about the loss to the copper companies, but also about the precedent that the Chilean action would set for the nationalisation of other big American interests throughout the developing world" (quoted in "Unpeople: Britain's Secret Human Rights Abuses", by Mark Curtis).

The Popular Unity Programme spelled out a mixed economy for Chile. It did not envisage wholesale nationalisation of every factory or every farm. And in fact the Government were fairly cautious in nationalising *latifundios*, only taking over those that were not being actively farmed. So certain actions by the ultra-left group, the MIR (Revolutionary Left Movement) which organised some *tomas* (seizures) of land and small factories, did nothing to help the Government's image, since they enabled the media to claim that this proved that Allende's socialist government had the aim of wholesale takeovers of all private property. It seemed to me that such *tomas* simply played into the hands of the Right.

In fact the Popular Unity Government never claimed to be a socialist government. Its Programme did, however, condemn the capitalist system. "What has failed in Chile is the system which does not correspond to the necessities of our time. Chile is a capitalist country, which depends on imperialism, dominated by sectors of the bourgeoisie intrinsically connected with foreign capital, which cannot solve the country's problems that arise precisely from their class privileges which they will never voluntarily renounce." That structure had to go, the Programme said, "in order to begin the building of socialism." That was enough for the Right to organise against it in whatever ways they could to prevent that happening. And the media played a crucial role in this.

As we now know from CIA documents released from the archives, CIA funding for the right-wing media in Chile had begun long before:

> "From 1953 through 1970 in Chile, the Station subsidized wire services, magazines written for intellectual circles, and a right-wing weekly newspaper. According to the testimony of former officials, support for the newspaper was terminated because it became so inflexibly rightist as to alienate responsible conservatives.

> "By far, the largest -and probably the most significant- instance of support for a media organization was the money provided to *El Mercurio*, the major Santiago daily, under pressure during the Allende regime. The support grew out of an existing propaganda project. In 1971 the Station judged that *El Mercurio*, the most important

opposition publication, could not survive pressure from the Allende government, including intervention in the newsprint market and the withdrawal of government advertising. The 40 Committee authorized $700,000 for *El Mercurio* on September 9, 1971, and added another $965,000 to that authorization on April 11, 1972. A CIA project renewal memorandum concluded that *El Mercurio* and other media outlets supported by the Agency had played an important role in setting the stage for the September 11, 1973, military coup which overthrew Allende." (US Department of State FOIA, Church Report (Covert Action in Chile)

Most people in Chile at that time did not own a TV set, but in the capital and in big towns, television was starting to play a big part in people's lives. By mid-1971, 500,000 sets were in use, reaching some 30% of families. The Popular Unity Government encouraged the manufacture of small portable sets, sold at a low price, and these were snapped up immediately by the population, whose purchasing power had increased significantly, since the minimum wage had been raised and special bonuses paid to the low-paid. Television in Chile had begun in the 1960s as a public service provided by the state and the two largest universities. So there was the Government channel, Channel 7, and two other channels, one run by the Universidad Católica and the other by the Universidad de Chile, called Channel 9.

The Government channel was certainly a big advantage for the Popular Unity Government and enabled President Allende to get the Government's policies over to the public, at least the part that had a TV set. But newspapers and magazines were of more importance at that time, and the Chilean press was diverse and increasingly more politically polarised as time went on.

Ricardo and I didn't have a television, mainly because we had such a busy life and did not spend much time at home. But we read the papers and magazines, and I found the variety and their diverse and overt political standpoints fascinating. *El Mercurio*, the main establishment newspaper, owned by the well-known Edwards family, turned from a fairly measured, serious newspaper into a virulently anti-Government and anti-Allende paper, ever more vitriolic in its attacks on the Government. At home we read *El Siglo*, which was the Communist Party daily – a very serious and dense newspaper – and sometimes *Clarín* or *Puro Chile*, which were left-wing, populist tabloids, which excelled in eye-catching headlines and popular language. There was also *Última Hora* which was a pro-socialist daily.

In June 1971, the man who as Christian Democrat Minister of the Interior had ordered the 1969 fatal raid on a squatters' camp outside the southern city of Puerto Montt, Edmundo Pérez Zukovic, was assassinated. Those responsible for the assassination turned out to be members of a shady so-called

"Organised Vanguard of the People" (VOP), a tiny, ostensibly far-left underground group. The Popular Unity parties condemned it as a provocation which only played into the hands of the Right. But the Right spared no effort in heaping the blame on the Government. Christian Democrat leader Eduardo Frei, who was in Europe at the time of the assassination, sent a message of condolence which clearly attributed the blame to Popular Unity:

> "this atrocious crime has one author: those who systematically lie, slander, incite to hatred, and are destroying Chile with impunity."
> (Quoted in "Allende's Chile", Boorstein, P. 169)

It all seemed intended to worsen the situation for the Government. And there were many problems, at local and national level, many caused by the years of underdevelopment and the sharply raised expectations of the people, who at last identified with a government which was trying hard to improve their situation. For some on the far left, however, whose position was one of critical support, the Allende Government was not being revolutionary enough.

Ricardo, in his role as Secretary-General of the University, felt this at close hand. The students at the University in Ñuble started a campaign for better student accommodation, which they sorely needed. The leadership of the Federación de Estudiantes (FECH), whose leader was a Communist, Juan Salas, went to see Ricardo, who had been made acting Vice-rector after Julio Stuardo had left for Santiago. Salas asked Ricardo to loan the FECH the University's bus, but with no questions asked concerning what they needed it for. Ricardo was in a dilemma, but trusting in the honesty and trustworthiness of the FECH leadership, he acceded to their request.

It turned out that the students had needed the bus to take over and occupy a building that belonged to the Ministry of Public Works, a ministry headed by a Communist, Pascual Barraza. The students then came to Ricardo to offer the building for the badly-needed University student accommodation. In fact, it was true that the ministry building had only been used occasionally by visiting ministry officials, so Ricardo had considerable sympathy with the students' action. Negotiations followed with the Ministry and it was agreed that the University's Welfare Service should take over the building.

But political opponents managed to get workers employed by the Ministry of Public Works to turf the students out and re-occupy the building. Ricardo accused them of opportunism, because until the students' action, they had displayed no interest in the building and had probably not even known of its existence. Eventually the Ministry in Santiago sent a representative to Chillán, and it was agreed that the University should have the building for student accommodation.

No sooner was one problem solved than another arose for Ricardo to deal with. The MIR decided they would now occupy a privately-owned building in the centre of the city. The province's *Intendente* had to intervene, since the action was illegal and against private property. It was a tricky situation, because if the *Intendente* were to send the police in to clear the MIR students from the building, it would have damaged the Government's image. Once again, Ricardo had to use all his skills of reasoned argument and persuasion, and in the end, the students agreed to leave the building on the promise of a room Ricardo offered them in the University itself. It was a compromise, and it won the day, both sides coming out of it with their dignity intact.

The MIR were a thorn in the side of the Government right from the start. They were not part of the Popular Unity coalition, and their programme was for out-and-out revolution, Cuban-style. They could not seem to understand that the Popular Unity Government was unable to bring about that kind of total revolution, because it had been elected with a narrow majority and because its pledge had been to follow the constitutional road. To me it seemed clear that the Government *was* introducing revolutionary changes; if it hadn't, the Right would not have reacted so vehemently against everything it did, and the CIA would not have got involved to try and bring the Government down. But the MIR continued to follow their own path, occupying small factories and farms, for instance, though they knew that the programme of the Popular Unity Government did not envisage nationalising small and medium-sized enterprises.

So whereas Allende had hoped to win over owners of small and medium-sized businesses – since, objectively, such people had nothing to lose from the Government's stated policies – instead, many of them became alienated and pushed into the arms of the Christian Democrats, as they saw small firms being seized illegally and occupied by "the workers". It seemed a suicidal policy to me, and I felt frustration and anger against the MIR for their short-sighted tactics.

In November the Cuban leader Fidel Castro came to Chile. One of the first things the Government had done after Salvador Allende came to power was to re-establish diplomatic ties with Cuba, which had been broken off by accord of the US-dominated OAS (Organisation of American States) in 1964. Re-establishment of Chilean-Cuban diplomatic relations helped to break the isolation of Cuba, which had arisen as a result of the stranglehold the USA had at the time over the countries of Latin America.

Our University organised coaches to Concepción, which was the nearest city to us where the Cuban leader would speak, at the city's biggest stadium. It was great to see Fidel standing next to President Allende, and to listen to him speak to the thousands of people cramming the stadium. There was such enthusiasm and warmth for the Cuban leader who had come to express his

86

support for a very different revolutionary process than Cuba's, but none the less real for all that.

It was a great occasion. I belonged to the University choir, and our choir sang a couple of songs, followed by other choirs from other universities and schools of the region. The acoustics were not very good of course, in the open-air stadium, and the music sounded distorted to me as we heard ourselves through the microphones. But it was a good feeling - that we had participated in that way in one of the big events of the Popular Unity period. It was a great privilege for me to listen to Fidel and see him in the flesh, and as always, he was an energetic and thoughtful speaker. In the years since then, my admiration for Fidel has remained undimmed: in his interviews with Gabriel García Marquez and in the recent book "My Life", based on Ignacio Ramonet's interviews with Fidel, he is confirmed to me as the greatest leader alive today, always visionary and with sometimes quite surprising and original views.

Ricardo and I had been teaching Russian since 1970 under the auspices of the Chilean-Soviet Institute, and eight of our students took the end-of-year exam. This merited a piece in the local paper *La Discusión*, and in general, the courses had proved quite a success in a provincial town of that size. Our friend Eduardo had started off on the course – for beginners, since it was the first time any Russian had been taught in Chillán – but he hadn't lasted long, since the pressures of being local councillor, then Mayor, at such a fast-changing time, obviously caught up with him. We were delighted to find, when meeting with him again in 1998, that he still remembered some Russian words and phrases we had taught him.

As relations between Chile and the USSR began to broaden, Chillán's town council decided to buy some snow-clearing equipment from the Soviet Union. I was asked to interpret for the technician who arrived in Chile together with the first of the machinery the council had bought. I spent a couple of days learning some new technical vocabulary fast, as we clambered over the massive vehicle, Igor Ivanovich patiently explaining the use of all the levers and buttons. It certainly made a change from my day job; whether the Chilean technicians understood anything of what I was saying, I never found out.

It's difficult to imagine poverty when you've never lived it. Of course, nowadays, we see plenty of scenes of poverty on our television screens, but even so, it is somehow sanitised by the fact that it's just on a screen, not right next to us. But in Chile, you were reminded of poverty everywhere you went, in the local markets, at the stations, and especially when driving in the countryside, passing little shacks, with fires burning in outdoor braziers, people barefoot and ragged, carrying heavy loads, or, in the case of the men, shuffling along, tipsy or drunk. I found the countryside very beautiful, but also rather sad, because of this.

Ricardo's father had been born and raised in Quinchamalí, a village about half an hour's drive from Chillán. It's a very small village, though it had one tarmac road running through it, with smaller dirt tracks running off in various directions from the main road. As you drive along towards the village you can see the snow-capped Andes in the distance jutting out into the intense azure sky, with rows of poplar and eucalyptus trees in the plains of the foothills. Most of the scenery you see in Chile from the main north-south highway, at least from Santiago going southwards, is like this, with the endless range of the Andes mountains to your left. It's quite easy, therefore, to get your bearings, you just look at the Andes and immediately you know where east and west are. Chile is so narrow that you can see the mountains from most of the main north-south highway. People would joke that the country's so narrow, you have to clap vertically when applauding!

Ricardo's father had moved away from Quinchamalí at seventeen, and became a policeman, but his sister, *tía* Albertina, still lived there. She had never married or had children, and lived alone in a small wooden house next to a dirt track. She had worked all her life in Santiago as a washerwoman for well-off families, carrying heavy loads on foot to and from the houses she washed for. Now elderly and retired, she lived in Quinchamalí in this small wooden house with no running water, and she cooked on an outside brazier, like most country-folk, though the house did have electricity. The john was an earth-closet some 50 metres away in the cherry-orchard to one side of the house.

Like many rural people born in the first decades of the twentieth century, Albertina had never had the chance to study or train for a career. At that time most villages like Quinchamalí or Cochamó, the nearest village to where Ricardo was born, did not even have a village school, and it was only during the first Popular Front government of President Pedro Aguirre Cerda, a former teacher (1937-41), whose slogan was "*Gobernar es educar!*" (to govern is to educate) that many rural schools were set up, for the first time enabling at least a basic education for the rural poor.

We would go and visit *tía* Albertina on a weekend sometimes. She led a rather solitary and poor existence, and we would take her fruit or a cake and spend a few hours with her. Ricardo knew she had had a hard life, and he was very kind to her. On one occasion we went to see her together with Ricardo's father who had come to see us, and a poet friend of Ricardo's who was visiting us. Renato Cardenas, though originally from an island in the south of Chile called Chiloé, now lived in Santiago and was a well-known poet. When we got to Quinchamalí, we found *tía* Albertina in bed, as she was unwell. I know she had neighbours and relatives there who looked after her to some extent, but basically she spent most of the time on her own. When *El Chico* Cardenas, as he was known by all and sundry in Chile, saw that she had a guitar hanging on the wall, he asked if he could play it. We sat in the adjoining room to Albertina's bedroom and *El Chico* sang lots of Chilean folk songs, accompanying himself on the guitar. *Don* Ricardo – Ricardo's father – and we joined in whenever we knew the words. He sang *cuecas* and sad songs like Violeta Parra's "*Arauco tiene una pena*" ("Arauco [the *Mapuche* indigenous region] is sad") and the *cueca* "*Hasta cuando está*" ("How long"), and other, jollier folk-songs. *La tía* Albertina clapped and laughed along with the rest of us, clearly cheered up enormously and told Ricardo as we were about to leave that she hadn't enjoyed herself so much in a long time.

Quinchamalí was famous in Chile for its folk pottery tradition. The local *feria* in Chillán was full of the typical black pottery with white etchings – vases, dishes, all sorts of animal shapes, three-legged pigs and goats, and most famous of all, the *guitarrera*, a graceful figure shaped a bit like a squash, the top part representing a woman wearing a flat brimmed hat and playing a stylised guitar. The *guitarreras* came in all sizes, from one you could put on your mantelpiece, to others that stood about two feet high. I loved them, and wanted to buy a big one, like the one our poet friend, Sergio Hernández, had standing in a corner of his living-room.

One day soon after we had bought our little white Fiat 600, we took Sergio to Quinchamalí for him to show us where the most authentic kinds of *guitarrera* were to be found. We passed the village of Quinchamalí and drove up into some hills, up a winding dirt track. Eventually we came to a hut with an old woman outside. We got out and walked up to her and Sergio started asking her about the old pottery traditions, as she was one of the oldest traditional potters thereabouts. She told us how the pots were made, how the white designs were etched on the clay, how the locals fired them and so on. Ricardo then asked the woman if there was any danger that this old pottery tradition, so specific to Quinchamalí, would die out, asking if the tradition was being passed on to the next generation. "Because," he added, "I suppose, *Señora*, you have children yourself...?" Her answer was somewhat disconcerting: "I wouldn't know, *señor*, I wouldn't know..." Sergio snorted behind his hand and had to turn away to hide his laughter, and we all had to stifle it till we were able to let go, after taking our leave.

Sergio Hernández was a bit of an eccentric. He taught Hispanic literature at the University, but in the main he was a bohemian and a poet. He used to walk the streets at night, and if he saw a light on in our house at midnight or even one in the morning, he would ring the doorbell and come in for a couple of hours over a drink or two. He was gay, though no one really talked about it. But once when we called in unexpectedly on him, he introduced us to a handsome young man who had obviously spent the night there. His colleagues knew that he would go to the railway station after midnight and meet potential partners there among the insomniacs, drunks and bohemians of that provincial city.

Our poet friend Sergio had a wicked sense of humour, always hitting the nail on the head in a very clever way. Once when some friends and I were at a big Socialist Party rally outside Chillán's Town Hall, another colleague, Alejandro Witker, a very prominent left-winger at the University, who had started off in the Communist Party, had then gone over to the MIR, and was now a Socialist Party member, was acting as compere at the rally. As music blared out over the loudspeakers, Witker was waving his short arms around wildly as if directing an orchestra – he looked for all the world as if he was some sort of crazy conductor. Later that evening, I was telling this story to Ricardo and Sergio, who hadn't been at the rally, and Ricardo asked me what music it was that was playing: was it the anthem of the Socialist Party or the National Anthem or what? Sergio commented drily: "The thing is, Witker tends to get his anthems all mixed up!" – an allusion to his somewhat erratic political party membership. Two years later after the infamous military coup against President Allende, Witker was imprisoned in the Quiriquina concentration camp together with Ricardo and many others, both from the Socialist Party, the MIR, the Communist Party and from no party at all, people who had simply been supporters of the Allende government.

Despite the problems the Government was having, there was enormous support for Popular Unity. Allende spoke at huge rallies in Santiago, where the whole breadth of the central streets was a sea of demonstrators, spread out in every direction, as far as the eye could see. It was great fun being at these demonstrations. Apart from the speeches, there'd be singing by the popular groups of the time, Inti-Illimani or Quilapayún, or Victor Jara, the famous Chilean bard whose songs infuriated the Right. One song he had written called on people to back the Government, not to stay sitting on the fence, but to take a stand. It went like this:

> Arrímese mas pa' ca
> aquí donde el sol calienta,
> si uste' ya está acostumbrado
> a andar dando volteretas
> y ningún daño le hará
> estar donde las papas queman.

Usted no es na'
ni *chicha* ni limoná
se la pasa manoseando
caramba zamba su dignidad.

La fiesta ya ha comenzao
y la cosa está que arde
uste' que era el más quedao
se quiere adueñar del baile
total a los olfatillos
no hay olor que se les escape.

Si queremos más fiestoca
primero hay que trabajar
y tendremos pa' toítos
abrigo, pan y amistad
y si usted no está de acuerdo
es cuestión de uste' nomás
la cosa va pa' delante
y no piensa recular.

Ya déjese de patillas
venga a remediar su mal
si aquí debajito 'el poncho
no tengo ningún puñal
y si sigue hociconeando
le vamos a expropiar
las pistolas y la lengua
y toíto lo demás.
(1970)

Neither Chicha[17] nor Lemonade

Come on over here
Where the sun is nice and warm.
Yes, you, who have the habit
Of jumping from one side to the other,
It won't do you any harm
To be here where everything's really happening.

---

17 *Chicha* is an alcoholic drink made from apples, a bit like a still cider. *Ni chichi ni limonada* is a saying in Chile meaning "neither one thing nor the other".

You're nothing at all,
Neither fish nor fowl,
You're too busy fondling
Caramba samba
Your own self-esteem.

This fiesta's already begun
The fireworks about to go off.
You, the most sluggish of all,
Now want to lead the dance.
Bloodhounds can always track down
A good thing by its smell.

If we want more fun and games
First of all there's work to do
And we shall make for all of us
Shelter, bread and friendship,
And if you don't agree
That's your own business,
This thing is going forward,
Don't think of turning tail.

Stop messing about
Come and make up for lost time.
Yes, honest, under my *poncho*
I've got no hidden dagger,
But if you go on mudslinging,
We'll have to expropriate you,
With your guns and your tongues
And everything else you've got.

Many of Victor's songs were equally combative and committed, which was why he was loved by all those who wanted to see the Popular Unity government achieve its aims of raising the standard of living for all those living in poverty or near-poverty. Victor Jara himself was from a poor peasant family, but he had had the chance to study and became Chile's leading singer/songwriter during this period. His LPs, like *La Población* or *Manifiesto* were imbued with his love and concern for the poverty-stricken people of the shanty-towns and poor rural areas of his country, as shown in the song *Luchín*, a little kid who played with a football made out of rags...

Luchín

Fragile as a kite
Over the roofs of *Barrancas*[18]
Little Luchín was playing
His hands blue with cold,
With the rag ball
The cat and the dog
And the horse looked on.

Green light was bathing
In his watery eyes
Bare-bummed and in the mud
His little life was crawling
With the rag ball, the cat and the dog
And the horse looked on.

The horse was another toy
In that tiny space
And it seemed the animal knew his job
With the rag ball
The cat and the dog
And with Luchín wet through.

If there are children like Luchín.
Who are eating earth and worms,
Let's open all the cages
So they can fly away like birds
With the rag ball, the cat and the dog
And with the horse as well.

I wasn't really familiar with any of Chillán's shanty-towns, but once or twice we drove to some activist's house in a *población* with makeshift shacks of sheets of corrugated iron and planks of wood and no paved roads, no electricity. They had standpipes here and there for people to fill their cans with water. Hordes of stray dogs would run after the car as you drove along the shanty-town's dirt roads, a cloud of dust kicked up by the car wheels. Dr Sheila Cassidy, in her book *Audacity to Believe* (Collins, 1977), did work as a doctor with patients from such *poblaciones*:

---

[18] *Barrancas* is a part of Santiago where several shanty-towns or *poblaciones* resulting from squatters' action can be found, such as Herminda de la Victoria (March 1967), Violeta Parra (February 1969) Montijo (August 1969).

"Later in the year when I worked in the ward for the under two-year-olds I saw cases of gross malnourishment – babies of a year who still did not sit up and who looked like little old men; babies with big, dark, sunken eyes and wrinkled skin who looked blankly into space and never smiled... Child medicine in the third world deals with children who are dying from malnutrition or from diarrhoea caused by unhygienic practices by ignorant parents in an area with poor sanitation. In summer the children died from gastroenteritis from infected milk and in winter from bronchitis and pneumonia because the house was unheated or from burns when the toddler upset the paraffin stove."

We and all our friends bought Victor Jara's LPs and you could hear the music playing in *peñas* and as you walked through the *feria* doing your shopping, or through windows open on summer evenings as you strolled along the streets. Of all the artists who supported the Government – and there were very many at the time – Victor Jara was certainly the most popular and the most combative. But Inti-Illimani, Quilapayún, Isabel and Angel Parra, Patricio Manns, Hector Pavez, Aparcoa, the Jaivas, Illapu and many others were also household names and very popular.

Ricardo was asked to run a radio programme on the local Chillán radio station *Radio Ñuble*. He had a weekly half-hour slot. Ricardo had done some media work before, when he lived in Temuco, where he was in charge of a quarterly newspaper both in Spanish (*"Recuperaremos la Tierra"*) and in the *Mapuche* language, *Mtutuain Mapu,* (*"We shall win back our Land"*) which was aimed at the indigenous *Mapuche* community who lived in that region. Now he was to launch into radio, with his own programme. He recruited Franklin Roach, another colleague from the university, to help him and together they ran a very interesting and varied programme until the military coup in September 1973, when it came to an abrupt end.

At the end of my third year in Chile we had a lovely camping holiday in Pichidangui together with Ricardo's kids – Ricky, who was sixteen, twins Claudia and Beatriz, who were fourteen and Daphne, who was ten. Pichidangui is on the coast north of Santiago, and the sea was wonderfully warm, the beaches golden and uncrowded, and the scent of eucalyptus trees wafted over in the balmy breeze. We swam a lot and sunbathed and played beach games. It was good to see how fond they all were of their Dad and I was much impressed with how well they all got on with each other. There was no quarrelling at all and they were such happy, well-adjusted children. I taught the girls to do handstands and cartwheels and how to dive down to the seabed. We used to go to an inexpensive transport cafe on the main north-south carriageway for lunch and eat wholesome fish soups or delicious conger-eel with salads.

On that holiday we took a tiny primus stove to heat water for making our morning tea. As it was heating up the water one morning, just outside our tents, the flame set alight some dry eucalyptus leaves from the tall trees among which the camp site was situated. The flames quickly spread to more leaves and twigs and all of a sudden we had a spreading fire on our hands. I dashed inside our tent, grabbed a blanket and rapidly smothered the fire, extinguishing it completely. Ricardo still marvels at how quick and practical I was. I put it down to my Brownie and Girl Guide training, which taught that kind of stuff, as well as knot-tying, first aid, how to put up tents and so much else that I've found of great practical use during my life.

It was a wonderful holiday and I felt for the first time that my relationship with Ricardo's daughters would improve with time – as it did, though it was a gradual process and took several years before we could say we became good friends.

As Ricky was the oldest, he often came to see his Dad on his own, and it was always nice to have him over at weekends and holidays. He was a serious, bookish sort of lad, tall and lanky, and very interested in history, politics and ideas, so our interests were similar too. He joined the Jota, the Chilean Young Communists, and would sometimes arrive for weekends proudly sporting the maroon shirt with shoulder flaps and breast-pockets which was a sort of unofficial uniform of the Jota, worn by both girls and boys alike.

All the parties of the Popular Unity coalition ran their own events and rallies, as well as joining in the united demonstrations in support of the Allende Government. In January 1972 there was a big Communist Party rally in Santiago to celebrate the fiftieth anniversary of the Party's foundation. It was an incredible feeling to be among 80,000 people there in the National Stadium where it was held. There was music, spectacle and speeches, and the air was electric with the excitement and fun of the occasion. The parties of the Left in Chile certainly knew how to organise mass events which were not just political, but also really enjoyable for families, since there was always something on the programme for children and young people too.

The youth movements of the Communists and the Socialists – the two biggest parties – grew fast during those heady days, when optimism was pervasive, and it seemed as if the Government would defeat the sceptics and those on the Right, whose voice in the media was still very powerful.

On 20 December 1971 there was a mass demonstration by Popular Unity in Santiago, against those forces that were trying to provoke a coup d'etat, as President Allende was warning. I wrote home at the time,

"...the Christian Democrats are joining with them (the Right, Ed.), forgetting their policies of social change, "communitarian socialism", etc. Class antagonisms are visibly sharpening, and people are taking their positions – either with the Government, or against the Government and together with the fascists – because the middle opposition road is fast disappearing."

Another, more sinister, youth movement had emerged earlier that year, in April 1971, called *Patria y Libertad* (Fatherland and Freedom). This paramilitary organisation was nationalistic and fascist in ideology and methods, as I was soon to find out for myself. It was responsible for acts of violence against Popular Unity supporters, and was bent on fomenting an atmosphere of chaos and panic in the country. It was discovered later, from official documents released in the US, that *Patria y Libertad* had been financed by the CIA.

The Government banned a *Patria y Libertad* parade planned for March 1972, after arms had been found at their headquarters in Santiago. With hindsight, it seems to me that *Patria y Libertad* should have been banned as an organisation, because it was paramilitary and unconstitutional. But the Government was all the time doing its utmost to act within the Constitution, so as to give no stick for opponents to beat it with.

A group of lecturers at the University in Chillán decided to organise an exhibition about the Vietnam war, which was raging at the time. Manuel Miranda, a Chilean writer who lectured in Hispanic literature, and I were in charge of it. We collected photographs and cuttings, and wrote a text connecting the pictures and posters, which I carefully wrote out with marker pen on big sheets of paper stuck to self-standing billboards.

It looked really eye-catching. I was quite a good artist, and the lettering was neat and easily legible. Years before, when I was in the Sixth Form in Britain, I had painted a big banner with a picture of Chesterfield's famous Crooked Spire, and the slogan "Better Bent than Bombed!" which I had carried on one of the Aldermaston peace marches held in the early Sixties.

Our Vietnam exhibition summarised the history and actuality of that dreadful war. Between 1965 when the USA invaded and 1975 when the war ended with Vietnam's victory, an estimated 3-4 million Vietnamese and 58,000 Americans had lost their lives. The USA was carrying out indiscriminate napalm bombing of rural areas, resulting in horrendous birth defects in Vietnamese babies born in subsequent years. Our exhibition was on the pavement just outside the main entrance to the University, and attracted quite a lot of attention, both from students and passers-by. Manuel and I put it up each lunch-time, and took turns in manning it for a couple of hours each day.

It was my turn that day. I was standing next to the billboards, handing out leaflets against the Vietnam war, when all of a sudden a group of about five or six youths wielding long poles rushed across the road from the central Square and started demolishing the exhibition before my very eyes. I was hit on the back of my leg with one youth's stick, as they ferociously and rapidly destroyed the whole exhibition. It was so rapid, and obviously so well-planned, that there was nothing I could do except flee for my life after I'd received the blow on my leg. It was all over in a matter of seconds, and I was left shaking uncontrollably, angry at my impotence in the face of their vicious attack, and hurting from the nasty blow on my leg.

It was my first taste of *Patria y Libertad*, and I was left in no doubt of the lengths to which such people were prepared to go. After all, our exhibition was perfectly legal and was on University ground, so there was no reason to attack it, other than to frighten people off and show their power to cause disruption and panic. It certainly made me aware, in a more visceral way, of the dangers Popular Unity at a national level was facing as *Patria y Libertad* became more and more brazen in their attacks and assaults, especially in Santiago.

The Government's pledge to introduce agrarian reform began to take effect. *Latifundios* which had been neglected or where the owners were abroad or away for long periods of the year were the first to be requisitioned and handed over to the peasants that worked on them. There was broad agreement in the country that some sort of agrarian reform was necessary, and many blamed the previous Christian Democratic government for failing to do enough to change the situation, keeping the poor peasants who worked on the big *latifundios* as virtual serfs, tied to their owners. Yet when Allende started to tackle the power of the *latifundistas*, he met with huge resistance from the landed gentry and their allies.

But another problem was that the peasants who lived on the newly-nationalised *latifundios* were suddenly expected to run the farms themselves. They had no expertise in management, finance, how to apply for credits or book-keeping. It was very difficult, and there were many ex-*latifundios* where production fell dramatically, either due to the peasants' ignorance in running farms or the feeling of euphoria, that having got rid of the bosses, they could take life easy at last...

One day the Popular Unity parties at our University organised a voluntary work day at one such farm in the province of Ñuble. We were to pick grapes on a former *latifundio* which produced wine. It was April, late for picking the grapes, and when we got there we could see that many of the grapes were rotting on the vines. Most of the *inquilinos*[19] were nowhere to be seen, and we University lecturers and students worked all day till late to pick the grapes

---

[19] Tenant farm worker, peasant.

that could be saved. It was an example of the new difficulties the people's government had to face.

Another time, during university vacations, we were invited by our friend Eduardo, the Mayor of Chillán, to a different *latifundio* which had recently been taken over by the peasants. The river Diguillín ran through the land, and there was a sandy beach near a wooded area, which we reached after quite a long walk from the road. The new managers, representatives of the former peasants, greeted us with great enthusiasm, and told us how they were running the farm to benefit themselves now. Several of them spent the whole afternoon with us, bathing and picnicking, and we all had a great time. But I couldn't help wondering how they were able to spend all that time with us on a weekday, when presumably they should have been working. We were on holiday, but they weren't.

It takes time to change people's mentalities. The new farm-managers were enthusiastic supporters of the Popular Unity Government, but it was another step entirely from that political support to their being willing to change their behaviour and work harder than ever so that the country's agriculture would improve for the good of the country as a whole. I soon saw in all sorts of ways that vocal political commitment was one thing, but true political consciousness was quite another.

By early 1972 it was absolutely clear that a process of destabilisation of the constitutional Government was underway. As documented in CIA documents which came to light in subsequent years, there was a carefully orchestrated campaign to bring down the Popular Unity Government by artificially causing problems, like shortages in the shops through hoarding, by terror attacks and provoking an impression among the populace of increasing chaos.

In October 1972 one of the worst events to hit the Popular Unity Government began - a transport strike. It was called by an organisation of lorry-owners, many of whom owned fleets of lorries. That's why in my articles and letters that I sent home at the time I always referred to the strike as run by the lorry-OWNERS, not lorry-drivers, as most British journalists writing about Chile at the time called them. It's quite different if a strike is organised by the *owners* of an industrial sector, than if it is the *workers* of that industry who are on strike for better wages and conditions, which is what is usually at the heart of most industrial disputes. This was, therefore, a completely different "strike" from any I had ever heard of, and "boycott" would have been a more accurate word to describe the action, which was aimed at paralysing the country and causing shortages of all sorts of goods and foodstuffs.

Chile is a long country, and at that time the rail network did not cover the north and many parts of the south, so lorries were essential to carry goods and foodstuffs up and down the country. And because Chile is such a long, snake-like shape, the main north-south highway is the arterial route for the entire country, making it relatively easy to block it at any point.

It was an ugly episode. The striking lorry-owners parked their lorries across the main north-south trunk road to block it at many points, resulting immediately in shortages of foodstuffs up and down the country. Suddenly all sorts of daily essential items became hard to find. You couldn't buy meat, sugar, oil and butter, then fruit and vegetables became scarce. The lorry-owners' action was quickly taken up by other right-wing sectors, such as the Chamber of Commerce, shop-owners, and some doctors, engineers and other professionals.

Yet the original demands of the striking lorry-owners had already been met by the Government: to be able to charge higher rates for transporting goods, to be given preference in buying new lorries imported by the Government, and more facilities in obtaining spare parts. So then the lorry-owners came up with new demands. This time, the demand was that the paper industry remain in private hands, so as to ensure freedom of publication for the right-wing newspapers. The Allende Government had done nothing to curtail the freedom of the press, so this was an overtly political demand. Then the lorry-owners demanded the temporary ban on one privately-owned radio station be lifted. This radio had been temporarily closed down on the grounds that it was issuing openly seditious calls to the public to bring the Government down. Lastly the strikers began to demand guarantees of "freedom" in general, as if that had somehow been in danger.

From an outsider's viewpoint, it seemed to me at the time that there was not so much freedom as licence. I don't think any government, acting within the Constitution and the law, as the Popular Unity Government undoubtedly was, would have put up with the insulting attacks on its leaders and overt sedition characteristic of the privately-owned press, radio and TV stations at that time. And these media were the vast majority, the left-wing press being much smaller, with much less capital behind them.

The Government started to requisition lorries and other vehicles in an attempt to ensure supplies got through. Our University mini-buses were requisitioned in this way, and used to transport goods that the lorry-owners wouldn't transport. But the strike was well-organised and did manage to paralyse the country to some extent, which in itself created panic-buying among the population. It is interesting that during this time not one factory went on strike, and out of 260,000 farms, only 107 stopped work, which showed that only the workers of an enterprise can halt production, not the owners.

The lorry-owners' strike was the first major action the Right staged against the Popular Unity Government and showed that they meant business. To create chaos, right-wing supporters of the National Party and *Patria y Libertad*, and even the Christian Democrats, stooped to tactics which can only be called terror tactics. Specially-made twisted nails, *miguelitos*, were produced and scattered on the trunk roads and on Santiago's main streets, to puncture the tyres of buses and lorries whose drivers had refused to join the strike. At least one child died after being injured in a road accident, when the bus taking him to hospital had its tyres punctured on the way, causing crucial delay.

Bombs were put on railway lines, in the ENTEL (Telegraph Company) tower and other key installations. The Government declared a State of Emergency and a night curfew was imposed. The Army was put in charge of the Zones of Emergency throughout the country. The Government called on its supporters to do voluntary work, organising them in Voluntary Work Brigades, to load and unload sacks of flour, sugar, powder milk, onions, potatoes etc, and the big food supermarkets that had been requisitioned carried on functioning as usual.

In Chillán most of the shop-owners had not joined the strike, so we had not suffered any major shortages, at least in food. As smaller shopkeepers and lorry-drivers began to ignore the calls of the Lorry-Owners' Confederation and Chamber of Commerce and go back to work, new broader movements of shopkeepers and of lorry-drivers were set up, along with a Patriotic Front of Professional People, and these organisations worked in those sectors to expose the real interests of those behind the lorry-owners' strike, and to bring together those who, whilst not necessarily supporting the Popular Unity Government, did not identify with the dangerous and increasingly unconstitutional tactics of the Right.

One of the most frightening incidents of my life, with the exception of the coup itself the following year, happened some months later. Ricardo and I had to go to Santiago on business, and we booked tickets on the new Japanese-made express train which had been imported by the new Government to improve the rail network. It did the journey in four hours instead of the seven or eight of the older trains. The *Japonesa*, as the people in Chillán called it, was sleek and elegant, with comfortable reclining seats, automatic doors, sealed windows and air-conditioning.

We were enjoying our journey, watching the rows of slim poplar trees and snow-capped Andes flash by as the train sped onwards towards Santiago. All of a sudden, the train stopped, not at a station but in the middle of nowhere.

We heard shouts in the distance, but thought nothing of it. Then people started running into our coach from the engine end of the train, shouting: "It's on fire! They've set the train on fire!" Then we saw smoke billowing past our window from the front of the train, and more and more people pushing through the gangways towards the rear coaches. Outside we could see some youths we took to be members of *Patria y Libertad* running about near the front of the train. They had set the train on fire deliberately as an act of sabotage.

One woman with a baby in her arms started screaming in panic. Everybody was pushing and shoving to get to the nearest door, before the flames spread to our coach. It was an air-conditioned train, so you couldn't open any windows. We managed to get to the door of our coach, Ricardo jumped down first and I was virtually pushed down by those behind me desperate to get out. It was a long way down to the ground, but Ricardo caught me, and dragged me away from the burning train.

We were in a field in the middle of nowhere, some 50 kilometres south of Santiago. Later we found out it was the Cajón del Maipo. All the passengers were running away from the train, in different directions. We were in a rough field of stubble, and I was stumbling as I ran, pulled along by Ricardo. I was afraid that the fascists of *Patria y Libertad* would shoot, since they were armed, or that the train could explode at any moment. All of a sudden shots rang out. I flung myself to the ground instinctively, shaking uncontrollably. More and more shots. But Ricardo was urging me up, saying "Come on, get up, we've got to run over that way!"

He dragged me up and we ran on, Ricardo half-laughing at me as he explained that the shots were tear-gas, fired by the police who had come to restore order. I had thought they were live rounds fired by the train-saboteurs, and that we were in danger of getting shot! I wasn't in much of a mood to see the funny side, I must say, though in later years, we have often had a good laugh over it.

Together with scores of other frightened passengers, we finally made it to a road, and hitched a lift from a farm truck-driver going to the capital. We rode in the back of the empty truck, bumping up and down along the unmade roads and in the cold air of the spring evening. It was dark by the time we got to the city centre. I was so cold and shaky I could hardly walk to our hotel, my legs ached and I still had a sick feeling in my stomach. It had been quite a day.

In the main, however, despite the worrying political situation in the country, our lives went on in a pretty normal fashion. We worked, we socialised with friends, we drove out into the beautiful countryside and swam in the rivers and at the coast. Sometimes we would go to a place called Confluencia, near

Quinchamalí, where the Itata and Ñuble rivers merge and where the waters were just deep enough to stand up in at the river banks. With its warm, flowing water, the river was ideal for swimming. Other times we would go to the river Diguillín, up in the mountains, where the icy waters from the Andes formed deep emerald pools among massive rocks on the riverbank. It was fun on a really hot summer's day to dive into these pools, if you could bear the sharp contrast of the freezing cold water on your sun-warmed body.

Once when we went up to that river in the lower reaches of the Andes, we took along the young Russian wife of a Chilean friend of ours, together with her little boy of about six. He was an adventurous little lad, and when clambering over some smaller rocks in a shallow part of the river, he stumbled and fell in. We had to laugh when we saw the shock on his face as his body registered the icy water. He soon got warm again under the blazing summer sun.

We enjoyed the freedom our little Fiat 600 gave us, and during the winter holidays drove to the south to the area where Ricardo's parents lived. Ricardo's mother, *Mamita* Santos, as everyone called her, whom he regards as his mother, though she was really his stepmother, was a religious woman, kindly and sweet-natured, but whose Catholic faith did not allow her to countenance separation or divorce. In view of this we felt it prudent that I should stay in a boarding-house in Puerto Montt, whilst Ricardo and his daughters, who had travelled with us, stayed at his parents' house. It was important not to offend *Mamita* Santos's sensibilities, and anyway, we were able to spend most of the daytime together out and about. Perhaps my good relations with her later on, when I *did* meet *Mamita* Santos, were a result of our being tactful then.

Ricardo's father had liked me from the moment we met. He had travelled especially to meet me quite soon after we had moved to Chillán, while we were still living in the boarding-house, and we had a very jolly meal together at a local restaurant. Being a bit of a ladies' man himself, he perhaps understood Ricardo's love for me, and he was always extremely supportive and understanding. For my part, I liked him very much. He was in his early seventies when I first met him, balding, stockily-built, and with a wide grin which seemed to stretch from ear to ear. He was an interesting story-teller, and was a good listener, too. Many years later, when we went back to Chile to celebrate his 100th birthday (he lived to 104) he was asking me about the geography of Great Britain and about life in the Soviet Union – as full of curiosity as a young person.

Politically, Ricardo's father did not support the Popular Unity Government, yet when Ricardo was elected Secretary-General of the University of Chile in Chillán, and then became Vice-rector a few months later, he was extremely

Local market in the Araucanian region of Chile, near Temuco

President Salvador Allende with Chilean poet and
Nobel Prize for Literature, Pablo Neruda

Casa Pangai, the remote spot housing nothing more than a police border post and a house or two, near the border with Argentina, where Ricardo lived from five or six years old

Ricardo was born in a little wooden house at this spot near Cochamó, in the south of Chile

Plaque commemorating the 1907 Santa María School massacre of some 2000 striking nitrate-workers and their families in the northern town of Iquique

Mural celebrating the nationalisation of Chile's copper industry in July 1971. The slogan reads: "Chile is putting on long trousers – now the copper is Chilean!!"

Above: 2012 mural at Temuco's Universidad de la Frontera, demanding university autonomy. "Co-government means a free university where staff, lecturers and students hold the power. Who pays? Who works? CO-GOVERNMENT NOW!"
Below: Mural photographed in 2012 in Antofagasta, showing a Mapuche figure on the left and pictures of Salvador Allende, Pablo Neruda and Victor Jara, with the slogan: "Long live Chile! Long live the people! Long live the workers!"

Above: Singer/songwriter Victor Jara with his wife Joan and
   daughter Amanda (on Joan's lap) and Manuela.
Below: Present-day statue of President Salvador Allende opposite
   the Moneda Palace where he died on 11 September 1973.

Above: Oxen carrying *cochayuyo*, an edible seaweed, delicious in salad with chopped onion!
Below: The hamlet of Petrohué, where Ricardo's father worked for many years. The *Todos los Santos* lake is usually a beautiful emerald colour

Above: The river Petrohué near Puerto Varas, southern Chile
Below: Todos los Santos lake

Above: Cochamó, the small town near where Ricardo was born and lived for his first five or six years. Below: Ricardo, in 2006, recalling the traumatic moment in his childhood, when at the age of five or six, he was separated for ever from his birth mother and put on a boat at this quayside, to travel to meet - for the first time - the father with whom he was to live from then on.

Above: Our student Carlos Lagos, with my little nephew Daniel, whilst staying with my brother and family to improve his English, 1971.

Below: Cemetery niches of Chillán's Mayor, Ricardo Lagos, his wife Sonia Ojeda and his 21-year old son Carlos Lagos, shot dead in their home a few days after the September 11th coup d'état.

Above: *Villa Grimaldi*, one of the Junta's infamous torture centres in Santiago, now a Peace Park of Remembrance.

Below: Present-day memorial in La Serena "for the disappeared and executed prisoners". Most towns now have a similar memorial.

La Torre (tower) in Villa Grimaldi, scene of the most barbarous tortures

La Serena memorial, with the name of Ricardo's old university friend, Jorge Washington Peña Hen, who founded and ran a children's orchestra in the city before the coup.

ESCOBAR ASTUDILLO SOFÍA
CHIARLEONI ... FÉLIX
FERNANDEZ LOPEZ VICTOR ...
FLORES ANTIVILO MARIO GILBERTO
GAMBOA PIZARRO LUIS ALFREDO
GUERRERO GUERRERO PASCUAL ANTONIO
GUZMAN SANTA CRUZ ROBERTO
HONORES AGUIRRE HERNAN DEL CARMEN
JORDAN DOMIC JORGE MARIO
LEDDERMAN KONOJOWSKA BERNARDO MARIO
MACARIAN JAMETT MANUEL JACHACLP
MOYA ROJAS MIGUEL ANGEL
OSORIO ZAMORA JORGE OVIDIO
PEÑA HEN JORGE WASHINGTON
PRATS GONZALEZ CARLOS
RAMIREZ SEPULVEDA MARIO ALBERTO
RIVERA RAMIREZ JOSE ANTONIO
RODRIGUEZ ACOSTA JOSE
RODRIGUEZ TORRES JOSE SEGUNDO
ROJAS CORTES JOSE EXEQUIEL
SILVA IRIARTE HECTOR MARIO
VASQUEZ MATAMALA JORGE MANUEL
VERGARA MUÑOZ GABRIEL GONZA

Originally, when this estate resembled a little paradise, there were sinks and showers in this room. Here, on a lovely summer afternoon, when the perfume of the Villa's five thousand rose bushes floated through the air and the bees and butterflies went about their business, guests could freshen up before or after an afternoon around the pool.

Years later, when the Villa Grimaldi had been seized from its rightful owner and no longer resembled a paradise but, rather, an inferno, agents of the DINA took it over, taking advantage of its installations to set up a photography lab used to fabricate false credentials used by its agents to impersonate employees of the gas, light and water companies and journalists in repressive operations.

The lab was also used to photograph prisoners, thus providing a record of the horror that reigned here.

At other times, it was used to keep the dogs who guarded the tower. Around the same time, a metal bed set up here and connected to the electricity was used to extract information from prisoners.

What it was not used for was for making false I.D. cards: they were not necessary, since the DINA had the full support of all of the state entities including the Civil Registry for setting up the massive apparatus used to repress, torture, murder and transport and bury the bodies of anyone who voiced opposition to the dictatorship.

Today, this room is a testament to the men and women who disappeared from here or who were executed here.

The objects on display here are original and remind us of aspects of life which are so simple that they are often forgotten.

The people who disappeared from here or who were murdered here loved, created, sang, prayed, cried, played, wrote, read and, above all, fought for a better world... In other words, they lived, just like you and the people you love do.

We invite you to enter with respect, so that you might learn something of their lives.

Villa Grimaldi wall plaque in English

The green linen suit I wore to petition the Junta's new military governor, Colonel Cristián Guedelhoefer (photo from before I went to Chile)

The handbag Ricardo made for me in prison, made of goatskin

Above: On one of the many solidarity events in Scotland – Edinburgh Miners' Gala, 1976. Below: Chilean exiles in Italy, post-1973, painting a mural typical of the Ramona Parra mural brigades

Left: My first meeting, after 25 years, with our dear friend Maruja Ferriere, in 1998

Below: Ricardo with Joan Jara, in front of the Victor Jara Foundation in Santiago, in 2012

The Moneda Palace today

The presidential Moneda Palace, bombed by military aircraft and burning on September 11th, 1973

proud of his son, even though he knew Ricardo's political views. He was also very happy that his son had come to live in the same area where he had been born – the village of Quinchamalí, near Chillán. He had been a policeman all his life, after leaving school at twelve, and had made his way up the ranks as far as he could without being an officer, which you could not be without going to Officer Training School. He used to refer to the rank he had reached as *general chico* (little general). It was the top rank for working-class or peasant entrants to the police force and the armed forces, and showed the class-based organisational structure of these forces. This class-based structure was no doubt a help during the 1973 coup in achieving almost total obedience from the lower orders to their superiors.

Don Ricardo did not belong to any party but broadly supported the Christian Democrats, though he, unlike his wife, was not a believer. In fact, he used to joke that, in his view, the sun was the only true god.

After retiring at an early age from the police, he went on to become the forest warden for the area around the lovely Todos los Santos lake, based in the remote hamlet of Petrohué, near Puerto Varas, in southern Chile's lake district. He was also in charge of the tiny post office there. It was an idyllic spot, and he spent several years there, mainly on his own, because *Mamita* Santos did not like living there in that solitude. Their family home was in Puerto Varas, a small town on the Llanquihue lake, and *Don* Ricardo would divide his time between there and Petrohué.

The Todos los Santos lake is a most unusual emerald green colour, and is framed by the volcanoes Puntiagudo (sharp-pointed) and Osorno. Ricardo spent many of his holidays there as a young man, camping, bathing and rowing out on the lake for hours on end. It is such dramatic scenery, the black volcanic soil contrasting with the pure white of the snow-capped mountains and the dark green of coniferous trees native to that area, against an often cloudless blue sky.

Ricardo's own family story, to many people in the UK, seems unconventional. But to many in the third world, where harsh economic facts determine reality, it was far from uncommon. He was born of a liaison between his policeman father and a local girl at one of the places where his father was stationed. His father had another two illegitimate children from other liaisons in other places, before marrying *Mamita* Santos and having three sons within the marriage – Ricardo's half-brothers. Ricardo's birth-mother, Manuela Villegas, lived in Cochamó and already had two other children by other fathers. Ricardo remembers that one day, when he was a small boy, a uniformed man on horseback rode up to him and asked him his name and where he lived. He then asked Ricardo: "And do you know who I am?" On hearing Ricardo's answer, "No", the man said: "And what would you think if I told you that I am your father?" Ricardo's response apparently caused the man on horseback great amusement, because the little Ricardo replied, "No, my father is much uglier than you!"

For his first few years of life Ricardo lived in a wooden house with his mother, his half-brothers and his maternal grandparents. When his grandfather, who was the main breadwinner, died, the family had to split up, as they had no means of support. When Ricardo was five years old, his birth mother met a man who apparently proposed marriage to her on condition that she left her children behind. Her two older children went to live with their respective fathers, and she contacted *Don* Ricardo to ask him to take responsibility for her third child, Ricardo. So it was that at five or six years old – Ricardo doesn't remember and his father couldn't tell us exactly when either – Ricardo was left in the charge of a female friend of his mother's, Ledesma Delgado, in a place nearby called Valle del Concha. He lived with her for a few months, after which time she put Ricardo on a boat which took him out to a steamer going to Puerto Montt, about fifty miles away. There Ricardo was met at the quayside by two strangers, one of whom was his father, *Don* Ricardo, and the other a brother of his future stepmother's, *Don* Gregorio. And so began a totally different life for a little boy whose earliest memories are of a loving, carefree existence in the countryside, with his mother, brothers and grandparents who had all lived happily together in a wooden village house. He remembers they had sheepskin bed coverings and slept on sheep's wool pallets on the earthen floor.

Illegitimate children were a common and accepted feature of rural life in Chile at that time. Villages and hamlets were often nothing more than isolated groups of houses, with no school, no cinema, no social life except what could be enjoyed in the beautiful countryside. Contraceptives were unheard-of, yet naturally, young men and women had the same needs and desires as everywhere and in all times.

Living with his father and stepmother proved to be a harsh awakening for the little boy. His father, schooled in the rigid discipline of the police force, and no doubt believing in the old adage "Spare the rod and spoil the child", set about curbing the free spirit the little boy had and bringing him to heel using the old-fashioned methods of a rural policeman of that time, the Thirties. Ricardo recalls many a beating, punishment and insults, such as "blockhead", thrown at him. His stepmother even intervened on one occasion to stop his father as he was punishing him. When his father lost patience with trying to teach the child to read (there was no nearby school in those remote mountainous parts – Casa Pangue[20], which was seven kilometres from the

---

[20] Casa Pangue is a tiny hamlet far up in the Andes. *Mamita* Santos remembered that Ricardo's initial impression as a little boy when he first arrived there was: "Is this the only little piece of sky we've got?"

border with Argentina – so Ricardo did not start school till he was nine), calling him a dimwit, his stepmother began to teach him in her gentle, gradual way, and soon he was reading. There was nothing wrong with his intelligence, but he could not learn under duress.

In later years, when his three children who were born inside the marriage were growing up, *Don* Ricardo became much mellower, and by the time his youngest, Jaime, was born, twenty or so years later, he never so much as lifted a finger to him. Ricardo, as the oldest son living in the family home, undoubtedly bore the brunt of the policeman's upbringing methods.

You might have thought that Ricardo in later years would bear a grudge at the harsh treatment meted out to him. It never failed to surprise me that Ricardo always talked of his father with affection and love, and didn't seem to hold anything against him. I suppose he understood that his father thought he was bringing him up in the best way, that he had punished him for his own good. And when he wasn't being so strict, he apparently did show love for his son, in his way: Ricardo fondly remembers the occasions when his father would talk and joke with him.

As Ricardo would explain to me later, his father's intellectual development had come exclusively from his police training. His mentality had been formed by that military discipline – and it *was* military, as the police or *carabineros* in Chile have always been armed, both with sabres and revolvers. In such an atmosphere of strict discipline, it was hard for Ricardo to love his father during those childhood years. But he loved his younger brothers and his stepmother, and certainly appreciated his father's intelligence and the efficiency he undoubtedly displayed in his work. He could also see that his father was dedicated to his family – his sons and his wife. And *Don* Ricardo was a highly respected person in that region of the south of Chile. Ricardo also learnt from him that poor people merited respect, no matter if they were poor, and always admired his father's teaching, that through hard work and study one could achieve success in life.

I had never found life so much fun as in those years with Ricardo during the early seventies in Chillán. I suppose it was mainly because we were in love, we had interesting jobs, a great group of friends, it was a new and beautiful country, and the political situation was fascinating and absorbing. I felt that I was growing to love this crazy country where people turned up at the most unlikely hours of day or night and where you could go for a *pichanga* at one o'clock in the morning. And there were always things to laugh about, like the following incident.

One day Ricardo had been to the local shop and bought some groceries and fruit. When he got to the front door of our little house, on the corner of

---

because of the fact that the high mountains rose up so steeply all around.

105

Bulnes and Independencia streets, he realised that he must have left his keys on the shop counter. He left his bag of shopping leaning against the front door, opened the wrought-iron gate and walked back to the shop, which was one block away, retrieved his keys and walked back. As he was approaching the house, he saw a man with a shopping-bag opening the wrought-iron gate and start walking away from our house.

"Who can that be?" Ricardo wondered. Then he realised that his bag of shopping had disappeared from where he had left it, leaning against our front door. He hurried up to the man who was walking off down the street, carrying the shopping-bag. "Hey, I think that's my shopping you've got there!" Ricardo told the man, "what do you think you are doing?"

"Ah, it's yours, is it?" the man said innocently. "You know, mister, you want to be more careful in future. Anybody could just make off with your things, you know!"

Ricardo was quite a celebrity in Chillán. Being Vice-rector of the region's University was an important position, and he frequently featured in the pages of the local paper *La Discusión*. He often had to officiate at big meetings and would be invited to official gatherings of different kinds to represent the University. One such meeting was a celebration of the anniversary of the foundation of Chile's police, the *carabineros,* where he was invited to speak. Ricardo spoke of the important role the police had at this historic time, keeping order in the country when sinister forces such as *Patria y Libertad* were doing all they could to subvert order and provoke chaos. He echoed President Allende's call for the police to remain loyal to the country's Constitution, which stated that the duty of the armed forces and police was to support the constitutionally-elected government of the day. He told the assembled police officers and other city dignitaries about his own background as the son and brother of serving policemen and how he had grown up in a *cuartel de carabineros*. He ended with a rousing call for the police to defend the new people's Government, which was trying, against tough opposition, to improve the position of Chile's poor. "The times of confrontations with the police have passed," Ricardo concluded, "and we look forward to the day when we can call you *"compañeros carabineros!"*

After the speech, which was met with enthusiastic applause by the rank-and-file policemen there, the commander-in-chief of the region's armed forces, Colonel Luciano Díaz Neira, strode up to Ricardo and spoke to him angrily. "If you had dared to give that speech in front of *my* men," he raged, "I would have walked out in indignation!"

The fact is that everyone was taking up positions. The Popular Unity Government left no one undecided. You were either with the Government and on the side of the poor and dispossessed, or with the ever more vociferous and audacious Opposition, increasingly backed by the Christian Democrats, who soon left their middle-of-the-road position and openly sided with big business and the *latifundistas* against the Government.

> "Covert American activity was a factor in almost every major election in Chile in the decade between 1963 and 1973. In several instances the United States intervention was massive.

> "In a sequence of decisions in 1971 through 1973, the 40 Committee authorized nearly $4 million for opposition political parties in Chile. Most of this money went to the Christian Democratic Party (PDC), but a substantial portion was earmarked for the National Party (PN), a conservative grouping more stridently opposed to the Allende government than was the PDC. An effort was also made to split the ruling Popular Unity coalition by inducing elements to break away."
> (ibid., US Senate Church Report)

One of the tactics the Opposition employed was to impeach Popular Unity *intendentes*, or governors, of the 25 provinces of the country. In our province, Ñuble, the way that power had been shared out by the Government among the six parties that made up the Popular Unity alliance was that Ñuble's *intendente* would be from the MAPU – United Popular Action Movement, which was a split-off from the Christian Democratic Party. One after another, the Opposition managed through a variety of different legal recourses to impeach our region's *intendentes*, the longest-serving of whom was a man descended from Scottish ancestors whose name was Santiago Bell.

Santiago was about Ricardo's age, then in his early forties, and had a great sense of humour. We once spent an evening with him and other city dignitaries at an official dinner, which began as one of those boring, formal occasions, but which ended in an intimate comradely gathering of those of us who were pro-Government supporters, and went on till the early hours. I remember Santiago, Ricardo and I staggering out on to the deserted pavement afterwards and laughing uncontrollably at Santiago's unfailing jokes and witticisms whilst endeavouring to hail a taxi to take us all home.

Later, Ricardo, together with Santiago Bell, was part of the same group of leading Popular Unity people from Chillán, *los peces gordos* (big fish) as the military called them, who were detained in the island concentration camp of Quiriquina after the military coup of 11 September 1973. Some weeks later, after horrible tortures like being submerged in a big barrel of water until the point of drowning, Santiago and the others were brought back to Chillán prison, Santiago taking solace in his bible and beginning to work in wood-carving. Later he would become recognised for his artistic talent in the UK, where he lived for many years as an exile before his untimely death in 2005 at the age of 73.

Several exhibitions of Santiago's wood carvings and sculptures were held during the 1990's in Tower Hamlets, where he worked for several years as part of a community arts project, and at Tate Britain and the Barbican. His carvings reveal his deep humanism and true Christianity, though he himself had endured the depths of man's inhumanity to man.

The Popular Unity Government remained popular among the masses. "The central objective of economic policy is to broaden political support for the government," Chile's Minister of Economics, Pedro Vuscovic, declared. And it is true that the Government's economic policies really had favoured working people: prices were controlled by the government agency, DIRINCO[21], unemployment went down and the standard of living of the working classes had improved dramatically in 1971. Industrial production rose by 13%, which was the biggest increase in ten years. The big wage readjustments and the increase in employment had shifted the distribution of income, and for the first time, many families could afford to buy meat and goods for the home.

But the Government encountered unforeseen problems, such as the fall in the price of copper in the international market, which reduced the country's income from her main export. At the same time, the prices of food imports rose sharply, which resulted in more capital leaving the country than was coming in. On top of this, US commercial banks and the Export-Import Bank, the World Bank and Inter-American Development Bank stopped giving loans to the Chilean Government.

It was all part of a deliberate conspiracy to bring down the Allende Government. The US Senate Select Committee report "Covert Action in Chile 1963-73" admits:

> "Eight million dollars was spent, covertly, in the three years between 1970 and the military coup in September 1973, with over three million dollars expended in fiscal year 1972 alone."

That report, usually known as the Church Report, named after its Chairman Franck Church, goes on:

> "What did covert CIA money buy in Chile? It financed activities covering a broad spectrum, from simple propaganda manipulation of the press to large-scale support for Chilean political parties, from public opinion polls to direct attempts to foment a military coup. The scope of "normal" activities of the CIA Station in Santiago included placement of Station-dictated material in the Chilean media through

---

21 Dirección Nacional de Industria y Comercio (National Board for Industry and Commerce).

propaganda assets, direct support of publications, and efforts to oppose communist and left-wing influence in student, peasant and labor organizations."

The infamous lorry-owners' strike (or more correctly, boycott), and later the shop-owners' boycotts, were financed and directed by the CIA, as the Church Report makes clear:

> "Did the U.S. provide covert support to striking truck-owners or other strikers during 1971-73? The 40 Committee did not approve any such support. However, the U.S. passed money to private sector groups which supported the strikers. And in at least one case, a small amount of CIA money was passed to the strikers by a private sector organization, contrary to CIA ground rules. Did the U.S. provide covert support to right-wing terrorist organizations during 1970-73?

> "The CIA gave support in 1970 to one group whose tactics became more violent over time. Through 1971 that group received small sums of American money through third parties for specific purpose. And it is possible that money was passed to these groups on the extreme right from CIA-supported opposition political parties.

> "The pattern of United States covert action in Chile is striking but not unique. It arose in the context not only of American foreign policy, but also of covert U.S. involvement in other countries within and outside Latin America. The scale of CIA involvement in Chile was unusual but by no means unprecedented."

When Ricardo and I went to Santiago one weekend in mid-October 1972 we found most of the shops closed. On our return to Chillán, we found almost all the central shops closed, except two where the shop's staff had voted against their bosses to keep their shops open. It was clear to any intelligent person that the only way that shop-owners would be prepared to close their shops, instead of doing business, was if they were being guaranteed income to offset their drop in sales whilst closed.

In an attempt to minimize the chaos caused by the transport and shop strikes, the hoarding of goods and *Patria y Libertad*'s increasingly bold activities, the Government temporarily put the Army in charge and imposed a State of Emergency. The Army ordered the biggest food stores to open, which alleviated the situation somewhat. I wrote back home at the time:

> "There are no vegetables in Chillán because the transport is paralysed, so imagine what it'll be like if the strikes go on for much longer."
> (Letter of 17 October 1972)

People were trying to buy up everything they could get hold of in the small local shops, I wrote, which were still open, in the main.

A few days later, I wrote to my parents:

> "We're still in a State of Emergency with night curfew; the shops are closed, except the big food stores that the Government has requisitioned, there are serious food and petrol shortages, but these are being overcome by voluntary work on a mass scale, loading and unloading food from Army lorries and public vehicles." (Letter of 23 October 1972)

The voluntary work seemed an almost spontaneous response by people to help the Government, increasingly beset by problems not of its own making. It was really encouraging to see so many people, especially students and young people from the shanty-towns, enthusiastically giving up their time to ensure that food supplies got through.

Although it was increasingly hard to concentrate on our work, we did continue to work as usual, teaching our students, preparing classes and marking homework. And we continued to enjoy a good social life, having picnics with friends, swimming in rivers and sunbathing, dining with colleagues and friends. About this time we began to see a bit less of our good friends Eduardo and Maruja, as Eduardo was extremely busy, of course, as the city Mayor. Eduardo was a great asset to the Left in Chillán and to the Communist Party – he had first been elected as a local councillor, then became Mayor, and was then chosen as the Party's parliamentary candidate, being elected Deputy to the Chilean Congress in the March 1973 parliamentary elections. He was immensely capable and hard-working and very popular in the city.

Some time during my first year in Chile, when I felt I spoke enough Spanish, I had raised the matter of my transfer to the Chilean Communist Party (PCCh) with the local leadership and had a talk with a man Ricardo had known from his years in Temuco. Juvenal Valdés was a small, stocky man with black bristly hair and a dark ruddy complexion. He had long been a Party functionary and was one of those people who had really committed their lives to the cause. He was serious, self-educated, and down-to-earth. It was he who had come to see Ricardo in 1969, when we still lived in the *pensión* , to ask him to be the Party's candidate to run for the new university post of Secretary-General. Juvenal clearly knew nothing about my request, and it was quite obvious from his attitude that it was not something he had much interest in. I did, however, finally get the transfer my Party had requested and began to be active in the PCCh by 1971. At the time it was a mass party, supported by most of the country's artists and writers, and with a vibrant, go-ahead youth movement.

Its share of the vote in national elections was up to 20%, and it had the backing of the trades unions and very broad sections of the populace.

To be fair to the Chilean CP, it probably did seem rather strange to them that a young woman from a leading developed nation like Great Britain should want to join their party. I probably seemed a queer fish to them, and some who didn't know me might even have suspected that I was some sort of "imperialist agent", since there was at that time a fair amount of anti-American feeling, and to a lot of Chileans, the *gringos* were all the same, whether you were American or British.

But once I became a member of the University academics' branch in Chillán, the local Party organisation treated me just as any other member. I was even entrusted with giving classes in rudimentary Marxism to peasants who had recently joined the Party in the rural areas near Chillán! I helped organise the ill-fated exhibition on the Vietnam war, which the fascists destroyed (see earlier), I gave Marxism classes and I was active in setting up a branch of the *Instituto chileno-soviético*, which was an organisation to promote friendship and cultural links with the USSR, with branches in Santiago and several cities.

I have already talked about our teaching Russian during our first year in Chillán. This continued in subsequent years with considerable success and formed a good starting-point for launching the *Instituto chileno-soviético de cultura*. We had a talk with some local people who might be interested, and soon found that there was certainly enough interest to get it off the ground. One of the people who became the President of the *Instituto* was the young city architect, a civil servant who worked for Chillán's Town Hall. He did not belong to any political party, but was generally supportive of the Popular Unity Government. Another was a lawyer, Mario Hermosilla, a man in his sixties who was prepared to put a lot of time in to make the venture a success.

Like our architect friend, Hermosilla did not belong to any party. But in his case, this was because the Communist Party would not allow him to join. The fact is that he had been a minister in a coalition government in the late forties, under Gabriel Gonzalez Videla. Gonzalez Videla, of the Radical Party, had been elected President of Chile in 1946 with the support of the Communist Party, which was the third force in electoral terms at the time, winning 16.5% of the vote in the 1947 municipal elections. However, once elected President, Gonzalez Videla, under pressure from the United States, turned on his former allies, so the Communists, who had three ministers in Gonzalez Videla's government, were obliged to withdraw their support for him. Furthermore Gonzalez Videla went on to enact the *Ley de Defensa de la Democracia* which outlawed the Communist Party altogether and even went so far as to take more than 20,000 known Communists off the electoral register. This was the situation which forced many leading Chilean intellectuals at the time, including the country's leading poet, Pablo Neruda, to flee the country, an episode described in some detail in the poet's autobiography, *"Confieso que he vivido"* (I Confess I have Lived). The Communists organised demonstrations against what became known as *"La Ley Maldita"* (the accursed law), there were many arrests and the Party was forced to operate clandestinely for the next four years. When the *Ley Maldita* was finally repealed in 1958 under the next President, Carlos Ibáñez del Campo, the Party came out on to the streets with the rhythmical chant: *"Y qué fue! Y qué fue! Aquí estamos otra vez!"* ("And so what! And so what! Here we are once again!")

Mario Hermosilla had been one of the Communist Party's three ministers in the Gonzalez Videla government. Another had been Miguel Concha, whose daughter Olivia joined the Communist Party when she came to work at our University in 1971, and who had been on our excursion to the coast together with muralist Julio Escámez, described earlier. When, after the *Ley Maldita* had been passed, the government ministers who were Communists had to choose between remaining ministers or remaining in the Communist Party, Miguel Concha chose to keep his post as Minister. Hermosilla, on the other hand, did the honourable thing, resigned as minister and was later imprisoned, simply because he was a leading Communist, in the infamous prison camp of Pisagua, in the desert north of Chile. But whilst being held prisoner there he subsequently succumbed to an amnesty offered by the Gonzalez Videla government to those willing to renounce Party membership in return for their freedom. At that point Hermosilla weakened. He was released from prison, and was subsequently expelled by the Communist Party. Thus began the personal tragedy of Mario Hermosilla. For decades afterwards, he regretted his decision, and tried to get the Party to accept him back into membership. But the Communist Party was adamant. He had done a treacherous thing in their eyes, and they would not allow him back.

But Hermosilla remained a Communist, though without a Party card, and did all he could as a supporter of the Party, which is why he readily agreed to take on the Chairmanship of the *Instituto chileno-soviético*. We worked very well together, and I liked him, with his funny snub nose and rather flat face.

The *Instituto chileno-soviético* did not manage to organise much before events overtook it. We had plans to hold lectures and film shows about the Soviet Union, and we received a gift of a brand-new music system with speakers and a typewriter from the USSR House of Friendship, which had links with all the friendship societies abroad. We also planned to hold another series of Russian classes, as there was a fair amount of interest in the language from students and some professional people in the city. One of my students of Russian was a local judge, a middle-aged woman who was independently-minded and did not belong to any political party. Another was a local shopkeeper, who owned the biggest clothing store on Chillán's main shopping street. But we did not manage to make the *Instituto* a big, flourishing concern as it was in Santiago and other bigger cities.

In March 1972 we first heard the revelations made by US journalist Jack Anderson concerning the involvement of the US company International Telephone and Telegraph Corporation (ITT) in the attempt to prevent Dr Allende becoming President in 1970. The material makes it quite clear that offers of financial aid aimed at preventing Allende coming to power were made by ITT's president Harold S. Geneen to the CIA in July 1970 and to Henry Kissinger's office in September that year (Paul E. Sigmund, "The "Invisible Blockade" and the Overthrow of Allende", *Foreign Affairs*, January 1974). It was yet another proof that there had been and still were conspiracies afoot to get rid of the Popular Unity Government by any means, fair or foul. Anderson's revelations about ITT came as no surprise to us, and we fully supported the Government's decision to "intervene" the ITT, which it did in September 1971. (It is interesting that after the military coup of September 1973, ITT was rewarded by the return of its holdings in Chile, presumably in gratitude for the multinational's efforts in bringing down Allende).

Further proof of US attempts to undermine the Allende Government can be seen in the following excerpts from Paul Sigmund's article:

"...the question of pressing Chile still harder, in fact of engaging in government-directed economic warfare, came up in October 1971 after the intervention of the Telephone Company and the announcement of the copper compensation decision. Two days after the Chilean announcement on October 11 that most of the expropriated copper mines would not be paid for, Secretary of State Rogers issued a statement criticizing the excess-profits deduction and warning that 'should Chile fail to meet its international obligations, it could jeopardize the flow of private funds and erode the base of support for foreign assistance.' A few days later, when Rogers held a meeting to discuss the situation with the principal U.S. companies with investments in Chile, ITT submitted to the State Department what it described as a Chile White Paper. This proposed a seven-point program which included an embargo on Chilean exports to the United States, a halt to all AID assistance in 'pipeline', a veto on Chilean loan projects before the Inter-American Development Bank (ITT memo-writers noted with dismay that after the July 1971 earthquake the Allende government had received additional IDB assistance from previously approved projects), the use of 'a U.S. veto or pressure' to shut off pending or future World Bank loans, and advice to the U.S.

banking community and 'if possible' to international banking circles to refrain from extending any further credits to Chile. (From *Multinational Corporations and the United States Foreign Policy, Hearings before the Subcommittee on Inter-American Affairs of the Senate Committee on Foreign Relations*, Washington, pp.946, 957 and 971)

Bank loans were cut, credit suspended:

"The Bank of America representative testified that short-term credits remained at approximately their 1970 level until December 1971, when following the debt moratorium announcement all such credits were suspended, to be resumed later 'on a lower level with selected borrowers'. Chase Manhattan testified that 'the Chileans made an honest effort to pay American banks in the year or so following the election' (i.e. between September 1970 and September 1971), but that 'because of our own appraisal of the deteriorating economic conditions in Chile' lines of credit were reduced from $31.9 million in the first quarter of 1971 to $5 million in the last quarter. (Op.cit. above)

Chile's Finance Minister, Orlando Millas, claimed in November 1972 that Chile's lines of short-term credit from American banks had been reduced by that time from $219 million to $32 million. It is significant that the only aid coming from the USA during the last two years of the Allende Government was that to the Chilean armed forces. The termination of Export-Import Bank loans and the reduction in short-term credits from US banks created serious problems in the availability of spare parts, which was clearly one of the factors contributing to the dissatisfaction of Chile's lorry-drivers, culminating in their paralysing strike of October 1972.

To me, as an observer from another country, it seemed that President Allende could have been tougher with the Opposition, whose calls to bring down the Government amounted to open sedition. I couldn't imagine that any British government would have put up with the kind of actions the Chilean Right and paramilitary groups like *Patria y Libertad* were organizing daily by 1972, like the lorry-owners' action which prevented supplies getting to shops and factories, like the criminal use of twisted nails (*miguelitos*) scattered on roads to paralyse traffic by deflating tyres, or like the gross insults thrown at the President daily by the right-wing press and media. Surely, I thought, something could be done about these sorts of things which would be within the existing law? Yet very little was done, and it seemed that Allende relied a lot on his ability to influence and convince people in high places – political leaders, the military high command, the Church.

As the actions by the Opposition became more and more ferocious, I felt sure that the Government would put some of the instigators behind bars, but this did not happen. Why, I can only guess. Allende had been elected by the constitutional path, and was determined not to do anything which would give the opposition grounds for a coup, or for impeachment. So he trod with care, trying to steer a path between the fascist fanatics on the far Right and the legal Opposition and those on the far left both within and outside the Popular Unity coalition, who felt that the advance towards socialism was not nearly fast enough. He put much reliance on his ability as a very experienced politician to keep the military onside, trusting their professed adherence to the doctrine of non-interference in politics and loyalty to the constitution. Perhaps too the fact that Allende was a Freemason could have led him to rely too much on personal links with other masons who were politically on the right.

The Communist Party was all the time trying to win over to the side of the Government the more left-wing elements of the Christian Democratic Party, but this task was made increasingly hard by what I saw as provocative actions by some of the ultra-left, who continued their policy of occupying small businesses and farms – something that was not envisaged by the Popular Unity programme, which aimed to nationalise and take over only big industries and *latifundios*.

On one occasion in Chillán, for instance, youth members of the MIR, MAPU and even some from the Socialist and Radical Parties staged a military-style show of force outside a Popular Unity women's rally, armed with sticks and some even with walkie-talkies. It was infantile gesture-politics at best, but had serious consequences for some of these young people some months later after the coup, when they were tortured to get them to confess to non-existent military plans, and specifically asked time and time again: "Where are your walkie-talkies? Who has got them, where are they being kept?"

The transport strike meant that there was no petrol to be had in Santiago, and there were acute shortages of vegetables and fruit which had to be transported from other regions of the long country that is Chile. The Opposition, composed of the National Party and the right-wing of the Christian Democrats, plus *Patria y Libertad*, organized marches where the women – mainly upper- and middle-class women from the affluent suburbs of the capital – took along saucepans and made a lot of noise as they banged their empty saucepans with spoons and shouted their slogans, that there was no food, their pots were empty, etc, etc. These demonstrations, whilst nowhere near as big as the pro-Government demonstrations that we had been on several times, and which filled all the central streets as far as the eye could see, were nevertheless quite effective, since the shortages were real, and obviously no-one wanted or expected to have to put up with that.

Yet the majority of the women on those marches never shopped or cooked in their kitchens, as they had maids who did that work for them. So it was a glaring example of hypocrisy, and they didn't get much sympathy from Chilean working-class and peasant women, who were used to having little to eat and little to cook, not because of shortages in the shops, but because they were always short of money to buy what food they needed to feed their families.

Women became a real force to be reckoned with during Popular Unity. I was surprised, coming from Great Britain, where even now there are so few women MP's, to find that there were quite a few women deputies and senators in the Chilean parliament. The Chilean Young Communists were led by a young woman, Gladys Marín, and she was subsequently elected to parliament as a Deputy. Mireya Baltra, a Communist Deputy who had worked for years in a newspaper kiosk, was made Minister for Work and Social Provision, and was responsible for getting more rights for domestic servants and ownership rights for shanty-town dwellers, like those of Nueva Matucana. Carmen Lazo had been a Socialist Deputy for many years, and one of the leading Socialists of the time. Both she and Mireya Baltra were working-class women who were fiery speakers and could really work a crowd. I remember when Mireya came to Chillán to speak in front of the Town Hall, all the nearby streets were packed with ordinary people who had come to listen, and she had a tremendous rapport with the people, in a speech peppered with laughs and cheers from the crowd.

There were many other leading women too, in all spheres of life. Julieta Campusano was a Senator, an imposing woman of the sort who didn't suffer fools gladly, then there was Carmen Lazo of the Socialist Party, Laura Allende, the younger sister of President Allende, who had been a Deputy in the Chilean Congress since 1965, and the Socialist Senator Dr María Elena Carrera. There were Christian Democratic women too, such as Juana Dip and Wilma Saavedra. There were women judges, women everywhere in the media (remember that in Britain it was 1974 before we had the first female TV newsreader, Angela Ripon), women heads of department at the universities. In short, I found that, despite the common conception that Latin American countries are "*machista*", in Chile women were more to the fore at that time than in my own country.

I have my own pet theory as to why this is. After five years living in Chile, and all the years since spending much of our social life in the company of other Chileans – friends and relatives – I have come to the conclusion that the developed western world has a misconception as to what "*machismo*" is. Whilst that term may describe a certain attitude and way of life of some Latin American men, it does not mean that women are considered second-class citizens. On the contrary, I have always found that Chilean men, if anything, put their womenfolk on a pedestal, and regard them as special, not inferior, but different. Whereas in Britain there always seems to be the attitude that if a woman wants to have a family, that's *her* problem, not that of society as a whole. I feel that a country should have an interest in enabling women – who are after all half of the population and the only ones who can give birth to the citizens of the country's future – to carry out that role with support both from the State *and* her workplace *and* her family.

In Chile all our friends had children and all the wives worked. It is true that the majority had maids, so their childcare arrangements were in that sense much easier than childcare arrangements in Britain. I always felt a great deal of respect from the male colleagues towards women colleagues at the University where we worked. And when I was elected Head of the Department of Languages, I felt only support and friendliness from my male colleagues. Women seemed to be accepted for what they are, rather than having to try to be more like men in an effort to advance in their careers, for instance, which is what often happens in Britain.

Ricardo was still Vice-rector of the University in Chillán, but there were to be elections in October 1972, when he hoped he would be free of the burden which the job had become. He had very little free time, having to go to Santiago for certain meetings of the University's *Consejo Superior* and to see different people at the University's headquarters concerning the purchase of land for the University in Chillán to have a campus of its own, or to do with salaries and a host of other issues, since our local University still depended in many ways on the national University of Chile in Santiago. In Chillán itself, he was in his office till late every evening, in interminable meetings, with colleagues and student representatives who had waited to see him about problems – anything from students' housing, to the financial problems of the canteen, to lack of rooms for staff to prepare work in, to problems of political machinations within the university as the different parties vied for popularity and influence.

The student canteen at the University where we worked was tiny, and ill-equipped to feed the hundreds of students who needed a lunch-time meal. It was run by a lovely kindly and plump woman whom everyone called *Señora* Olguita, who worked all hours to ensure that a good hot meal was provided once a day. We would sometimes eat there ourselves, and found the food wholesome and tasty, as well as very reasonably priced. *Señora* Olguita was very popular and well-loved by the students, who could see that she provided a service against all the odds – a tiny kitchen and inadequate finance. She was very fond of Ricardo, and whenever we appeared, she would come and make a fuss of us, always saying the same thing to Ricardo: *"Tan linda ella...!"*

(She's so pretty...!) – something Ricardo always teased me about later when we were on our own.

The issue of a campus of its own for the University was pressing: under Popular Unity, student numbers had swelled, yet the buildings we had at our disposal were cramped and in some cases, unsuitable. Ricardo started negotiations with a local landowner, a prominent Christian Democrat called Fernando May, over a house he was selling and some adjacent land which he might be willing to donate to the University, as a local benefactor. Initially May was trying to sell the property, a big country house, at an exorbitant price, and his idea was to throw in six hectares of land as a bait, no doubt with the idea of thus appearing as an important local benefactor. This was the proposition Ricardo was first presented with. Gradually Ricardo, with much persistence, managed to convince May that the University needed more land, because the house itself would not be suitable as the main building for the University. New, much bigger, buildings would be needed which would require at least 25 hectares.

After prolonged negotiation, and trips back and forth to Santiago to check that the necessary finance would be forthcoming, it was finally agreed that the University would buy the house Fernando May was selling, but that he should donate 30 hectares, not the six that he had initially offered. This was quite a coup for Ricardo, since the landowner had clearly thought originally that a donation of six hectares would be enough to ensure himself a venerable place in local history. I think Ricardo managed to pull the deal off by a mixture of his powers of persuasion and diplomacy.

The local newspaper *La Discusión* of 7 October 1972 carried the following news report:

> "Yesterday, at 17 hrs, in the Vice-rector's office of the University of Chile in Chillán, the agreements and pledges were signed for this University *sede* to acquire the buildings of *El Mono* estate for one million *escudos* from its owner, Fernando May Didier, together with Mr May's donation, at the same estate, of 29.25 hectares, on which the definitive buildings of the University will be built.

> "Present at the signing ceremony were the well-known landowner, Fernando May Didier, and the Vice-rector of the University of Chile in Chillán, Ricardo Figueroa..." Then the report goes on to mention other local and University dignitaries.

May's country house was converted into a student hall of residence and building work on the new University campus started in 1973. As the news report of 7 October 1972 pointed out, the city's University at that time had 15 degree courses and 2,400 students. The fact that the new campus of the now re-named University of the Bío-Bío has been built there, on the land donated (or, more accurately, sold) by Fernando May, is almost entirely due to Ricardo's efforts, though up to now there is no official recognition of this, as I mentioned earlier in the book. It was to be Ricardo's most important legacy from the 18 months he spent in the post of top authority of the University in Chillán.

In October 1972 there was a huge demonstration in Santiago to protest at the US Kennecott copper company's seizure of a ship carrying Chilean copper. What had happened was this: the Kennecott Copper Corporation had obtained a French court order blocking payment to Chile of $1.4 million owed by French manufacturers for copper produced at Chilean mines, now nationalised, that Kennecott had previously owned. Then a court in the Netherlands ruled to allow Kennecott to seize a ship from Chile loaded with 1,250 tons of copper. (P.296, *We Must Make Haste – Slowly*, David J. Morris, Random House, 1973). Since copper was Chile's main source of income, this was a serious setback, and seemed grossly unfair to all of us in Chile who supported the Popular Unity Government and who were trying their hardest to make the process a success.

It showed once more the power of the big US multi-national companies, that they were able to exert such influence on European governments, to the detriment of Chile. In a letter I sent back home at the time, I wrote:

> "The giant Kennecott company is attacking Chile because their economic interests have been drastically affected by the Popular Unity Government's nationalisation of Chile's copper in July 1971, especially since they have received no compensation from the Chilean Government, whose legally established Copper Tribunal (composed of all the different political sectors of the country) laid down that there could be no question of compensation being paid, in view of the excessive profits the US copper companies obtained during decades."

By 1972 we were not seeing much of our friends Eduardo and Maruja Contreras, as I've said earlier, because Eduardo's increasing political role left him no time for socialising. But we still saw Maruja, a lovely gentle person with a very sweet nature, who was a student of Ricardo's in her final year. We had numerous other friends, some of them lecturers who had joined the University's staff more recently. Juan Gabriel Araya and his wife Maruja Ferriere were two of our closest friends. Juan Gabriel taught Latin American Literature and Maruja taught Nursery Nursing. They had come to Chillán from Angol, further south, and had a house in Chillán Viejo, which, as its name suggests, is the oldest part of Chillán and is where the Chilean mother of Chile's great nineteenth century independence hero, Bernardo O'Higgins, came from.

Readers might well wonder how a Chilean Independence figure comes to have such an un-Chilean name. Bernardo O'Higgins was born to a Chilean woman, Isabel Riquelme, when she was only in her teens. She had met and become pregnant by Bernardo's father, an Irishman, Ambrose O'Higgins[22], who was in his fifties, and who was later to become Viceroy of Peru for the Spanish crown. Her illegitimate son, Bernardo, became Chile's most famous son because of his role in gaining Chile's independence from Spain in 1818, after eight years of fighting with nationalist forces, finally joining forces with the famous Argentinian liberator, José de San Martín. Bernardo O'Higgins thus became the first national leader of newly-independent Chile and ruled for six years before being deposed in a coup by the conservative land-owning class in January 1823.

People from Chillán Viejo are very conscious of this history, and there is a monument to Bernardo O'Higgins in the Plaza Mayor Isabel Riquelme, a mural featuring his exploits and a mausoleum containing the remains of his mother, Isabel Riquelme, and his sister, Rosita. Those whose families had long lived in Chillán Viejo even considered it to be a separate place from the city of Chillán itself, because of its older history and its connections with Bernardo O'Higgins.

I only found out much later that in Richmond, London, there is a bust of Bernardo O'Higgins in a square named after him, and a blue plaque at Clarence House, where O'Higgins lived when studying in London.

---

22 O'Higgins, Ambrose (c. 1721-1801), governor and captain-general of Chile, later viceroy of Peru. O'Higgins, who was Irish, went to Spain around 1751 and worked for the Irish merchant firm of Butler in Cádiz, on whose behalf he undertook a commercial journey to South America in 1756. In 1761 Ambrose O'Higgins was back in Spain, where he joined the army as 'ingeniero delineador' (engineer draughtsman), with the rank of lieutenant. Three years later he was sent again to South America and on his first journey across the Andes, O'Higgins conceived the idea of improving the route by constructing a chain of brick-built shelters, and by 1766 a year-round postal service was operating between the Atlantic coast and Chile. He returned to Spain and wrote the *Description of the Realm of Chile*, a memorandum containing recommendations about the indigenous population, agriculture, trade, and administration.

Back in Chile in 1770, Ambrose O'Higgins was named captain, lieutenant-colonel, and field-marshal. In the 1770s his troops were engaged in wars with the Llanos and Pehuenches, indigenous people of the region, and he was twice wounded. In 1780 he was appointed commandant-general of the Spanish army in Chile, defending the town of Concepción against the attacks of the British army. O'Higgins' highest titles were attained in 1787 as governor and captain-general of Chile, and in September of 1795 as viceroy of Peru, a post he held for nearly 5 years. Among his most important achievements was the abolition in 1789 of the cruel 'encomienda' system, whereby landowners kept indigenous labourers in conditions close to slavery. He also pushed reforms in the Catholic church to benefit the poor, eliciting the antagonism of the reactionary local elite. Ambrose O'Higgins never married and his titles died with him. In his late fifties he had a romantic liaison with María Isabel Riquelme de la Barrera, an attractive eighteen-year-old Chilean woman from a well-known local family. Their son, Bernardo O'Higgins, was born in Chile and was educated by his father, whom he never knew. He died on 19 March 1801 in Lima, Peru. (Ref: Edmundo Murray, in Dictionary of Irish Latin American Biography).

Anyway, to get back to our friends Juan Gabriel and Maruja, who lived in Chillán Viejo. (Incidentally, years later, Juan Gabriel, who became a well-known writer, published a novel about Isabel Riquelme, entitled *Primera Dama*). They had two daughters when we first became friendly with them, and later Maruja gave birth to their third daughter. They had a maid, Lydia, who had been with them for years, and as is so often the case, she was a single mother from the countryside. We spent many evenings having dinner together, both at their place and ours, sometimes with other friends, like Oscar and Sylvia, another couple from Angol.

Juan Gabriel is a tall, lanky fellow, who spreads his long body at various angles over furniture. The furniture we had in our living room was the inexpensive but attractive cane and wicker furniture you could get from the local *feria*. And to accompany it, I had made a piece of furniture I'd seen in a magazine to act as a sort of two-person seat, which consisted of a longish varnished board placed horizontally on top of two smaller vertically-placed boards slotted together to form a perpendicular diagonal-shaped cross at either end. Then on top of the board was an oblong piece of foam covered in some bright red checked material I had bought and sewed. The board was longer than the mattress and was meant, according to the design I had seen in a magazine, to project some nine inches at either end, so you could put your cup of tea down on one of the ends, or your glass of wine, or some ornament or other. We had it against the longer wall in our tiny living/dining room and it looked quite smart, with bright cushions on it against the wall.

On each occasion they came to visit, Juan Gabriel would gravitate towards that home-made seat, his long legs splayed out in a variety of directions. As he talked animatedly and laughed at anecdotes being related, his body would jerk and twist around and the board of the seat would gradually edge further and further away from the wall. He was usually oblivious, until it would get to such an extent that a big gap between the seat and the wall had opened up, and he found he no longer had any back support to rest against, at which point he would utter some expletive. Then he would stand up, cursing and laughing, and we'd have to push the contraption back against the wall.

On such occasions, we would laugh a great deal over the meal, and a fair amount of wine would be consumed. The conversation would go on late into the night, since they didn't have to worry about baby-sitters as Lydia was a live-in maid. But eventually Maruja would gently remind Gabriel of the time and that perhaps they should think about making tracks. So they would stand with coats on, and Ricardo would invariably call out, "Ah, but you must have the stirrup drink!" and proceed to pour out another glass of wine. "*El trago del estribo*" ("One for the road") is a Chilean peasant custom, and was

121

traditionally the last drink before putting your foot in the stirrup and hoisting yourself on to your horse to go home.

One night, after one such convivial evening together at our place, Juan Gabriel and Maruja had been standing in their coats near the front door for some time, but Juan Gabriel kept thinking of something else to say, some funny story to relate or comment to make and we all remained standing, they poised to leave but never managing to leave. Juan Gabriel always remembers how after some time like this I apparently burst out: "Well, if you're going to go, for goodness sake, go!" Everybody found that so funny.

Maruja herself would never have said anything as rude as that. She was from a Swiss French family of immigrants to Chile who had lived and farmed the agricultural area near Angol. She was very pretty, with the most unusual blue-grey eyes and fair complexion. Juan Gabriel adored her, and they were a lovely family. Once we went with them to visit her brother, who lived in what had been their parents' home in the Nahuelbuta mountains near Angol. Her parents had died by this time, and her brother lived there with his family. Her brother suffered from cerebral palsy, and was in a wheelchair outside the entrance as we drew up in the car after a two-hour drive from Chillán. It was a beautiful day, sunny and warm, and the hills all around the house were lush and green, with tall trees and winding dirt-tracks going off into the distance. In front of the big wooden country house his three small ginger-haired children played around happily while his wife, a small woman with thick dark-red hair, served us *chicha*[23], which they made on their farm. In fact we learnt that that was how they made a living, and though his speech was hard to understand and he had all the problems associated with cerebral palsy, we were impressed that he managed to bring up a family and run a successful *chicha* business.

The political situation in the country, with the lorry-owners' strike, the State of Emergency and the extremist actions of some sectors of the Right meant that practically everybody in the country took a stand: you were either with the Government or against it. Among our colleagues there were very few whose politics or political stance remained unknown. We had one colleague in the Department of Languages who had done a postgraduate degree in the USA, who made it clear that he did not support the Popular Unity Government, but he never entered into any discussions and kept himself very much to himself. But the majority of staff were pro-Allende, even if they were not members of any particular political party.

---

23 *Chicha* is fermented apple juice, not clear and sparkling like cider, but cloudy and still. It's just as potent, however.

Chile's great poet, Pablo Neruda, wrote a poem about the country's increasingly polarised situation, which was put to music and became one of Victor Jara's best-known songs:

I do not want my country to be divided,
I do not want it bloodstained by seven daggers,
I want the leafy light of Chile to shine
On the new house that we have put together.
I do not want my country to be divided,
I do not want it bloodstained by seven daggers.

I do not want my country to be divided,
There is room for all of us in this land of mine,
And let those who feel themselves to be prisoners
Take that old melody and go far away.
The rich were always foreigners amongst us,
Let them go off to Miami with their aunts.
I do not want my country to be divided,
Take that old melody and go far away.

I do not want my country to be divided.
There is room for all of us in this land of mine.
I am staying here to sing along with the workers
In this new history and geography.
I am staying here to sing along with the workers
In this new history and geography.

We were always very busy. Ricardo was still Vice-rector of the University in Chillán, and I was Head of the Department of Languages and in charge of the Language Laboratory. I managed to finish my book on Chile in May 1972 and sent it off for publication, which was a huge burden lifted from my shoulders. The book came out later that year in Britain. In Chile it also received some publicity and an interview with President Allende himself was promised me, so that I could present him with a copy in person. Unfortunately this never happened: events took over and with all the problems the Government was facing, a meeting with me was not likely to be seen as a priority by those who ran his schedules.

Despite all the problems, most of our colleagues backed the Government because they saw that election promises had been carried out – copper had been nationalised, iron and steel, coal mining and textiles likewise. Banks had been nationalised and systems of credit introduced to favour small business and farms. Workers had been brought both into the Government and on to the boards of nationalised industries, unemployment had been cut from over 8% when Allende took office to just over 4% in February 1972. They saw that the cost of living, which had gone up by 36% in 1970, had risen by only 23% in 1971. GDP had increased by nearly 8% in the same year. Food prices had remained low and real wages had increased by 30%. The lowest-paid had had their wages raised, old-age and widows' pensions had gone up. Pension schemes were extended to include sectors that had not previously had access to them, such as shopkeepers and the self-employed. The Government had expropriated 1,300 *latifundios* in its first seven months of office, as compared with 1,200 farms expropriated in the whole of former President Frei's six-year term.

Though inflation was high, the Government introduced regular *reajustes*, or inflation compensation bonuses, to recompense workers for the rise in the cost of living – something previous governments had also done, but never so fully.

On a personal level, we teachers had more money in our pockets than before. We had the money to buy a small TV and even (by instalments) a little car, which was something the majority of colleagues could only dream of before. Food shortages began in 1972, but we supporters of the Popular Unity Government felt sure that these were being artificially orchestrated by *latifundistas* hoarding food or selling it abroad, by shop-owners hoarding fridges, washing machines and cookers to create artificial shortages. The Government set up neighbourhood committees to distribute basic foodstuffs such as meat, eggs, flour, cheese, fish, rice, oil and these JAPs[24] played a very important role in ensuring that people from the *poblaciones* and shanty-towns did not go without food, since if you were registered as a resident of a particular neighbourhood, you had a ration-card enabling you to buy these foodstuffs without any problems.

So there were plenty of reasons for working people to support the Government and to condemn what were seen as increasingly flagrant attacks on the Government by the Opposition. But the shortages and the atmosphere of constant attacks and terrorist acts by *Patria y Libertad* began to take its toll. Whilst supporting the Government's aims, many non-political people began to wish for an end to the apparent chaos, for order to be restored.

The lorry-owners' boycott lasted 19 days, but it was like a declaration of war on the Government. Railway tracks from Santiago to Valparaíso and transmitting towers were blown up. Industrial premises were set on fire and *miguelitos* on the highways became frequent. The Government responded by imposing a State of Emergency, and briefly took over radio stations in the capital. President Allende was faced with an increasingly uncontrollable

---

24 Juntas de Abastecimiento y Control de Precios (Supply and Price Control Committees).

situation. The lorry-owners' and employers' strike ended with Allende deciding to bring into the Cabinet top military men to head three of the most important ministries – the Interior, Mining and Public Works.

This was a logical move, from the President's point of view, since his whole strategy was to inch the revolution forward but always within the confines of the Constitution, which meant keeping the military onside. At the same time Allende brought in the head of the CUT (Central Unica de Trabajadores, equivalent to the British TUC), Luís Figueroa, as Labour Minister, and another workers' leader, Rolando Calderón, as Minister for Agriculture, probably in an attempt to counteract the influence of the military and keep onboard the unhappy far left, both within the Socialist Party and the MIR. Once again, it was a balancing act.

I was very uneasy about the decision to bring the Armed Forces into the Popular Unity cabinet. From all that I knew about the Chilean army's training in the USA, I could not imagine that they would ever be on the side of the people. At the time I wrote home:

> "The incorporation of the Commander-in-Chief of the Army, General Carlos Prats, (successor to René Schneider, assassinated by ultra-right elements in October 1970), a Navy Rear-Admiral and an Air Force General to the Popular Unity Government's Cabinet is probably difficult to understand unless one understands the particular characteristics of the Chilean Armed Forces. The tradition which is deeply implanted in the Chilean Armed Forces is one of allegiance to the legally constituted government, the Constitution and laws of the country. This was the concept firmly upheld by the late Commander-in-Chief of the Army, General René Schneider, and which has come to be known as 'The Schneider Doctrine'.

> "This tradition of professionalism, non-interference in the political issues of the day and the concept of merely accomplishing professional duty has meant that the Armed Forces have acted, since the Popular Unity Government came to power two years ago, on the side of the Government and have consistently rejected all attempts to get the Armed Forces to act against the Government. The faithful allegiance to their historical tradition has won them all kinds of insults and abuse from the right-wing elements in the country, who previously considered the Army as 'theirs' and have been bitterly disillusioned to find that the Army is neither 'theirs' nor anybody's – that is, the Armed Forces maintain an attitude of impartiality, but at the same time, one of strict allegiance to the Constitution and the established laws of the country. As it is the Popular Unity Government which is abiding by

the Constitution and the laws, and it is the Opposition who are resorting to tactics which are illegal and unconstitutional, the Armed Forces, to be true to their tradition, must obviously act in favour of the Government at the present time."

I can remember clearly that I did not feel as confident as my words suggested at the time. But neither did there seem to be any other way to proceed. I did not see how you could start arming the part of the population that supported the Government, as the MIR was calling for, since that would surely just bring forward the time when the military would step in and organise a coup d'état. As one of the Chilean Communist Party's top leaders, Volodia Teitelboim, put it, in his colourful popular language, "You can't swap horses in the middle of the river!" In other words, if you're on the constitutional road, you can't suddenly change to a different path.

It was estimated at the time that the lorry owners' and shop owners' boycotts had lost the country some $200 million. But much had been learned, not least the capacity for organisation of ordinary people in the shanty-towns and *poblaciones*. Thousands volunteered for all sorts of jobs, loading and unloading goods brought by requisitioned transport and distributing them to local shops and the JAPs. It was quite a learning process.

But because the situation was becoming increasingly tense and a military outcome of one sort or another seemed to be looming large by the end of 1972, the parties of the Popular Unity started to organise self-defence brigades and began to man important buildings during the night, so as to guard them against any attack. Ricardo and I went to self-defence classes, where we learned how to divert a fist coming at you, how to trip up your attacker, how to knee him in the privates and so on. It was all good fun, but personally I couldn't for the life of me see how that was going to help in defending the country if there was a coup. Similarly manning during the night the buildings of the University or the headquarters of the Popular Unity parties seemed pretty pointless to me. I did it a few times, together with other colleagues, but the only thing that came out of it was feeling shattered the day after, and still having to teach the next morning.

Two of Ricardo's brothers were officers in the *carabineros*[25]. We had a visit from one of them, Sergio, who lived in Santiago, together with his wife, Marlis, and their two sons, who were about ten and twelve. I remember that we had a discussion over a meal in our little bungalow, when Ricardo expressed the opinion that their job as police officers was now more in keeping with the "law and order" aspect of their job, since they no longer had to repress the people as they had had to do under previous governments. Sergio admitted

---

25 police.

that this was true but at the same time expressed his misgivings about how the public viewed the *carabineros* nowadays, saying that he felt that they were losing respect, because every Tom, Dick and Harry now felt they had a role to play in governing the country. It was all very well the people feeling backed up by the Government, he said, but the constant demonstrations, the seizures of small businesses and farms and increasing chaos were all leading to an impossible situation for the police. Ricardo argued that the *carabineros* were better paid than before and that the Government had done nothing to contribute to any lack of respect by the populace – quite the opposite. But in a sense I could see what Sergio meant. It was evident that for the first time in Chile's history, the common people really had come to the fore and were playing a leading role in many areas in Government, where there were worker ministers, in the JAP's, in state organisations like CORVI (State Housing Corporation), as well as in the six political parties that made up the Popular Unity. And the *carabineros*, like the officer corps in the Armed Forces, were not at all used to that – they were used to being the boss and acting as such.

However, Sergio and Ricardo parted on good terms, though that was to be the last time they saw each other until many years later, in 1989 – Ricardo's first visit back to Chile after the tragic coup d'état which deprived him of his homeland for sixteen long years.

The Left pinned much hope on the forthcoming March 1973 parliamentary elections. It had become patently obvious that having only one part of the power – the Executive, i.e. the Presidency – was not enough to be able to advance further in implementing the Popular Unity Government programme. Ministers were being impeached, *intendentes*[26] of the provinces were being arbitrarily dismissed from their posts, bills were blocked in parliament because the Opposition had a majority in the Congress and the Senate – the two houses of parliament. The Popular Unity alliance had 17 senators and 57 deputies, whereas the combined opposition (mainly Christian Democrats and the National Party) had 32 senators and 93 deputies.

In Chillán, the *intendentes* of Ñuble province, who belonged to the Christian MAPU (a breakaway from the Christian Democrats) were impeached one after another, on spurious grounds. Ricardo was later to find himself in the company of three of them in prison after the coup. At national level, the impeachments took up time and prevented the Government from getting on with the business of governing. Since the start of 1971 up to the end of 1972 some sixteen different bills introduced to Congress by the Government had been blocked by the Opposition majority.

---

[26] Governors – direct representatives of the Presidency in the provinces, appointed by the President under the Constitution.

At the same time the inspectors of the Government body DIRINCO (National Board for Industry and Commerce) were finding stockpiles of goods that had disappeared from the shops up and down the country – beef, rice, sugar, tea, coffee, flour, detergents, toilet paper, toothpaste, cooking oil, cigarettes. All these were produced in Chile, not imported, but they were being illegally hoarded with the double aim both of provoking shortages and selling at inflated prices on the black market.

The Government controlled about 20% of the distribution network, the rest was owned privately. The Opposition controlled some 65% of the radio and TV channels, and they lost no opportunity to attack the Government for the shortages and growing chaos. The Government wanted to bring in a law to outlaw economic crimes like hoarding and black market sales, but it was rejected by the Opposition majority in Congress. Increasingly, it seemed that the only solution was for Popular Unity to gain a bigger majority at the March 1973 parliamentary elections. For the Opposition's part, they hoped to win two-thirds of the seats in those elections, as that would give them the possibility of impeaching the President himself.

In the event, despite all the problems, shortages and increasing atmosphere of chaos caused by the deliberate destabilisation of the Government, Allende's Popular Unity coalition did manage to increase its vote, from 36.2% in September 1970 to 43.2% in March 1973, in the elections for the Congress and Senate. This was a tremendous victory: normally sitting governments *lost* popularity as time went on, whereas the Popular Unity Government, despite all the problems, had actually *gained* seven percentage points. But it was still not enough for an outright majority, and so the stand-off remained. What's more, the informal cooperation between the more working-class and peasant sectors of the Christian Democratic Party and Popular Unity, which had been demonstrated during the October 1972 lorry-owners' strike, for instance, dwindled as the leadership of the Christian Democratic party allied the party with the right-wing National Party, forming the *Confederación Democrática*, or CODE.

CODE was a political alliance formed in July 1972 with the express aim of gaining the maximum vote in the forthcoming parliamentary elections in March 1973. Whilst the right-wing National Party and the so-called *Democracia Radical* stated that CODE was "the most efficient way of defeating Marxism once and for all", the Christian Democrats and two other smaller parties saw the formation of CODE as a means simply of exercising control over the Popular Unity Government, but within the confines of the law. The Christian Democrats' General Secretary, Belisario Velasco, said at the time about CODE: "Christian Democracy has made a big sacrifice because we understand that the interests of the country come before the party's interests.

An eventual Popular Unity majority in the Congress would be intolerable for Chileans. Freedoms would be totally threatened and repression would replace the law." (quoted in *Historia Política Legislativa del Congreso Nacional de Chile*).

Thus the Popular Unity Government became increasingly paralysed, unable to pass any new legislation which would have helped it to overcome the situation. It later came to light that the CIA had paid some $8 million to right-wing opposition groups to "create pressures, exploit weaknesses, magnify obstacles[27]" – in other words, to destabilise the Allende Government, something many of us suspected must have been going on.

In June 1973, just three months after Allende's Pyrrhic victory in the parliamentary elections, the military of one regiment staged a trial coup, known in Chile as the *tancazo*, meaning tank putsch. An army lieutenant colonel by the name of Roberto Souper led a column of sixteen armoured vehicles, including tanks, into the centre of Santiago and surrounded the Moneda presidential palace and the Ministry of Defence. His tanks opened fire on these buildings, resulting in a number of deaths and several people wounded. This putsch was instigated by *Patria y Libertad*, the extreme right-wing paramilitary group. However, it failed, as it was not supported by the top military as a whole at that time. The Army's Commander-in-Chief, General Carlos Prats, went to the scene, faced down the mutinous soldiers, and by 11.30 a.m. it was all over. But this coup attempt showed how potentially easy it would be to take the presidential palace, and no doubt gave heart to all those in the military and on the extreme Right who wanted to see an end to the Popular Unity Government.

The failed *tancazo* was an ominous warning to the whole country, and sent shivers down our spines. Meanwhile the Communist Party of Chile kept warning of the dangers of a civil war, and once more, I found myself at odds with the party line, because it seemed to me that the real danger was a *coup*, not a civil war. How could the supporters of the Allende Government fight against the Armed Forces, when they did not have weapons, for instance? And why did the Party assume that part of the armed forces would take the side of the Government in any military conflict? I could not see how or why that would happen, given the Chilean Armed Forces' history and training, where obedience to superiors was paramount.

The parties of the Popular Unity could not openly arm their members, since that would have been to give the green light to the pro-coup people within the military, who would be able to claim that the Government was acting outside the Constitution. But because of the political impasse and the increasingly seditious actions by the Opposition, the Popular Unity parties

---

[27] CIA 2000 report, p. 12, National Security Archive, George Washington University.

knew they had to do something to be ready in case the worst happened. So the Socialist and Communist parties began clandestine moves to acquire arms. I was not aware of this personally until after the coup, when Ricardo swiftly took out of the house a big box that had been on top of a wardrobe and drove off. Fortunately he never breathed a word of anything to do with this to me, so as not to incriminate me.

It must have been about this time that our friend Eduardo, ex-Mayor, who in the March elections had been elected to Congress as a Communist Deputy for our province of Ñuble, dropped in to see us with a new acquaintance. They ended up having supper with us, and it turned out that his companion was a lieutenant in the Army. We had an interesting conversation over a long meal, as is the Chilean custom. Eduardo argued passionately that the Armed Forces had to back the Government and clamp down on *Patria y Libertad* and anti-Government acts by extremists, since the Government was merely carrying out its programme, which it had been elected to do, and that programme was in favour of the majority of the people, not the rich. He argued that most of the military came from the working class, peasantry or middle classes, so they should not ally themselves with those who only wanted to benefit the rich.

The lieutenant, a tall, European-looking man, whose name was Andrés Morales, appeared to agree with much that we said, and we had a friendly evening together. At one point Eduardo got out a tiny pistol from his belt, Morales got out his, and the two of them were comparing the two weapons and talking technical know-how. I remember that Morales said at one point: "But you have to know, Eduardo, that much as you and I are friends, if it came to the crunch and there was a war, I would be on one side and you would be on the other." And he added: "I would be bound to kill you, and that's the nice thing about it!" He repeated that last phrase several times: "*Y eso es lo bonito!*" What he found *bonito* was that each of them would be bound to defend their own cause to the point of accepting that it would in that case be ethical to kill one's friend. There was laughter and it was all said in a mood of camaraderie. It seemed to us at the time that it was no bad thing that leading Government politicians like Eduardo had amicable contacts like this with officers in the armed forces. And we thought no more of it.

After the coup, when Ricardo was being held as a "prisoner of war" on Quiriquina Island, our friend Mario Hermosilla, who was charged with storing explosives for President Allende, warned Ricardo never to breathe a word of this conversation or this episode to anyone. If any of the Junta's interrogators had known of it, Ricardo is certain that he would have been sent to his death.

In April 1973 the copper miners of El Teniente went on strike. The copper workers were the best-paid section of the Chilean working class, and formed a sort of elite. Because of their privileged position, in terms of wages and conditions, many of them identified with the Christian Democrats more than with the Popular Unity Government. The strike lasted till June. One weekend that month Ricardo set off to Temuco to see his children, but had to turn back at Los Angeles, about an hour's drive from Chillán, because the north-south highway *La Panamericana* was blocked by pro-Government supporters who were determined to stop a caravan of lorries from getting through, because they were taking food to the striking copper miners of El Teniente, in the north. In a letter home at the time, I wrote that it was obvious that the strike was "artificial and completely political". Since when, I asked, did striking miners anywhere ever receive whole lorry-loads of food? It was all part of the Right's strategy to cause maximum problems and destabilise the Government.

Conditions worsened in June, July, and August, as middle- and upper-class business proprietors and professionals launched another wave of workplace shutdowns and lockouts, as they had in late 1972. In addition, there was another strike by the lorry-owners timed to coincide with the copper workers' action.

Meanwhile I was having nightmares and sleepless nights due to the worrying situation, as I explained to my family in Britain at the time:

> "We live a tenseness which can't be good for us. At times I think it'll be impossible for the Government to win through, with this kind of opposition organised by the Right, with all the power they still have."

And later, in the same letter:

> "It's difficult to see what will happen. The Right is really desperate, that's for certain."

By August 1973 the country was in the grip of a constitutional crisis. The Supreme Court issued a declaration saying that the Government had shown itself incapable of enforcing the law of the land, and in Congress, the Christian Democrat and National Party majority accused President Allende of acting outside the Constitution and called on the military to enforce constitutional order.

In reply, President Allende declared:

> "Chilean democracy is a conquest by all of the people. It is neither the work nor the gift of the exploiting classes, and it will be defended by those who, with sacrifices accumulated over generations, have imposed it ... With a tranquil conscience ... I sustain that never before has Chile had a more democratic government than that over which I

have the honor to preside … I solemnly reiterate my decision to develop democracy and a state of law to their ultimate consequences … Parliament has turned itself into a bastion against the transformations … and has done everything it can to disrupt the functioning of finances and of institutions, stifling all creative initiatives."

He concluded by calling on the workers, all democrats and patriots to join him in defending the Chilean Constitution and the revolutionary process.

Confrontation and seditious calls became commonplace. Street demonstrations both by Popular Unity supporters and the Right were frequent, almost daily, events and increasingly violent. *Patria y Libertad* openly called for a coup to "restore order". The far left group MIR called on Allende to carry out a pre-emptive coup of his own which would wrong-foot the right-wing forces and prevent his being toppled. Workers' defence committees started to be formed in the *poblaciones* and in workplaces to defend the Government and their gains.

I wrote an article, despatched on 5 September 1973, which was published in *Labour Monthly* (October 1973) in which I wrote:

> "The opposition majority in Congress is continuing its obstructionist attitude. The bill for the annual 'readjustment' bonus awarded to all wage-earners as compensation for the loss of purchasing power due to inflation, was passed by Congress, but without the necessary financial backing. Thus the government has been obliged to issue more paper money to cover the readjustment bonus, which in turn means increasing inflation.

> "Similarly, the opposition have prevented a bill being passed to deal with the black marketeers and speculators, and so the problem continues to exist and grows, since there is no adequate legislation to make these offences punishable by law. The public has to pay double or even treble the official price in order to obtain the articles which are in short supply.

> "In short, the opposition has consistently opposed every initiative the government has presented in Congress.

> "One of the most sinister acts of the opposition was the recent so-called 'Agreement Bill' passed by the opposition majority in Congress, which sets out to prove that the government has acted unconstitutionally and is practically illegal, and pretends to force the resignation of the President on these grounds. Whilst this bill has no legal validity, since Congress can only oust a president if there is a two-thirds majority in favour, it is nevertheless important in the sense

132

that it is intended to cause confusion amongst the armed forces. The right-wing newspaper, *El Mercurio*, in its edition of August 26, put it this way:

> 'The most significant thing in the Agreement Bill is that, after the solid reasons given in parliament, the President cannot continue to use the obligation of military obedience to make the armed forces collaborate in carrying out his programme.'

"The tactic of the right is clear, to make the armed forces feel that they no longer owe allegiance to the government because this government has been 'proved' unconstitutional, i.e. to prepare the ground for a coup d'état."

It began to seem obvious that the military were preparing for a coup, because raids on the *poblaciones* began, ostensibly to search for arms among Popular Unity's supporters, using the Law on Control of Firearms. The armed forces even carried out searches in the headquarters of the Popular Unity parties. In Valparaíso, for instance, some Party members were detained in one such raid. One worker in the state-owned Lanera Austral factory in the southern city of Punta Arenas was killed when troops with tanks and machine-guns carried out a military operation, forcing workers to lie face down on the ground and destroying machinery during the raid.

As I wrote at the time,

> "This is indeed one of the contradictions of the 'Chilean Road'. The left is in the government, and yet it is the left who are suffering from the searches... The right are carrying out terrorist acts every day, and practically nothing happens to them." (Labour Monthly, Oct. 1973)

While all these anti-Government actions were going on, we at the University continued to do our jobs to the best of our ability. Classes were held, students' work got marked, seminars and tutorials went on as normal and the Language Laboratory had its usual number of students using it. Yet there were many disruptions, for demonstrations, or due to students not being able to get to the city from where they lived because of road blocks or other transport problems. And food and other shortages meant more time had to be spent trying to buy than before. So life was not easy. I wrote home at the time:

> "We are living a very tense and nerve-racking period which makes me very unsettled. I've got lots of academic work to do, marking, etc., which I just haven't got down to, not only because of lack of time. I'm not sleeping well, again I put it down to the situation, because I have the most horrible dreams, with war scenes and me alone looking for someone I know..."

In August 1973, a friend of ours had given birth to a baby. Soon after the birth she was told that the baby was ill and was not likely to live long. She was devastated. We did our best to comfort her and show her all our support. As it happened, she lived on the same street as us, and we had gradually got to know her better through neighbourhood activities. Irene was an attractive woman in her late thirties, separated and with two school-age children, who lived with her in a bungalow similar to ours just down the street on the other side.

Ricardo and I went to see Irene after she brought the baby back home. She was sad, but her demeanour was very calm and practical. The baby was very small, and the cry emanating from the little cot at the foot of Irene's bed sounded almost like a cat's mewing. I admired Irene's resourcefulness, as she made up feeds in a baby bottle and sat there in bed, feeding her baby, not a trace of feeling sorry for herself, just a matter-of-fact attitude that this was her lot and fate or God would decide what would happen.

In early September, President Allende was preparing to call for a national plebiscite to resolve the impasse between his Popular Unity Government and the Opposition – something allowed for by the Constitution. But this was never held, since the military, under the recently appointed army commander-in-chief, General Augusto Pinochet Ugarte, who had taken care to purge any officers who were sympathetic to the President or the Constitution, acted first, on 11 September 1973, staging the bloodiest coup in history against a constitutional government.

CHAPTER FOUR

".....And one morning all that was burning,
one morning the bonfires
leapt out of the earth
devouring human beings –
and from then on fire
gunpowder from then on,
and from then on blood.
....

Treacherous
generals:
see my dead house,
look at broken Spain:
from every house burning metal flows
instead of flowers,
....

And you will ask: why doesn't his poetry speak of dreams and
leaves and the great volcanoes of his native land?

Come and see the blood in the streets.
Come and see
the blood in the streets.
Come and see the blood in the streets!"

(Explico algunas cosas (I explain a few things)
from *España en el Corazon* (Spain in my Heart),
by Chile's great poet Pablo Neruda,
Nobel Prize for Literature,1971)

The morning of 11th September was bright and sunny, a typical spring morning. I had early classes that day, at 8 a.m., at the Department of Languages, which was about eight blocks from our house, beyond the main square. I set off in our little white Fiat 600 and was surprised to see military personnel and armoured vehicles stationed in front of the *Intendencia* facing one side of the main square. But since this was the time of repeated states of emergency, due to the situation in the country, I did not think much of it and simply drove past. It wasn't until I got to the Department that I learned that there had been a coup d'état and that the TV and radio were all broadcasting military declarations and martial music. There would be no classes that day, nor ever again, for me or Ricardo, at the University of Chile in Chillán.

I drove back home immediately, my heart racing. Could it really be true? Was it really possible that the solid institutionalism of Chile – so untypical of other Latin American countries where coups and military dictatorships were commonplace – had crumbled that easily? What had happened to President Allende? What should we do now? So many questions raced through my mind as I sped back home. I found Ricardo still in the bathroom, getting ready. He told me that a comrade of his had called and had had to knock on the little window of the bathroom, which was close to the front door, to make Ricardo hear. With typical Chilean working-class humour, even on a day like that, Humberto had shouted through the little window: "What the f....! The country's in the deepest shit, and you're having a shower!" He had given Ricardo the dreadful news about the coup, and told him to meet him in an hour or so at one of the local factories.

Ashen-faced, Ricardo left hurriedly in the car to meet Humberto at the agreed rendezvous. But when he got there, he found out that his comrade had already been detained by the military. I meanwhile was frantically listening to the radio to find out what was going on. Between martial music, the radio was announcing a long list of people who, it said, had to present themselves to the local headquarters of the army regiment. So far, neither of our names figured in the list.

We heard with growing dread and cold fear of the bombing of the Moneda Palace in Santiago, and the death of President Allende in the Palace. We heard that the military were rounding up thousands of Popular Unity supporters from the factories and workplaces, from the streets and *poblaciones*. We heard that many thousands detained in this way in the capital had been taken to the *Estadio Nacional* (National Stadium) and the *Estadio de Chile*. We heard that in Valparaíso soldiers with blackened faces had disembarked from ships to raid the factories and detain thousands of workers. It was terrifying news. And the more we listened, the more terrifying and hopeless we realised it was.

I don't know whether it was that fateful day, or the next, that we decided to walk down to the main square to try and meet anybody, any comrade from our Party or colleague from the University who might know more than we did. We had to be back home before the curfew, imposed by the Junta throughout the country, which was to begin at 3 p.m. We met a comrade and colleague of ours, Fernando Guajardo, who was from a small town outside Chillán, San Carlos, walking through the square. He had been in the Party for decades, and had been a clandestine member of the Communist youth when the party had operated underground during the rule of González Videla in the Fifties. We asked him what the Party's instructions were, did he know anything? He knew no more than we did, and just recommended keeping our heads down and staying put until the situation became clearer.

Our only source of outside news was the radio. It was so frightening to listen to the lists of wanted people, who were supposed to present themselves to the local regimental headquarters, among whom were our friend, Chillán's current Socialist Mayor, Ricardo Lagos, and Eduardo Contreras, our friend who was a Communist Deputy to parliament, which, of course, had been suspended on the very day of the coup. The lists of wanted people were seemingly endless, and announced in a sombre, official way which struck fear in our hearts, as well as despair, as the hours went by and there was clearly going to be no chance of a fight-back against this well-organised and executed coup d'état.

We heard rumours that the man who had recently resigned as President Allende's Commander-in-Chief of the Chilean armed forces, General Carlos Prats, was on his way with a column of tanks to crush the coup-makers, or another, that the Soviets were sending troops and moving up towards Santiago from the south... It was all wishful thinking, borne of desperation at the cruelty and injustice of the coup, which in one day wiped out the hopes and dreams of countless Chileans who supported the Popular Unity Government's programme to transform the country in favour of the ordinary working people.

General Carlos Prats had been Commander-in-Chief of the armed forces until he resigned on 23 August 1973, just three weeks before the coup. He was also at the time Allende's Minister of the Interior and was the most prominent of those military people who followed the "Schneider doctrine" of obedience to the constitutionally-elected government of the day, the so-called "constitutionalists". Under the Chilean Constitution, the armed forces owe allegiance to the president of the republic. On 22 August the wives of some of the military had held a protest rally outside his home, calling him a coward for not acting to restore civic order to the country. This action was clearly the catalyst for him resigning.

His resignation removed the last obstacle for the coup-plotters, since the person who took over from Prats was his second-in-command, a general who had been thought to be loyal to the Constitution – General Augusto Pinochet. General Prats fled Chile five days after the coup, for Argentina, where he lived in exile with his wife, until a year later when they were both killed outside their Buenos Aires apartment by a car-bomb, victims of Pinochet's secret police agents, the DINA[28].

As the *bandos militares* (military edicts) boomed out over the radio – one of which said that if a weapon of any kind were found in anyone's house, all the people in the house at the time would be summarily shot – we, like all our friends, feared for our lives. Though we were calm in the knowledge that we had never done anything wrong or illegal, it was not enough to make us feel secure, since all the normal laws and rules that existed in Chile had been suspended and terror reigned supreme.

Ricardo and I talked over endlessly what we should do. He was worried sick for his children in Temuco, with no telephone contact, and because of the long curfews, no possibility of going there. We knew that his son, Ricky, had been active in the *Juventudes Comunistas* there, but their mother was a well-respected secondary-school teacher at the *liceo*, and Ricardo did not think that they would be in imminent danger. Nevertheless, it was a huge worry.

We debated whether we should stay in Chillán or flee to Santiago, where we would not be known. But we couldn't see how we would live – where, on what money – since our only source of income was our University salaries, and anyway, we thought it would be dangerous for Ricardo's brothers if they took us in. And Ricardo felt that, since his eminence in Chillán was solely due to his having been Vice-rector of the University, he would not be in the military's sights. So we stayed put, listening to the motors of the military's stationary armoured cars purring outside our windows after curfew hours, not knowing what would happen or what to do for the best.

The University was closed until further notice by the military. The Junta appointed a military Director. Women staff were told not to wear trousers, and men told to cut their hair short and shave off beards. The university was to be "reorganised".

On 16 September, six days after the coup, we heard that our friend Ricardo Lagos, Mayor of Chillán and long-time member of the Socialist Party, had been shot dead in the patio of his home in Chillán Viejo, together with his wife, Sonia Ojeda, who was seven months pregnant, and younger son Carlos, who was a student of ours on the English degree course. The radio said it had been an armed confrontation, but witnesses say it was nothing of the kind – they were simply shot in cold blood during an armed police raid on their house.

---

28 Pinochet knew that Prats, in exile, was writing his memoirs and had refused warnings to desist. Pinochet described Prats as "a dangerous man for Chile", because he knew that as a constitutionalist, Prats would be able to reveal much about the machinations against Allende within the armed forces. (*The Condor Years*, The New Press, by John Dinges, pp.72-77).

It's difficult to convey the shock and terror this news caused us. Carlos' death in particular was hard to take. He was twenty years old, and it had only been the previous year that I had arranged for Carlos to stay with my brother and family in Chesterfield for a few weeks, to help him improve his English, and I had received lovely letters from him full of his impressions of England. He was such an attractive young man, courteous, thoughtful, serious and unselfish, who had so much to give his country and his people. His letters exude concern for his people and the people of Latin America as a whole. I had also had the unenviable task, during the weeks that Carlos was staying with my brother and family, of telephoning Carlos in England to give him the tragic news that his beloved mother Victoria had died. Yet now, on hearing of his cruel killing, I couldn't weep for the deaths of the Lagos family: I was too angry inside, and too frightened[29].

Twenty five years later, on my first visit back to Chile since leaving in 1974, Ricardo and I went to the cemetery in Chillán to find the grave of our friends Ricardo Lagos and his son Carlos, who had stayed with my brother Joe and wife Shirley in England in 1972, and who had been so brutally murdered, at home, in this way.

It was so sad to see their niche at Chillán cemetery, with the inscriptions of the whole family – father Ricardo Lagos, his wife Sonia, and 20-year-old Carlos. Carlos's older brother Ricardo, who was detained in Santiago, became one of the "disappeared", whose body has never been found. There were fresh flowers in the niche then, perhaps left by Carlos's grandmother, or by friends or comrades.

Later still, on our next visit to Chile, in April 2006, we once again went back to the cemetery, this time accompanied by our son Victor and his partner Marcela. This time the Lagos niche, high up on the cemetery wall, had no fresh flowers. We bought some flowers at the cemetery entrance, got a ladder, and Victor climbed up and left our flowers in the Lagos family niche. It was a very emotional moment, both for Ricardo and me, and for the younger generation, who had not, of course, known Carlos and who were at that time a little older than Carlos was when so unjustly killed 33 years earlier.

The following day, 17 September 1973, was an even worse day. We had walked into the town centre to try and find anyone who might give us news as to friends and colleagues, and because there was nothing else to do, since the University was closed and staff suspended. In the eerie calm of those

---

29 In August 2008 we received news that the police colonel who had been in charge of that "operation", Luís Gajardo, was sentenced to 5 years of "*libertad vigilada*" (supervised freedom) and Lieutenant Colonel Patricio Jeldrez was given a sentence of three years. It was our friend Eduardo Contreras who, many years later, had instigated legal proceedings against those responsible for the Lagos family deaths. On hearing the light sentences handed down in 2008, he roundly condemned Judge Joaquín Billard for "failing to do justice and fostering impunity".

post-coup days we walked here and there, did some shopping and walked back home again, not daring to go and see any of our friends, for fear of incriminating them, since most of them had not had such a prominent role as Ricardo.

We met Fernando Guajardo, the comrade whom we had met the first day after the coup, and who lived outside Chillán. He had been the comrade responsible for all the Communists in the University, and Ricardo thought that he would be a likely target to be detained, because of this. But he told Ricardo: "You'll be the one who'll be arrested, not me!" He seemed confident of his unassailability, which seemed strange to us, except that later I recalled the occasion when I had spent Christmas with him and his family in San Carlos. While I was there, he had received a visit from a local landowner at his house, and afterwards had explained to us that he had friends both from the Left and the Right, because of his being from an old San Carlos family. It seemed he was now confident that these contacts, built up over years, would save him from being a target.

Looking back, it seems naive of us to have stayed in our little house, as if, just because we knew our only "guilt" consisted in having supported and worked for the legal, constitutional Government of Salvador Allende, that of itself would save us from the clutches of the military. With the benefit of hindsight, and especially recalling Fernando's words of warning that it would be Ricardo who was more likely to be detained than himself, I am certain that what we should have done was to have left for Santiago immediately and stayed as long as our money lasted, by which time the Junta authorities in Chillán might have forgotten about him.

We thought of it, we discussed it that day, but Ricardo didn't feel he could go because that would mean being even further away from his children, without knowing what had befallen them there. And I did not even consider leaving Ricardo and going on my own. We could have gone to Santiago to the British Embassy or any of the other embassies which were taking in asylum-seekers, like those of Sweden, Mexico or France. We learnt that this was what our friend Eduardo, on orders from the Party, had done.

On the day of the coup, 11 September 1973, Eduardo had been driving down to the capital early in the morning, together with his fellow Deputy from the Socialist Party, Rogelio de la Fuente, to take part in parliamentary proceedings as usual, it being a Tuesday. Congress was due to discuss the question of holding a plebiscite, in an attempt to end the political stalemate. Eduardo was stopped a few times by military roadblocks, but – and these are the strange things that can happen in this sort of situation – the soldiers manning the blocks saw his official pass showing that he was a member of parliament, and simply waved him on. In this way he was able to reach the capital, and once in touch with the Party there, it was quickly arranged that he be taken to the Panamanian Embassy to seek refuge there.

Eduardo then spent several years in exile, in Panama, Mexico and Cuba. As soon as he could he returned to Chile and it was he who in 1998 filed the first lawsuit against General Pinochet for causing the deaths and disappearances of so many innocent victims of the bloody September 1973 coup d'état. In July 2000 on the eve of a high-profile legal victory against Pinochet in the courts, he and his second wife Rebeca were victims of an assassination attempt, when, after stopping to help someone who had flagged them down, their stationary car was hit at high speed by a jeep coming the other way in a deliberate "accident". Rebeca suffered horrific injuries and spent months in hospital recovering, whilst Eduardo, who, unusually for him, had been in the passenger seat, was luckier, suffering only bruises from the impact. The details of this dreadful incident, whose perpetrators have still not been brought to justice, are described in Eduardo's book *"El Desaforado"* (Stripped of Immunity).

That evening, 17 September, we were back at home long before the curfew, and we received a visit from Irene's 12-year-old son Jorge, from across the street. Ricardo and he started a game of chess – we had to do something to try and defuse the terrible tension and fear somehow – and the game was still going on after the curfew had begun. Dusk fell, and Jorge was still there, but we did not feel unduly worried, since Jorge's house was only a few metres away on the other side of the narrow street, so he wouldn't be noticed as he slipped home, once the game was over.

Suddenly we heard a loud rap on the front door, which opened straight into the living room. Ricardo went to open it. There stood two soldiers – officers – who demanded he step outside. Ricardo did as he was bid, upon which he was promptly frogmarched off to a waiting lorry with an open back, which was parked at the corner of the street, on the other side. I hurriedly went to the door and was just in time to see Ricardo being shoved up into the back of the truck, and I saw that there were other prisoners already in the truck. We didn't manage to exchange even a good-bye, nothing. It was over in a flash, and the lorry had driven off, who knows where.

Jorge and I were as if frozen to the spot. I had to get him home, as his mother would be worried, so I checked that there were no vehicles or people about, saw him across the street and watched as he reached his house.

A cold and paralysing fear spread within me. I knew that this was the worst sign – to be taken after dark, after curfew, when there were no witnesses, no proof that he had been detained. I had to do something immediately to ensure that he would not be killed that very night. I grabbed a warm jacket and ran across to the house of another neighbour, a lecturer from the *Escuela de*

Agronomía which belonged to the University of Concepción. We had a common friend and had socialised with him on a couple of occasions, but I did not know him well. They had a telephone, and I knew that if I could phone some authority, I might be able to save Ricardo's life.

The neighbour very reluctantly let me in and allowed me to phone. He was obviously scared of what the repercussions might be for him. I got the number of the local Regiment, and phoned, demanding to know what had happened to Ricardo. I told them I was British and that I would be letting the British authorities know what had happened to him. I told them how and at what time he had been detained, giving all the information I could, including Ricardo's academic status, and my (foreign-sounding) name and position, insisting that they relay the information so as to ensure his safety.

I thanked our neighbour and left, furtively crossing the street after making sure no one was about to see me, and reached home safely.

But it was no longer "home" without Ricardo. I paced the house, hot drink in hand, not wanting to sleep, not able to sleep, my mind furiously working out all the things I had to do the next day to kick up a stink and get Ricardo out. My fear and dread was that he could be killed that very night, since I knew from all that we had heard since the coup that many people were killed immediately. Thousands of people had already been killed. The National Stadium in Santiago was full of prisoners. Torture was widespread, and every day you heard of more and more deaths in "confrontations with the military". And the way that Ricardo had been picked up from the house after dark was ominous. But I finally slept a few hours, comforted in the knowledge that I had done all I could do that night to keep him alive.

The next day, 18 September, was Chile's National Day, ironically. There were going to be no celebrations this year. I woke up early, a sick feeling in my stomach. I literally did not know, nor had any means of knowing, whether the man I loved was at that moment alive or dead. It was a horrible, sickening feeling. Yet my mind was clear and sharp, and I started racking my brains to think of all the things I could do to ensure Ricardo's safety, in the event that he was still alive, and get him released.

Before I could do anything, there was a knock at the door. When I opened it, my heart sank. The group of soldiers thrust their way past me into the house. One of them I recognised as the lieutenant who had come with our Deputy friend Eduardo that evening not long before and had ended up having supper with us – Andrés Morales. The soldiers went into our study, which had bookshelves along one entire wall, and started pulling books off the shelves and putting some aside in a heap. The conscripts doing the job were having a hard job knowing what to take, I could see. They took anything with Marxism or Lenin in the title and all sorts of other books, even novels, that had anything like "red" or "revolution" in the title. Their officer, Morales, stood guard, barking orders at them, and himself going through the numerous drawers of our enormous double-sided desk. I was glad that I had had the foresight as soon as Ricardo had been detained the previous night to hide our Party cards. We had a manual floor-polisher which had a metal upper part that screwed on to the lower part. I had unscrewed this and carefully placed the cards between the two metal plates, screwing them back together again. I was pretty sure no-one would think of looking there.

It was all a stupid charade, I thought. We had never hidden our affiliation, and the Communist Party and all the parties of Popular Unity were legal parties which had formed the elected Government. My heart was full of hatred, and of fear, and yet, as I looked at the young conscripts, I knew that they weren't enjoying what they were having to do. We knew that during the first few days after the coup there had been several examples of military men disobeying the Junta's orders, and being shot or imprisoned as a result. We were aware of the example of General Alberto Bachelet, an Air Force general whom President Allende had put in charge of the JAP (Supply and Price Control Committees) and who was arrested the very day of the coup and imprisoned in the Air War Academy, charged with treason[30].

I can't remember how long the raid lasted. It was terrifying. The soldier standing guard, gun at the ready, the barked orders, the rifling through documents and the piles of books taken away, the fear of the unknown. All of a sudden, Morales told them to leave, and the soldiers left. He gestured for me to go into the bedroom next to the study. He stood against the wall at the door and simply said: "Don't worry, nothing's going to happen to Ricardo! I just wanted you to know that." And at that he nodded stiffly to me, and left.

Once they had gone, my whole body began to shake uncontrollably. I had held it together whilst they were in the house, somehow knowing that it wouldn't do to show fear or weakness, but now I collapsed. I remember trying to make a cup of tea and my hand shaking so much that I spilt the hot water all over the place. Yet despite everything, I felt another slight glimmer of hope, recalling Morales' words that Ricardo would not be killed. Yet how could I trust someone who was taking orders from the Junta?

I decided the first thing I had to do was to go and see the military governor who had been put there by the Junta immediately after the coup to rule the province of Ñuble. It had to be done as soon as possible – it was literally a matter of life and death.

---

[30] General Bachelet died on March 12 1974, from a heart attack as a result of the torture he was subjected to. After Chile's return to democracy, his daughter, Michelle, became Minister of Defence in 2002 and was elected President of Chile in January 2006.

143

The military provincial governor the Junta had appointed was called Cristián Guedelhoefer. I guessed from his German-sounding name that he would be from the wealthy classes, and decided to use my Englishness, my English looks and background to get him to agree to an interview. The Chilean upper classes identified totally with Europeans and Americans, and the more light-skinned you were, the more blond and blue-eyed you were, the more you fitted into that upper-class "ideal" physical type.

I had a green linen suit that I had bought for my first job interview at Imperial Chemical Industries and had never worn in Chile, because it looked too formal. I fished it out, ironed it and put it on. I also had a pearl necklace, one of only two items I inherited from my grandmother, and which I had never previously worn, so I put that on with the suit. Now I looked a bit more like a member of the Chilean ruling class, I thought. I looked the part, no matter what I was feeling inside.

I walked the four or five blocks down to the *Intendencia*, which was thronged with military uniforms of all kinds and smart young women in high heels scurrying to and fro. I marched straight into the office of Guedelhoefer's secretary and, adopting a deliberately foreign accent in Spanish, as if I were an Englishwoman who did not know the language very well, requested to see Lieutenant Colonel Guedelhoefer. I don't know how I managed to keep my cool, but I did, and it worked. He clearly felt he could not refuse a citizen of the British Crown, and agreed to see me. As soon as I entered the room, I was faced with the dilemma, to shake his proffered hand or not. Politically, I couldn't. He represented all that was loathsome and despicable. But I was there to plead Ricardo's case, not to make a political statement. So I shook his hand, and accepted the seat offered.

Guedelhoefer had been put there immediately after the coup, and was not from Chillán. So he did not know much about the Popular Unity supporters in the city. Perhaps that was why I was able to get away with my role-play as a young and innocent Englishwoman caught up in this dreadful situation, the man I loved – who was a good man – taken away from me and languishing who knows where... I looked the part, with my crisp linen suit and pearl necklace and my long auburn hair tied up at the back, and I acted the part. Guedelhoefer treated me with courtesy, listening to my description of Ricardo as essentially an academic, whom I had met and fallen in love with in Europe, and that was the reason I had come to live in Chile. He promised to look into Ricardo's case.

I felt a sense of triumph as I left the *Intendencia*. Again, I knew that I had done as much as I could on that day, and that if anyone could save Ricardo, Guedelhoefer could. And whatever he thought of me, the fact that he had agreed to see me, I was sure, meant that at the very least, he now knew he was dealing with a British citizen and that Ricardo's fate would become known in Britain, not just in Chillán. So I felt fairly confident of two things: first, that Ricardo must still be alive, otherwise he would surely not have agreed to see me; and second, that Guedelhoefer would be likely to give orders that Ricardo should not be killed, because of the British connection. The Junta knew that their bloody coup had been given a terrible press throughout the world.

I found out that Ricardo was being held in Chillán's prison. As it happened our little bungalow was only four blocks from the square where the prison is. The next day Ricardo managed to get a message to me to take him a mattress and a sleeping bag, if possible. I was not able to see him, but I was allowed to hand these things in to the prison for him. It was a huge relief to know that he was still alive, and physically nearby. The prison, which had formerly been solely a place for delinquents and common criminals, suddenly found itself the busy hub for huge numbers of political prisoners, both from Chillán and from surrounding rural areas.

Several of our friends had been arrested and were being held there. Some, like *Chepo* Sepulveda, our veterinary friend, had been detained the same evening as Ricardo, and then found themselves in prisons and detention centres miles away. Other friends, like Franklin Roach, a lecturer at the University, Franklin Carpenter, along with several of his brothers, Abraham Cuervo, another University colleague and Juan Salas, a student leader there, and several other friends and acquaintances, were being held in the local prison. Another colleague, Francisco Sánchez, had been detained and "disappeared".

The night Ricardo was arrested he had been taken to the Regimental headquarters in Chillán, together with all the detainees in the truck who had been snatched from their homes that night. There he saw several people he knew. After hours at the Regiment, some of the prisoners, including Ricardo, were transferred to the local prison, spending that first horrific night huddled with dozens of other detainees in a cramped cell. But for Ricardo it was something of a relief to find himself in the prison, after the long hours at the Regiment, which everyone knew had been the scene of many executions. From our house you could hear gunshots during the nights in the first weeks after the coup, coming from the direction of the Regiment.

On the second or third day after Ricardo's arrest, while he was being held *incomunicado* in the prison, I went over to our neighbour Irene's house. She suggested we could send Ricardo a flask with what looked like milky coffee, but instead he would find *malta con huevos*. This was a drink made of a Chilean kind of stout, whisked up with egg in a liquidiser. She had a liquidiser, whereas I did not. The prison authorities would never guess, she said, and it would be a nice surprise for Ricardo.

It was while I was with Irene in her kitchen making this drink that the military arrived to raid her house. She was a well-known teacher with many left-wing friends. The officer yelled at us to face the wall and put our hands up above our heads against the wall. Even Jorge, Irene's 12-year-old son, who was in the house at the time, was forced to do the same. While we were in that position, they started to search the house. Irene's newborn baby, who was sick, was mewling pathetically in his little cot. I was terrified, remembering the *bando militar* on the radio that if any weapons were found in a house, all the occupants would be summarily shot. I hoped to God that Irene wouldn't have been stupid enough to get involved with weapons, but I couldn't be sure. I had a sudden sinking feeling that this was where my beautiful life was going to end.

To my amazement, Irene took her arms down from the wall and went over to her baby, explaining to the soldiers that she couldn't leave the poor mite crying like that. She then began to flirt outrageously with the captain in charge, flashing smiles at him and chatting inconsequentially about this and that as if this were the most normal thing in the world. Irene was a primary-school teacher, but clearly had great acting ability, which she put to very good use here. She was a very attractive woman with a good figure. Men found her sexy, and this Captain was no exception. She sidled up to him, fluttering her eyelashes and all the while assuring them they wouldn't find anything in her house: did they really think she would put her own children at risk by hiding weapons there?

It was a master class. I was amazed at her cool and her acting. She pulled it off, and after a quick look round the garden, the soldiers left. Irene, Jorge and I looked at each other in disbelief, then we all hugged each other and started laughing and crying, all mixed up together. It was the relief, and the pent-up emotion. Poor Jorge was the worst affected, I think: he was really scared, his face as white as a sheet.

Our friends Juan Gabriel Araya and Maruja were caught up in a different way. They were at home with their three young children when the police burst into their house one night soon after the coup and dragged Juan Gabriel out of his bed. They beat him up savagely there in his own home, in front of Maruja and the children. Since it was the police who had just shot dead the entire family of Ricardo Lagos, the Mayor, also in Chillán Viejo, he was "lucky" to escape with his life. We were very surprised at what had happened to Juan Gabriel, since he was not a leader or prominent person at all, and was not well-known in Chillán, having moved there from Angol only two or three years before. He himself never knew why he had been targeted: the only likely explanation seems to be that the Junta was bent on fostering a climate of terror in every town and village throughout the country.

When the air force bombed the Moneda Palace, for instance, on the morning of the coup, it was more to do with terrorising the population than any need to subdue the occupants of the Palace, as there were only a few of President Allende's personal armed guard (the GAP) there. As a military operation, it was unnecessary.

Poor Maruja was severely traumatised by this episode. From being a fairly plump woman she became a skeleton in a few weeks, due to her fear and the worry for her young family. I had never seen someone change so much in just a matter of weeks. When there are children involved, the worry in situations such as ours was multiplied a thousandfold.

For myself, although I had started to wish over the last year or so that Ricardo and I could have a child together, probably because I had reached that age when many women start to feel that as a strong desire, I was glad that I did not have a child to worry about in this nightmarish situation. I felt very lonely, though, because in the immediate aftermath of the coup I had no contact with most of our close friends, as we all knew that it would be dangerous to incriminate others by socialising with them. So this was a very lonely time for me, and it was fortunate that I was able to keep myself extremely busy, writing letters to my family in Britain, to Ricardo's children in Temuco, going to see officials and organisations to try and get news of Ricardo and to get him released.

I received news of Ricardo's son, Ricky, who was eighteen at the time, that he had been detained by the military in Temuco. He had his head forcibly shaved (that was a favourite occupation of the military during the post-coup period), was roughed up a bit and then released after a few hours. It was a very frightening experience for him and his mother and sisters. Fortunately nothing happened to them until much later, when his mother was arrested and imprisoned in the women's jail for several months, only to be released, like most people, without charge. What charge could there be? She, like hundreds of thousands of others, was merely "guilty" of supporting the constitutional Government of Salvador Allende.

The University was closed down, and staff were told that it would not reopen until the following academic year, beginning in March. It was to be "restructured", the military authorities declared. On 28 September male lecturers were ordered to give in their identity cards to the military representatives at the University and report to the Regiment for interrogation. Some had their identity cards withdrawn, others had them returned. That day female members of staff had to form long queues outside the bank, where our salaries were due to be paid, and give our personal data to the soldiers on duty there. We were each asked what our political affiliations were. I asked the lieutenant on duty: "What is the purpose of this humiliating procedure?" He replied:

"It's to see who are the good people and who are the bad people in the University."

A couple of days after the military raid on our house, soldiers returned to demand my passport. They took it away, which was very unsettling, since I knew that my British citizenship was at least some sort of guarantee of security in the lawless climate of those days. I had a visa which depended on my contract with the University. This was due to expire in December, the end of the academic year, and the visa and contract had up to now been automatically renewed each year. I feared that without my passport I would have difficulty in renewing my visa, especially since it seemed that I, like all the left-wing staff, would be unlikely to get their University contracts renewed now that the University was under military control. The last thing I wanted was to be forced to leave Chile while Ricardo was imprisoned.

One of the most upsetting things I found about the period immediately after the coup was the way fear made people change. Some people on the left, when they met each other on the streets, started to say things like: "Ah well, it's not surprising so-and-so's been detained – he was very involved!" That phrase, *estaba muy metido,* really irritated and annoyed me enormously. Instead of feeling proud that we had been on the side of a project to win a better life for the majority of Chileans, these people seemed to be judging their erstwhile friends and comrades by the sinister yardstick of the military – to what extent people had been politically involved in the Popular Unity project. It really made me see red, and I remember snapping at one Socialist Party colleague who said it in my presence with reference to Ricardo. I was walking along a street when I met this colleague, together with a friend of his. I told them that Ricardo had been detained, and that was what he said. Firstly, I thought it was pretty insensitive to say that to my face – as if to say, "well, what do you expect, of course he'd be arrested because he was really *metido,* wasn't he?" The implication being that therefore Ricardo would be likely to be either killed or sentenced to years in prison. And secondly because I knew that none of us Popular Unity supporters had anything to feel ashamed about; quite the opposite, we should feel proud that we were involved in trying to make the Popular Unity project succeed. I told him as much, in no uncertain terms, and turned away in disgust to return home.

In Chillán prison Ricardo was being held *incomunicado,* so I could not see him and neither were we allowed to send any letters or messages to the prisoners. But I remember one day, I was walking near the prison, looking up at its high-sided walls and wondering how Ricardo was, whether he was being tortured, like so many we were hearing about from snippets of information that leaked out, when I was approached by a young lad in shoddy clothes and sandals made of car tyre rubber. He told me that he had just been released

148

from prison, where he had been a "common criminal" and he had a message from Ricardo that I shouldn't worry, he was all right. Presumably Ricardo had been able to get a message to this lad, and had asked him to look out for me. I was a pretty conspicuous figure around the prison, as the only English-looking person around.

It is hard to transmit the sick feeling of fear that we all felt during those first days and weeks. The radio was all the time playing martial music and they would interrupt programmes with news of this or that person's arrest, this or that person's death while "trying to resist arrest" or in "armed combat". Frequent radio broadcasts warned that if the military found arms in any house, all occupants would be summarily shot, whether they were resident in the house or not. It was terrifying and chilling to hear. Meanwhile the news from Santiago and the rest of the country was dire. We heard that the immensely popular singer/songwriter, Victor Jara, had been arrested and tortured at the Chile Stadium, that his torturers had broken the bones in his hands and taunted him to play the guitar with his broken hands. Between savage beatings, Victor had managed to write a last poem on a scrap of paper and secretly pass it to a fellow-prisoner before being taken away to be shot:

There are five thousand of us here
in this small part of the city.
We are five thousand.
I wonder how many we are in all
in the cities and in the whole country?
Here alone
are ten thousand hands which plant seeds
and make the factories run.
How much humanity
exposed to hunger, cold, panic, pain,
moral pressure, terror and insanity?
Six of us were lost
as if into starry space.
One dead, another beaten as I could never have believed
a human being could be beaten.
The other four wanted to end their terror
one jumping into nothingness,
another beating his head against a wall,
but all with the fixed stare of death.
What horror the face of fascism creates!
They carry out their plans with knife-like precision.
Nothing matters to them.
To them, blood equals medals,

slaughter is an act of heroism.
Oh God, is this the world that you created,
for this your seven days of wonder and work?
Within these four walls only a number exists
which does not progress,
which slowly will wish more and more for death.
But suddenly my conscience awakes
and I see that this tide has no heartbeat,
only the pulse of machines
and the military showing their midwives' faces
full of sweetness.
Let Mexico, Cuba and the world
cry out against this atrocity!
We are ten thousand hands
which can produce nothing.
How many of us in the whole country?
The blood of our President, our compañero,
will strike with more strength than bombs and machine guns!
So will our fist strike again!

How hard it is to sing
when I must sing of horror.
Horror which I am living,
horror which I am dying.
To see myself among so much
and so many moments of infinity
in which silence and screams
are the end of my song.
What I see, I have never seen
What I have felt and what I feel
Will give birth to the moment...

Estadio Chile
September 1973

The poem was interrupted when guards came to get him. Victor Jara's body was found on Sunday, 16 September, together with five others, in the working-class district of San Miguel in Santiago. They had all been machine-gunned. Day after day, the radio gave constant updates as to who among prominent Popular Unity figures had been arrested or killed, and the news sent a shiver of fear down my spine every time I listened. The sick feeling in my stomach would not go away.

FEAR FOR SAFETY OF CHESTERFIELD WOMAN IN CHILE

By a staff reporter

THE husband of a Chesterfield woman has been arrested by the new military junta in Chile and thrown into an island prison.

And relatives were making desperate efforts from London today to get in touch with her at her Chile home, 200 miles south of the capital, Santiago.

They heard of the arrest in a midnight phone call from her in Chile last night.

She is Kathleen Figueroa, formerly of Old Whittngton, near Chesterfield.

Her brother, Mr. Joe Clark, a director for the Clay Cross engineering firm of W. R. Clark and Co., said: "My father is visiting the Foreign Office to find out ways we can get in touch with Kate."

RICARDO FIGUEROA

Her husband, Ricardo Figueroa is a lecturer at the University of Chile in Chillan. He has been charged with incompetence in his former job as the University College's Vice Rector.

After he was arrested, Mrs. Figueroa had to wait se n days before she was told where he had been taken — and why.

The family are also worried for Kathleen's safety.

"What worries us is that the communications between the two countries are almost non-existent. It is almost impossible for us to find out how she is or where she is.

"There is a lot of anti-foreigner feelings being generated in Chile. We only hope that Kate doesn't fall

KATHLEEN FIGUEROA

foul of that," Mr. Clark added.

The couple met while Ricardo was doing post graduate work at Manchester University. They have lived in Chile for almost five years. Kathleen is also a university lecturer.

Life in Chile — as seen by a Stretton woman

A STRETTON woman and former St. Helena School pupil, now teaching in Chile, has just had a book published in England dealing with the current situation in Chile.

She is Miss Kate Clark, daughter of Mr. and Mrs. W. R. Clark, Highstairs Lane, Stretton. Her book, "The Reality and Prospects of Popular Unity", was published in December.

She studied for an honours degree in Russian at Manchester University, and then won a British Council scholarship which enabled her to study for a year at Moscow University.

She has now been living and working in Chile for four years and lectures on English at the University of Chile and in Russian at the Institute of Soviet Studies.

At Christmas, Kate's family sent her a handkerchief decorated with a hand-drawn picture of the Crooked Spire and greetings from over 70 friends and acquaintances in the Chesterfield area.

She hopes to return to England in the near future to study comparative linguistics, a subject in which she has become increasingly interested as her studies in five languages have developed.

Copies of her book have been sent to President Allende and leaders of the Chilean Government.

The UK press published news of Kate Clark's book in the situation in Chile. A year later, they reported accounts of Ricardo's detention

el proceso CHILENO en un libro INGLES

Día a día crece el interés internacional por el proceso de cambios que Chile está viviendo. Es así como aumenta la demanda por la información sobre lo que pasa en nuestro país, a la par con la solidaridad de los otros pueblos.

Reality and Prospects of Popular Unity

KATE CLARK

★ El Partido Comunista Inglés, interesado en responder a la creciente inquietud de su pueblo por lo que sucede en Chile, solicitó a la corresponsal de su diario, "Morning Star", en Chile, **Kate Clark**, que escribiera un libro sobre la Unidad Popular. El resultado es **"Reality and prospects of Popular Unity"** ("Realidad y perspectivas de la Unidad Popular"), con prólogo de **Jack Woddis**, responsable del Departamento Internacional del Partido Comunista Inglés.

★ KATE CLARK, joven de 30 años, ya lleva cuatro años en Chile como corresponsal del "Morning Star". Es profesora de fonética inglesa de la Universidad de Chile-Chillán. Ha tenido un contacto muy directo con el pueblo chileno a través de estudiantes, obreros y campesinos, en especial. Ha conocido la cuenca carbonífera del Bío Bío, las organizaciones campesinas, los sindicatos de diversas industrias.

★ El libro es un intento de explicar algunas cosas fundamentales para el público inglés, aunque esas mismas sean aquí bastante conocidas. El primer capítulo muestra qué es Chile, su geografía, su situación económico-social. Luego explica la trayectoria del movimiento obrero y el movimiento popular desde Recabarren, el desarrollo de la Izquierda desde sus orígenes, es decir, todo lo que es básico para entender el triunfo de la Unidad Popular.

★ Continúa presentando el Programa de la Unidad Popular, destacando la nacionalización de las riquezas básicas y los aspectos que ya se han cumplido. Finalmente, señala las perspectivas de la Unidad Popular.

★ El prólogo de Woddis pone de relieve la difícil empresa acometida por el pueblo chileno al dar el triunfo a la Unidad Popular y seguir avanzando en el camino de los cambios.

★ "Reality and prospects of Popular Unity", a juicio de los ingleses, contribuye a llenar un vacío, producto del desconocimiento de América Latina y de Chile en particular. Este libro deja en evidencia la necesidad de proseguir informando sobre los últimos acontecimientos.

★ Kate Clark opina que es muy rápido el desarrollo de la lucha de clases, los antagonismos, el perpetuo cambio y que las perspectivas de la Unidad Popular dependen de lo que el Gobierno y el pueblo de Chile hagan desde ahora en adelante, en los próximos 3 años.

★ Para el pueblo inglés, la experiencia chilena es apasionante, pues su propia perspectiva de llegar al socialismo sólo es posible dentro de las vías constitucionales, por un camino similar al que está siguiendo Chile.

"El Siglo" 25·III·73

Kate Clark's book received enthusiastic coverage in the Chilean newspapers - this is an example, from *El Siglo*, published on 25 March 1973, shortly before the *coup d'etat* in September.

The Letters

Como voy a aceptar el ofrecimiento de
mi familia en Inglaterra, mientras tú estés
allí?! Quien le llevaría al puffin el tabaco,
el chocolate, etc. a la Isla Qu.? Además así
yo voy a poder ayudar a los cabros, por
si el asunto sale para largo. Hasta ahora
estoy bien y con buen ánimo, considerando
todas las cosas.

Pienso mucho en ti y en todos los que
están allá. Me pregunto como estarán, que
estarán haciendo, como estará el ánimo.
Este tipo de período es como una prueba para
toda la gente, no?

From Kate's letter of 29 Sept. 1973

How can I accept the offer of my family in England while ever you are there? (in detention on Quiriquina Island, Ed.) Who would take the puffin (pet name, Ed.) tobacco, chocolate etc on the island? Also, this way I can help the kids, in case this situation goes on for a long time. So far I am holding up and in good spirits, considering everything.

I think a lot about you and all the other prisoners there. I wonder how you all are, what you are doing, whether you're keeping your spirits up. This is a testing time for us all, isn't it?

These are three of the tiny notes that Kate put inside the screw top of the thermos that she took each day to Ricardo when he was held incommunicado in Chillán jail. No translation needed

From Kate's letter of 29 September 1973

Lots of my students have come to see me, which gives me confidence that they can't just sack me willy-nilly from the University. I told them (the military interrogators, Ed.): "You ask my students, and they'll tell you that I'm an excellent teacher." A bit big-headed, wasn't it!

P.S. Recibí tu libreta de cheques sin dificultades.
Martes, 2 de Octubre de 1973.

Mi querido Negro,
Como estas tu, en este día nublado y frío? Parece que el animo se pone al tono con el tiempo. Si es posible, escribame frequentemente aun si son esas notitas no más. Tu tienes papel, sobres y estampillas, pero supongo que no estas permitido de escribir cartas, sino habrías escrito.
Ojalá que recibiste todas las cosas que llevé el Domingo pasado a Talcahuano. Con las cosas para Germán, además, mis brazos me dolían cuando llegué al portón de los leones! Pero vale la pena si te hace la vida mejor allá. Mi Negro, no esté triste, por favor. Yo estoy bien y creo que los de Tco. también, así que en ese sentido no te preocupas. Los amigos están portandose macanudos conmigo.

From Kate's letter of 2 October 1973

My dear *Negro* (nickname in Chile for anyone who is dark-skinned and with black hair)

How are you, on this cold, cloudy day? It seems as if the weather is in tune with our spirits. If you can, write to me frequently, even if it's only those notes. You've got paper, pen and stamps, but I suppose you're not allowed to write letters, otherwise you would have written.

I hope you received all the things I took to Talcahuano (nearest port to the Quiriquina Island, Ed.) last Sunday. With the things I took for Germán too, my arms were aching when I got to the entrance gates! But it's worth it if it makes your life a bit easier. My love, don't be sad, please. I am all right, and I think those in Temuco (Ricardo's children, Ed.) are too, so in that sense don't worry. Our friends are being a great support to me.

Te mando esta fotografía que tuve que sacar para el asunto de la visa, para que te reconforte cuando te sientes algo triste.

Hoy en la mañana fui a un notario y me hizo un poder que tu tienes que firmar en presencia de militar de la isla, quien debe escribir dejar constancia, abajo de tu firma, de que tu firmaste en presencia de el. Una vez hecho eso, tu debes mandarme el poder de nuevo.

From Kate's letter of 11 October 1973

I'm sending you this photo that I had to have taken for my visa, so as to comfort you when you're feeling a bit low.

This morning I went to see a notary and he prepared a power of attorney for you to sign, in the presence of a military officer on the island, who has to testify, below your signature, that you have signed it in his presence. Once that's been done, you're to send it back to me.

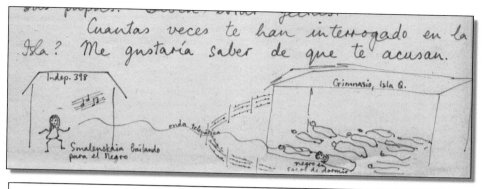

Cuantas veces te han interrogado en la Isla? Me gustaría saber de que te acusan.

Indep. 398

Smalenskaia bailando para el Negro

onda telepática

Gimnasio, Isla Q.

negro en saco de dormir

From Kate's letter of 14 October 1973

How many times have they interrogated you on the island? I'd like to know what they're accusing you of.

Kate's drawing of her dancing for Ricardo, a wave of telepathy, and Ricardo (*el Negro*) in his sleeping bag on the floor of the gymnasium (where the prisoners had to sleep on Quiriquina Island, Ed.)

Como tú, yo también sueño, sobre nuestros tiempos felices, sobre el futuro. No concibo de un futuro separados. Aún si la detención se prolongára, yo esperaré y después estaremos juntos en alguna parte. Aún en mis momentos más pesimistas no concibo no estar juntos en el futuro. Lo que no sé es cuando ese futuro se hará realidad.

From Kate's letter of 17 October 1973

Like you, I also dream about our happy times and about our future. I cannot conceive of a future without each other. Even if your imprisonment goes on for a long time, I'll wait for you and then we'll be together somewhere. Even in my most pessimistic moments I can't imagine not being together in the future. What I don't know is when that future might come true.

From Kate's letter of 22 October 1973

Kate's drawing of her flying from their house on Independence Street to Ricardo asleep on the floor of the gymnasium.

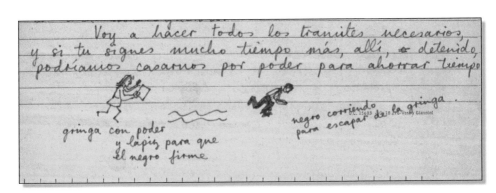

From Kate's letter of 27 October 1973

I'm going to make all the necessary arrangements , and if you are still being held prisoner for much more time there, we could marry by proxy, to gain time.

Kate's drawing: *La Gringa* (Kate) with pen and power of attorney for *el Negro* (Ricardo) to sign – and Ricardo running away to escape from her.

> *Me he sentido bien hoy y con mucho mejor ánimo, debido a haberme dormido mejor anoche, parece, y después, haber recibido tus cartas. Sueño tanto sobre nuestro futuro. De tantos sueños lindos, como no va a realizarse por lo menos uno?*
>
> *I love you,*

From Kate's letter of 27 October 1973

I have been feeling good today and in better spirits, due to having slept better last night, I think, and after receiving your letters. I dream so much about our future. Of so many sweet dreams, surely at least one of them must come true?

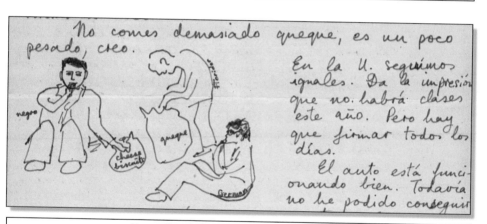

> *No comes demasiado queque, es un poco pesado, creo.*
>
> *En la U. seguimos iguales. Da la impresión que no habrá clases este año. Pero hay que firmar todos los días.*
>
> *El auto está funcionando bien. Todavía no he podido conseguir*

From Kate's letter of 31 October 1973

You'd better not eat too much of the cake, as I think it's a bit heavy.

In the University it's all still the same. I have the impression there won't be any more classes this year. But we have to keep signing in there every day.

Kate's drawing: Ricardo eating the cheese biscuits she had made for him, with fellow prisoners Floridor (with the cake Kate had made for them) and Germán

19th November 1973

19th November 1973

For the attention of MR. BUTLER

Dear Sir:

Since writing my letter of November 14th on
the subject of my daughter Kathleen and her husband
Ricardo Figueroa, we have had a letter which tells
us that Ricardo has been transferred from the island
to the prison at Chillan.

He is being held in solitary confinement,
and although Kathleen had been told that she would
probably be able to see him last Wednesday, she had
still not been able to see him when she telephoned on
Friday.

I know that everything that can be done by
your office will be done, and that the new circumstances, including Kathleen's having been dismissed
from her University post, cannot affect your efforts,
but naturally I want to keep you properly informed
as news comes to hand. As she is quite alone, it
will be appreciated how desperate she must feel in
such a situation.

                    Yours truly,

The Foreign and Commonwealth Office,
Consular Department,
Clive House,
Petty France,
LONDON, S.W.1.

Kate's father's letter to the Foreign and Commonwealth Office.

Consular Department
Foreign and Commonwealth Office
Clive House Petty France London SW1 H 9HD

Telephone ~~01-353~~ 01-930 2323 Ext 1306

W R Clark Esq
W R Clark & Co (Engineers) Ltd
Bridge Street
Clay Cross
Chesterfield

Your reference

Our reference
GK/362/2/1
Date

23 November 1973

Dear Mr Clark,

Thank you for your letter of 14 November about your daughter Kathleen
and her family in Chile.

While I have very great sympathy with the problems your daughter must
be facing and fully understand your worry about her husband's
safety and well-being, I am afraid there is virtually nothing we
can do to help. Mr Figueroa is a Chilean citizen and we could not
properly intervene with the authorities about the treatment of their
own nationals. It could indeed even be harmful to his interests and
possibly those of his family were we seen to be attempting to do so.

I am sorry I cannot let you have a more encouraging reply.

Yours sincerely

M K Butler

P.S. I have now received your further letter of 19 November

Foreign and Commonwealth Office reply to Kate's father.

From Kate's letter of 2 November 1973

Kate's drawing of her preparing to pack possessions away for sending to England.

Nº 4

PARA: my darling Kate
DE: Ricardo
ENCARGOS: 1 refill para escribirte.
1.- Cepillo dientes (3ª carta en q' te
2.- lo pido) Jabón para la soap-dish
3.- Recibí libros: Chaplin, Benedetti
4.- Anouille (?), Cortazar (Rayuela)
5.- Coraje: todo saldrá bien al final.

RECADOS A:
Te mando carta Nº 3 y en el
sobre te incluyo cartas para:
1) Roberto y Edith 2) Miguel y Ivan,
3) Poli y 4) The Clark family. No
sé si ésta será autorizada por
ir en inglés. Pienso escribirle
a Jaime Mejía, a Antonio, etc.
Ya se me está parando la sor-
dera. Quiere decir que estaré bien
Pero si tú no estás bien ¿de qué sirve?
SALUDOS A: Pamela, Natacha, Andrea,
y progenitores. ¿Cómo está Maruja?

ISLA QUIRIQUINA. 22 de Octubre de 1973.—

Ricardo's note of 22 October 1973 sent to Kate from Quiriquina Island.

(List of things needed, and letters for friends and relatives).

Courage: everything will be fine in the end.

My deafness is getting a bit better. So I think I'll be all right. But what is the point of that if you're not feeling all right?

> Mañana voy a ir a un notario a hacer la cuestión del poder ese para # que pueda cobrar tu sueldo para mandar dinero a tus hijos. Parece que nos adelanta el

From Kate's letter of 11 October 1973

Tomorrow I'll go to see a notary in order to get a power of attorney so that I can collect your salary to send money to your children

> Ricky en su carta dice que están todos bien y que no han recibido noticias tuyas desde que dijiste que iban a interrogar a todos los de Chillán a lo mejor habrán recibido algo más de ti ahora. Yo contestaré la carta de Ricky hoy. Mañana supongo que podré cobrar tu sueldo ahora que tengo el poder, y mandaré la misma suma que en Sept.

From Kate's letter of 21 October 1973.

Ricky (Ricardo's son, Ed.) says in his letter that they are all fine but that they haven't had any news from you since you told them that all the prisoners from Chillán were going to be interrogated. Perhaps by now they will have received something more from you. I'll reply to Ricky's letter today. I expect I'll be able to collect your salary now that I've got the power of attorney, and I'll send them the same amount as in September

"cucharita pero de plástico.
En ningún caso de metal.
Gracias por la foto. Estás
tan linda que podría jurar
que no eres mi hija... Yo
duermo con ella. Be
cheerful, mi pequeña. Besos
SALUDOS A: Van firmados los
poderes

ISLA QUIRIQUINA, 16 de Octubre de 1973.-

From Ricardo's note of 16 October 1973 sent to Kate from Quiriquina Island.

... a little spoon, but of plastic, it mustn't be a metal one.

Thanks for the photo .... You look lovely. I sleep with it. Be cheerful, little one. Kisses ....

Patchwork pictures were made by prisoners' relatives to highlight their plight and to raise funds. This one says: "Bread has gone up".

Visiting the prison became a daily activity. I would prepare a *vianda*[31] and take it to the prison at lunch-time. The prison authorities gave the prisoners only the barest of rations - either beans or lentils - so most people who had outside contacts asked for food to be handed in for them. Since the University was closed and I had nothing to do except try to get Ricardo released, the daily *vianda* and excursion to the prison became something to focus on and keep me busy. Sometimes I would see a military vehicle draw up at the prison steps, dispensing bloodied and ragged prisoners who stumbled painfully up the steps and back into the prison. They had been for "interrogation" at the local Regiment.

An article years later in the local newspaper, *La Discusión* (2 December 2004) entitled "The Hidden Story of 'The Sheraton' and the stables of Mountain Infantry Regiment No 9, Chillán" describes how this was one of the main detention centres in the area. Prisoners were taken there from the prison, blindfolded and held *incomunicado*, only taken out of the cells to be tortured, by beatings, electric shocks, suspension by the hands, submersion in water and other barbarities. This was apparently carried out in *Guardia No. 2*, which was commonly known as 'The Sheraton', or down in the basement cells. Other detainees were taken to a military training camp in Quilmo *latifundio*. From 1973 to 1975 the Regiment was under Commander Guillermo Toro Dávila and later under Lt. Colonel Cristián Guedelhoefer.

Whilst Ricardo was in Chillán prison I made some new friends among the wives, mothers and daughters who were also taking food to their loved ones. I got to know a young woman called Ana, who was the wife of Germán Gajardo, a young man who had been a trade union leader for the region. I used to take her to the prison and back by car, as she had a baby of a few months old and a little girl of about five and lived in a *población* some way from the prison. She was so young and innocent and somehow puzzled as to how Germán had got caught up in all this. She was not at all political and did not seem to understand at all why this dreadful thing had happened to her little family. How would the family survive, if Germán were killed or given a long prison sentence, I wondered.

Letters were not allowed, so I devised a method of getting messages to Ricardo. One of the most ingenious was to write tiny notes and put them inside the screw top of the thermos flask I would hand in. Ricardo told me later that he had found them, and they had cheered him up enormously. But usually the empty flask came back with no note from R – he did not have a pen, as he was *incomunicado*.

---

[31] A ready-made, usually hot, meal placed in special 2 or 3-tiered saucepans with a handle for carrying. It was a common practice for busy professional people to buy a *vianda* service from a local woman, who would bring a prepared meal to your house during the working week.

Ricardo was held in the local prison for three days. I could not see him – no visits were allowed – but I took him some food on the 20th, so I knew he was still there then. But I found out later that on the 20th, an army patrol came to take Ricardo and a group of detainees to two different interrogation centres. It was there that they first heard of the "charges" against them. They had to sleep that night on wooden benches in a police cell. The following morning this group were ordered into a van and told to crouch down on the floor between the seats. On both sides of the driver there were soldiers pointing their machine guns at them. Once the van had left behind the noises of the city and seemed to be driving along an open road, Ricardo feared that they might be being taken to the mountains to be shot. But in fact the van was heading the other way, in a westerly direction, towards Concepción. They arrived at the Chacabuco Infantry Regimental headquarters in that city, where Ricardo had done his national service twenty years earlier. The officer there apparently told the army officer accompanying Ricardo's group of detainees that there was no room for them there, so the van set off again, finally reaching the naval base of Talcahuano the evening of the 22 September 1973. From there the prisoners were transferred by naval motor launch to the Quiriquina Island, which was also a naval base.

I had never heard of such a place, before all this happened. For the hundreds of prisoners held there, as for their families and for me personally, "*la Quiriquina*" was now to become seared in our consciousness for the rest of our lives.

CHAPTER FIVE

"Upon my bed at night
I sought him whom my soul loves;
I sought him, but found him not..."
(Song of Solomon, 3.1)

When you spread out the bed like a map
folding the sheet in the South
organising your hair in the North
when you open the bed
which your hand
embroidered with flowers

when I stretch
your long
and narrow strip
of skin
and kisses

with no central in the valley
as if making room for me in the West
Chilean pacific ocean maid
your islander compatriot
seeking you in the dark
on that couch far inland
-no lighthouse to guide –
and cannot find you and cannot talk to you
because they've extinguished the light
and silenced us all
here in the gaol."

(*Goodnight, love, don't sleep, just dream,* by Floridor Pérez,
poet from Los Angeles in southern Chile,
imprisoned with Ricardo on Quiriquina Island)

On 22 September, five days after Ricardo's arrest, he was transferred to a detention centre on the Island of Quiriquina, near the city of

Concepción. I found out when I went to the prison with my daily *vianda* for Ricardo and was told at the gates that he was no longer there. My heart sank. It was ominous news, since many of the top Popular Unity people were being held on Quiriquina Island, or on Dawson Island much further south, and the papers were full of news of people who had been sentenced to death there. I found out that he was part of a group of some twelve men from Chillán, among whom were four ex-*Intendentes*, including Luís Quezada, Juan de Dios Fuentes, our friend Santiago Bell, and an ex-Minister of Agriculture, Pedro Hidalgo. Also in this group were Germán Gajardo, a trade union leader, Isidoro Manríquez, an agronomist, together with other leading officials of the CORA (Agrarian Reform Corporation) and lawyer Mario Hermosilla, my colleague on the Committee of the *Instituto chileno-soviético de Cultura*, who was charged with harbouring explosives. The military authorities in Chillán apparently referred to this group as *los peces gordos,* the big fish.

The Quiriquina is a tiny island just off Talcahuano, where there was a naval base. Some 552 prisoners were packed into the island's gymnasium which was 50 by 25 metres, surrounded by barbed wire and heavily guarded. There was a dry outdoor swimming pool, where the detainees were herded to be hosed down with icy cold sea water at dawn. There were no beds or mattresses. Thirty-three women prisoners were also held there, in a separate room. Held on Quiriquina were the *Intendente* of Concepción, Fernando Álvarez Castillo, and dozens of city and regional leaders, including miners' leaders from the nearby mining region of Lota.

And so began our long correspondence, me from our little house in Chillán, which had seemed so cosy when we lived in it together, but which was now merely somewhere where I slept and did the job of working out what to do to get Ricardo freed, and Ricardo from the Quiriquina Island detention centre, where he had to sleep on the bare wooden floor of the gymnasium, together with hundreds of other detainees from the Concepción region, each fearing the frequent loudspeaker announcements summoning detainees to the doors to an uncertain fate.

At least we could write to each other while Ricardo was on Quiriquina Island, something that had not been allowed during the few days that he had been held in Chillán's prison. To me that was a great relief, to have some tangible communication with him. We are fortunate that most of that correspondence has survived, and is certainly witness to our enduring love during that testing time.

A day or two after Ricardo's transfer to Quiriquina Island we heard that Pablo Neruda had died, on 23 September 1973. Though he was already ill with the cancer that would finally kill him, the cruel coup d'état must surely have hastened his end. A poet's soul cannot bear such an inhuman blow. As

I write these lines forty years later, judges in Chile have ordered the exhumation of Neruda's body, after claims by the poet's chauffeur, Manuel Araya, that he did not die naturally, but was injected with some lethal substance to silence him so that he, as an internationally famous public figure, would not be able to tell the world what was happening. "I believe that Pablo Neruda was murdered, because Pablo Neruda was a very relevant figure in history, as much in this country as in the world," Araya told CNN Chile. "He was going to go into exile on 24 September and they silenced him before then."

Earlier that year, when Neruda, already ill with cancer, returned to Chile from Paris where he had been President Allende's Ambassador, I had been promised a meeting with Neruda, to present him with my recently-published book "*Chile: Reality and Prospects of Popular Unity*". But that much-desired meeting never took place. The infamous Junta of Generals betrayed Allende, and Pablo Neruda, already ill, could not withstand the immense tragedy that had befallen his people, dying less than two weeks later. Many of us felt that his death marked, as it were, the death not only of Chile's much-loved poet, but of Chile's attempt to chart a different future for herself. His death marked the death of the country's burgeoning democracy, and thousands of people disobeyed the curfew to attend his funeral in Santiago, in defiance of arrests, deaths and disappearances which were already the hallmark of the military Junta's regime. Neruda's funeral was filmed and became the first public protest of many against the Junta.

The Quiriquina prisoners were allowed to write short notes on specially printed small papers, with the headings:

From...................
To......................
To bring..............
Requests.............
Greetings to..............
Isla Quiriquina ....of.............. 1973

On one of these notes Ricardo told me that I would have to write in Spanish, so that the military censors would be able to do their work. Obviously he could not tell me in the few notes that he was able to write me during the months he was imprisoned there what conditions were like – but we all knew that there were people who had been sentenced to death there. This is from an account Ricardo wrote later, in exile:

"Because the world should know.

The loudspeaker was not just one more kind of torture in the Quiriquina Island Concentration Camp, but something worse,

155

although every syllable emitted by that hard metallic voice was like an invisible bullet drilling through our brains day and night, each day and every day. That's why nobody wanted to hear it, the loudspeaker, but we realised that behind every "Attention!" there could lurk some fatal message for any one of us. That's why we had to listen to it, just as we had to keep a watch on the door of the gymnasium. It was part of the torture we had to suffer as condemned men, because that place, full of hidden dangers, was haunted by the malevolent face of death.

"This, the presence of death, made us forget other suffering, like our permanent hunger, for example, or our thirst, that would have been bad enough in themselves in other circumstances. It's true that our relatives – those who were in a position to do so, which was not the majority – could send us food from time to time. This policy was in the interests of our executioners since it lowered the costs of the repression. But our relatives could not send us water to drink, and there was a dangerous shortage of drinking water on the island, something which must have helped to make our complaints – constipation, for instance – much worse. But the door and the damned loudspeaker made us forget it, because there it was only possible to do that – to forget our lesser evils.

"We could consider a lesser evil the fact that there were only five outside latrines, near the empty swimming pool in the open air, for the 500 or so prisoners shut up in a gymnasium. For each person three minutes were counted out in military style and under the aim of machine-guns from various sides."

One of the prisoners with Ricardo on Quiriquina Island was Mario Hermosilla, my colleague in the *Instituto chileno-soviético*, also one of the group of the "big fish" whom I've mentioned before. He was charged with keeping explosives, at the direct request of Salvador Allende himself, at a country cottage he owned near Chillán. When the military raided the house and found the explosives, Hermosilla was not there. And so he escaped being shot on the spot, as many others had been, including our friend Ricardo Lagos and family.

One of our colleagues at the *sede*, Alejandro Witker, who was the Socialist that Ricardo had "unearthed" when we had first arrived in Chillán, told a joke in his book *Prisión en Chile* about the time that all of them had been together in Quiriquina concentration camp after the 1973 military coup. All the prisoners were herded together in what had once been the gymnasium of the island military base. Every so often, over the loudspeaker, a voice would announce a prisoner's name, then the words: "To the doors!" followed by the ominous words, "together with all his belongings!" This usually meant, not that so-and-so was going to be freed, but that he was being taken out to be shot, and they wouldn't see him again. The prisoners grew to dread that announcement. According to Witker, in Hermosilla's case, the announcement would be: "Mario Hermosilla, to the doors, together with... all his explosives!"

Humour in Chile was never far from the surface, even in those terrifying days and weeks after the coup. Amid all the beatings and tortures, prisoners returning to the gymnasium after "interrogation sessions" with bruises, gashes and broken limbs, one of the detainees would be sure to turn whatever he could into something for having a laugh. Mario Hermosilla, a man by now in his sixties, although he had a lawyer's bearing and gravitas, had a rather snub nose. So the joke ran round the other prisoners: "Don't go thinking his nose is like that from being hit in the face by a rifle-butt. No, he's always been like that!"

Ricardo told me later that at first when the prisoners heard the announcement: "So-and-so, to the doors, together with all his belongings!" they thought it meant that the person was going to be freed, and prisoners applauded. But soon it became clear: they were taken to be interrogated under torture, and some died from the torture. Sometimes it meant a prisoner's change of place of detention, but more often than not it meant summary execution.

Once I knew that Ricardo was on the Quiriquina, I found out that no visits were allowed, and, because it was a three-hour journey from Chillán just to hand food in, I realised I would not be able to go more than once a week at most. And anyway, I felt with even more urgency than ever that I had to pull out all the stops to get his case known about and get him released. I phoned my parents in England, who had of course been very worried, since they had only received an initial telegram from me saying that we were all right. They, I knew, would already have been writing letters to the Foreign Office telling them about our case, and publicising it in the newspapers.

I travelled to Santiago to the British Embassy to ask for their help. I was received sympathetically enough, and was given an official letter with an impressive embossed seal at the foot of the page, which pointed out to the Chilean authorities that I, the bearer, was a citizen of Great Britain, and requesting I be treated as such. This letter was worth its weight in gold, and certainly proved so on a number of occasions during the troubled months that followed. But when it came to my urging that the Embassy intercede on Ricardo's behalf, I was met with a stone wall. Nothing could be done, I was told, because we were not legally married. "But we have been living together since 1968!" I protested, "surely you can do something!" "I'm afraid not," came the polite but firm reply, "we can only deal with married partners of British citizens."

I wrote to Ricardo's father in Puerto Varas to see whether he, as a former policeman, could do anything. I had no idea what Ricardo's two brothers, who were both police officers of more senior rank than their father, were doing or what their attitude to the coup had been. I hardly knew one of those brothers and had only met the other a couple of times. They made no contact with me, though I was sure they must have known, through their other brothers, that Ricardo had been arrested. That did not surprise me, however, because we all knew that any military people who had spoken out against the coup would have suffered the same fate as General Bachelet. So the most likely thing would be that they would keep their heads down. On Quiriquina Island Ricardo met a former policeman who had been arrested and sent there for having disobeyed orders on the day of the coup. He was a fervent Protestant, which was perhaps what saved him from being shot, since he always insisted he had had to follow his religious commandment not to kill.

I wrote to Ricardo's former wife and children in Temuco, and managed, with considerable difficulty, to arrange to collect Ricardo's salary and send it to her. Fortunately at that stage we were still being paid, and anyway she had not been sacked from her teaching post as she was not marked as a political activist. Ricky wrote to me telling me their news so that I could pass it on to their father, and they too began to write to him on the island. Schools had begun functioning again after the military coup, so the children were all busy with their studies as the school year drew to a close.

Ricardo's father came to Chillán, hoping to see his son, but too late – he had already been sent to Quiriquina Island. I felt sorry for *Don* Ricardo: he had been so proud of his son when he had become Vice-rector of the University and now a terrible thing, shameful in his eyes, had happened to him. He was very concerned about the situation and kept repeating that he couldn't understand how it had come to this. He was also concerned about his two sons who were serving police officers, since he knew that for them, any association with known left-wing people would be dangerous or, at the very least, not beneficial for their careers.

The day after Ricardo's father arrived, 27 September 1973, I left him in the house after breakfast telling him I would be back in an hour or so. I went to the Police Headquarters, a few blocks away, to the Department for Foreigners, to see about renewing my visa, which was due to expire in December. Once there, I was taken to a room for questioning and treated as if I was under suspicion. "We know what you have been doing!" I was told by the Chief Inspector, "you have been teaching English in the Communist Party Headquarters!" If I hadn't been so scared I would have laughed out loud! The thought of that being the worst thing they could come up with was simply ludicrous and showed the paucity of their military intelligence.

They could have accused me of teaching Marxism-Leninism to the *campesinos* in rural localities of Ñuble province (true), or of having attended self-defence combat classes (true), or of being secretary of the *Instituto chileno-soviético de Cultura* (true), or of having taught Russian at the Town Hall (true), of having published a book in Great Britain on the Popular Unity process (true) or just of having been a Chilean Communist Party member (true)... but teaching English to Party members in the Party's headquarters – wow, some crime!

But it was no laughing matter. I was whisked away in a police van, under arrest, but with no charge, and soon found myself in the headquarters of the Regiment, where we knew so many prisoners were being taken daily for interrogation and torture. I was told to stand against a wall, with two armed conscripts facing me across the corridor. I was scared, but determined not to show it. So I looked all around me and concentrated on trying to see what was going on and to think of what I would say when my turn came to be interrogated. I had with me the letter I had managed to obtain from the British Embassy and felt pretty sure that that would help.

By now it must have been about 11 a.m. I worried about *Don* Ricardo at home on his own, not knowing where I was or what had happened to me. I thought about my own dear *compañero* Ricardo, somewhere on a cold gymnasium floor with no mattress or pillow, not knowing what fate awaited him. I worried about his hearing, which had not improved since his operation in Santiago in 1971, and which would surely deteriorate with the icy-cold seawater hosing-down the detainees were forced to undergo at dawn. Whatever happened to me, I thought, could not possibly be as horrible as his sufferings.

The hours went by. The conscript guard was changed every hour or so, but still I was made to stand. I asked for a drink, but my request was ignored. Standing in one place for a long time becomes increasingly arduous, as was no doubt the intention. It's not "torture", but it certainly adds to any "softening-up" process. Yet strangely, although I was sick inside with fear, I did not feel that I was in danger of breaking down in tears or saying anything I would later feel ashamed about. I felt strong and firm in my convictions.

As the day went on, I became increasingly hungry and thirsty, and worried about *Don* Ricardo. I was still being forced to stand, and all I could do was to shift my weight from one foot to the other, but there was little respite. I tried to speak to the soldiers on guard opposite me, but was told I had to be silent. I concentrated on what I would say when eventually I would be taken somewhere for interrogation.

After several hours I was taken into an office and told to sit down. It was a great relief. I took out my letter from the British Embassy and handed it to the official in charge of my interrogation. He did not look best pleased. I answered all his questions truthfully, and was glad I had not been involved in anything illegal. Why had I come to Chile, what was Ricardo involved in, why had he stepped down from being Vice-rector of the University – he must have been assigned to more important, secret work inside the Party, that's right, isn't it? Isn't it? *Isn't it?* The officer's voice got louder and louder, more and more insistent. And you, why are you always going to the Communist Party headquarters? What do you do there? You are a foreigner, you have no right to be meddling in Chilean affairs!

I told him I had the right to vote and engage in Chilean affairs as long as this was within the law, which it was. I told him I had been living and working in Chile for five years and was highly respected as an academic and by my students – ask any of them, I said brazenly. As for Ricardo, he was totally innocent, of that I was sure, and the authorities in Britain were already working to get him freed, which is something you should know about, I said. I told him it was unforgivable that I, a British citizen, should have been treated in this way and made to stand for all those hours with no food or drink. I insisted that they let me go, to join Ricardo's father who would be most worried about me by now.

It was dusk by the time they let me go. I was escorted under military guard to the gates of the Regiment and seen through the gates. Trembling all over with relief after my ordeal, I walked the six or so blocks to our house, feeling weak and shaken. When I got home I saw that, as I had feared, *Don* Ricardo was very worried, and had not known what to do, since he had no house key and could only imagine what could have befallen me. He had had no lunch, all the time expecting me back at any moment. Like most people, we had no telephone, so all he had been able to do was to sit and wait.

I could see that for *Don* Ricardo, a man who all his life had had a deep admiration for the German people of the south[32] and, by extension, for all Europeans, whom he saw as hard-working and honest people, unlike the Chilean *campesinos* whom he regarded as lazy and uneducated, was deeply upset that a young woman like me – an *Englishwoman*, to boot – could have been put through an experience such as I had gone through that day. I think it was a real lesson for him in understanding what this coup d'état meant for all of us who found ourselves on the 'wrong' side of it.

---

[32] In the second half of the nineteenth century the Chilean government arranged for settlers from Germany to come to Chile to farm large tracts of land in the south of the country. The land had not previously been put to agricultural use, as those were largely unpopulated areas, so the early settlers had to work very hard to farm the land and make it productive. They formed a community in the regions from Valdivia to the north down to Puerto Montt to the south, continuing to speak German among themselves and setting up German schools, churches etc. for their community. Ricardo's sister-in-law, Marlis, is the daughter of such immigrants, who settled in Osorno. She and her sister always spoke German at home to their parents who had both been born in Germany.

The military official at the Regiment had told me that I would most likely be deported, but then I was told that the matter was awaiting a decision by the *Comandancia* of the region. I had to go from one office to another to try and get my visa renewed. I was afraid that I might get deported, which would have meant leaving Ricardo to an unknown fate. That was the last thing I wanted. Meanwhile when I tried to collect Ricardo's salary, which Ricardo had asked me to do, so that I could send it to his former wife and children, I was told I could not do so, because I was not his legal wife. I would have to get a power of attorney from Ricardo in order to be able to collect any future salary. I did, however, manage to get authorisation from the *Comandancia*, as a special dispensation, to collect his September salary, and sent it with *Don* Ricardo, who was going to stop off in Temuco to see his grandchildren.

It was very encouraging that, whilst some of our close friends did not feel able to come and visit me, because it would have been incriminating for them[33], many of our students did come to show me their support. One lad, who lived a few blocks away on the same street, was a first-year student of Ricardo's. He came to the house one day, and after we chatted a little about Ricardo's situation and his studies, we started talking about music. He asked me if I had the record of Vivaldi's Four Seasons. I told him I knew the work, but no, we did not have the record. Next day he knocked on the door with that and other classical music records under his arm, for me to borrow. These visits made me feel a little less lonely, and helped the day go a bit faster.

On Sunday 30 September I travelled to Talcahuano to take Ricardo some things. I also had a small parcel for the young trade unionist leader, Germán Gajardo, from his wife Ana. I had to take a bus from Chillán to Concepción, then a local bus from Concepción to the naval base of Talcahuano. That was where we had to hand in the parcels and bags with the prisoner's name. It was a long trek which took all day, and you couldn't even get a glimpse of Quiriquina Island from the bus terminal at Talcahuano or from the naval base gates. Ricardo could have been a million miles away.

How did I spend my days? Going from one office to another, trying to get my visa sorted, trying to get a power of attorney to send to Ricardo for him to sign, receiving visits, writing long letters to Ricardo and to my family in England, and going to see a very few friends – people who were not known in Chillán because they had arrived there quite recently, like our friends Oscar

---

[33] My letters to Ricardo on Quiriquina Island show that I did not always understand this at the time. Whilst in one I write that "our friends are being very supportive and nice", in another I write: "It's depressing how some people have turned so cowardly. It's comforting to know that you are not like that and that you will be able to face up to things with the courage that your clear conscience gives you. I too feel serene and am facing up to the situation calmly." And in another: "I've discovered who our real friends are. In this sort of situation you soon find out where the solidarity is. I don't condemn those I used to think of as friends, but I feel pity for them."

and Sylvia, or those who had not been at all involved in politics. One of these was a colleague, an art teacher at the University, called Gladys Bornand[34], the wife of our veterinary friend *Chepo*, who had been detained the same time as Ricardo. *Chepo* was being held in the Regional Stadium in Concepción. Just as in Santiago, football stadiums up and down the country were being used to hold the thousands of political prisoners detained after the coup.

Gladys was seven months pregnant and, because of a previous miscarriage, had been told to rest as much as possible during this pregnancy. I found her very sanguine about the whole situation, confident that *Chepo* would soon be released and that this nightmare would not last very long. I was glad to see her so positive, but could not share her optimism.

The University continued closed and in early October a Police Colonel, Mario Alvarez Molina, was put in charge of the three universities in the province.

The local newspaper carried an advertisement for a Committee for Help to Foreigners in Chile, in Concepción, under the auspices of the United Nations, I believe. I decided to go there to put our case. After explaining my situation and that of Ricardo, the woman in charge there told me much the same as the British Embassy – that they could help *me* leave Chile, yes, but they would not be able to help get Ricardo released so that he could leave with me, because we were not married. She advised me to do everything possible to get married. This would help me, she said, to be able to stay in Chile even if I were not granted a renewal of visa, and would possibly act as some small guarantee for Ricardo, in the sense that he would be married to a British citizen[35].

I was not at all sure that Ricardo would agree. It is true that we were both very much in love – of that I had no doubt – but he had already been married and had children, and he also knew that I had never shown any interest in being married. He had, however, always been keen to have his first marriage "annulled", which was the only sort of divorce that was possible at the time in Chile, and I knew that he had done everything needed from the legal point of view to get that annulment document. For my part, I had always had a strange and unusual attitude to marriage, probably because I saw that my

---

34 In Chile, and in general in Latin America and Spain, married women do not change their surnames after marriage. Some women in Chile would add "de + the surname of their husband" after their own surnames, but this was not particularly common, and it was mainly confined to rather upper-class women. I was always known as "Clark" in Chile, and I decided to keep my own surname after we came to Britain to live.

35 The famous and much-loved singer/songwriter Victor Jara had a British wife, as we found out a few months later in London, when I met Joan Jara for the first time. The fact that he was married to a British woman had not saved Victor – his combative songs and outspoken support for the Popular Unity Government had made him a particular target for the Junta, as Joan makes clear in her moving autobiography "Victor - An Unfinished Song" (Bloomsbury, 1983). Victor was detained on the very day of the coup, savagely tortured and killed a few days later.

own parents' marriage was far from happy. My mother was quite a feminist in her own way and never wore a wedding ring, which was most unusual for the forties and fifties. I had felt that since Ricardo had been married before, there was no real point in us going through the legal procedure of marrying.

But obviously there was a different situation now. I went to see Gladys Bornand upon my return from Concepción, and she was emphatic. "But of course you must!" she declared. "It's the logical thing to do! What possible doubt can there be?" I came away from her house deep in thought, for the first time seriously entertaining the idea that we should get married after all, despite all our previous attitudes and opinions.

The Junta called all the detainees "prisoners of war". It was spine-chilling to hear this terminology over the radio and in the press. What war? The only "war" was that unleashed against its own people by a small clique of military men. I felt the grim satisfaction of knowing that my gut instinct all along these last few months had been right – that the danger came from the military as well as the political Right and that the danger all along had been that of a coup, not a civil war, as the Party had led us to believe. Whilst backing the so-called "constitutional road" charted by the Popular Unity Government, I had become convinced ever since the lorry-owners' strike, or boycott, in October 1972, that the military could not be trusted to back a left-wing government, even if that government did abide totally by the Constitution. The Chilean military had long been sending its officers for training at the infamous "Escuela de las Americas"[36] run by the United States.

It is true that there were officers and even top generals, like Commander-in-Chief Rene Schneider[37], General Carlos Prats[38] and General Alberto Bachelet[39] who had always maintained loyalty to the constitutionally elected government, no matter what colour that government was. But the rapid polarisation of political views from 1970 onwards saw a shift towards the

---

[36] School of the Americas graduates are responsible for some of the worst human rights abuses in Latin America. In 1996 the Pentagon was forced to release training manuals used at the school that advocated torture, extortion and execution.

[37] Commander-in-Chief of the Armed Forces at the time of Salvador Allende's election in September 1970. He opposed intervention by the armed forces to block parliament's ratification of Allende as President, and argued that the military should guarantee any constitutionally-elected government. This became known as the Schneider doctrine. In a clear attempt to prevent Allende coming to power, Schneider was assassinated on October 25, 1970, aged 56.

[38] Commander-in-Chief of the Armed Forces and served for a time in Allende's cabinet. He resigned on August 22, 1973, being replaced by General Augusto Pinochet, who at that time was thought to be loyal to the Constitution. After the coup on September 11, 1973 Prats fled to Argentina, where he was assassinated, together with his wife, by a car bomb in Buenos Aires on September 30, 1974, aged 59.

[39] An air force general who opposed the military coup of September 11, 1973. He was arrested the day of the coup and died of heart failure as a result of torture on March 12, 1974, aged 52. His daughter, Michelle, became Chile's first female President, in January 2006.

right on the part of many people who had previously held centrist positions or were simply non-political, and the military were no exception.

Yet after the coup we heard of instances of people in the armed forces and police, some conscripts, others even officers, who, although not prepared to risk their lives by taking a stand against the new Junta, did try to help individual prisoners in small ways. By no means all the uniformed personnel supported the coup, but the command structure within the services was such, and the coup so well-prepared, that any opposition to the Junta's seizure of power was futile.

I began a routine of travelling to Talcahuano every Friday, which was the only day allowed for relatives to take food, clothes or other articles to the prisoners. One day when I got there with a heavy bag of food, including fruit which I guessed they would not be getting in their diet, I was told they had stopped allowing food of any kind. It was a windy, rainy day, and, somewhat dispirited, I decided to catch a bus back to Concepción and walk to the Regional Stadium where our friend *Chepo* was being held, and hand in for him all the food I had taken for Ricardo. That was typical of those months – arbitrary decisions changed at whim, with no thought for the poor relatives, sometimes elderly mothers, who had trekked miles from rural locations to hand parcels over for their imprisoned sons or daughters.

There was nothing else to do except write letters, read the papers, which was horribly depressing, and rack my brains incessantly to think what else I could do to get Ricardo released. The University, which had been painted a clinical white on the orders of the military, was closed, but I learned that the military authorities had now appointed a new Vice-rector and Secretary-General from the existing staff – two lecturers who had been opposed to the Allende Government. Would I be officially sacked, as Irene, our neighbour, had been, I wondered.

Not only our University building was painted a cold uniform white. Much worse was the fate of the giant mural painted by our friend Julio Escámez on the wall of the entrance hall of Chillán's Town Hall. He had begun it, at the invitation of the city's Mayor and councillors, early in 1970 and it took him till June 1972 to complete the work. The mural reflected the struggle between the different antagonistic social classes and how, out of this struggle, there emerges a better, more humanistic and happier world. It was such an important event in the artistic life of Chile that President Allende himself came to Chillán to attend the inauguration of the mural in August 1972. Soon after the coup the Junta ordered the mural not merely to be painted over, but completely destroyed, by partially demolishing the wall on which it had been painted.

It has been reported (in Chillán's local newspaper *La Discusión*, 11 December 2008) that after the coup the Junta had even wanted to destroy the world-famous David Siqueiros mural in the *Escuela de México* in Chillán, but that the Mexican authorities got wind of their intentions and intervened to prevent it. After the destruction of his mural, Julio Escámez feared for his life and left Chile for Costa Rica, where he continued to live and work during the long dictatorship years.

One of the many people I went to see during the months that Ricardo was held on Quiriquina Island was a Catholic priest who had latterly been a student of mine on the English course. José Luís Ysern was a Spaniard but had lived several years in Chile. I told him I wanted to see Ricardo, especially after receiving a couple of worrying letters from him, and asked for him to intercede. He told me he did not think it would be possible unless the military authorities gave all prisoners visiting rights, as they had begun to do in the local Chillán prison, but he would have a word with the chaplain of the island concentration camp. José Luís added that he did not think Ricardo would be held much longer, since the only accusation against him was that he had been the University's Vice-rector. He knew, he said, that Ricardo was considered a good academic and was highly thought of by his students.

Father Ysern could not know that what Ricardo's interrogators actually accused him of was of being directly involved in the so-called "*Plan Zeta*" (Z Plan), supposedly a sinister plot hatched by the Left to overthrow the constitution of Chile and seize power by force of arms. The military interrogators told Ricardo that since he had not been his Party's candidate in the second elections for Vice-rector of the University, even though he was already acting Vice-rector, ipso facto he must have been designated some other, more important, secret work within the Party – the *Plan Zeta*.

Of the few friends who continued to see me in those first post-coup months, Edith Miranda and her husband Roberto Aravire were the most constant. They were Maths lecturers from Antofagasta in the far north of Chile and were not particularly well-known at the university. They were about my age, and we had spent quite a lot of our free time with them. They had supported the Popular Unity Government, but had not joined any political party, so I suppose they felt that continued friendship with me did not put them in much danger. Edith travelled with me to Talcahuano a few times, and it was good to have someone I was close to by my side during that difficult time.

On one of our visits to hand in a parcel for Ricardo we learnt that the rules had changed again: now they were once more allowing food to be handed in. So Edith and I traipsed back from the naval base to the centre of Talcahuano to buy some cheese, salami and biscuits, and then back again to the naval base at the port, to make sure Ricardo (and Germán, whose wife Ana could not make the journey since she had two small children) would get a food parcel, as well as letters, tea bags, cigarettes and pipe tobacco. It was comforting to know that soon he would receive something nice that I had taken for him, and that he would know that I had been there that day, so close, yet so far away from him.

One of the people I decided to go and see during this time, because I thought he might have some influence with the military authorities, was the man Ricardo had had negotiations with and had managed to persuade to donate land for a new campus for our University – local landowner and Christian Democrat, Fernando May. I had not met Mr May during the time that Ricardo was busy with the negotiations regarding the land donation. But when Ricardo was in the Quiriquina Island concentration camp, I found out where he lived and went to see him to ask him to intercede on Ricardo's behalf, since I knew he was an influential local person from an old-established and well-respected family. He listened to me courteously, in the old-fashioned but elegant drawing-room of his rather grand house, and seemed troubled by what I told him of Ricardo's fate. I left with his promise to do whatever he could to help Ricardo's situation ringing in my ears, not knowing whether he spoke genuinely, or whether it was merely his polite way of getting rid of an irksome visitor.

On one of my weekly trips to Talcahuano to take Ricardo a food parcel, I met a woman who was frantic for news of her son, a teenager, being held on the island. She had had no news of him since his detention, and was sick with worry. She was a simple peasant woman, who, like many poor rural people who could not afford dental treatment, had gaps in her teeth which spoiled her otherwise pleasant face. I was happy to learn, when I saw her again on a subsequent visit that she had finally heard from her son, by letter. It was touching to hear her love and concern for her son, who was so young. She would go to the Naval base gates two or three times a day to see if there was any note from him, all the way from her home in Hualpencillo, outside Talcahuano. My friend Edith and I would help her read the lists pasted up at the gates, of those for whom there were letters or messages, for she had difficulty in reading.

On one of the visits Edith and I made together we went on afterwards to see our muralist friend, Julio Escámez, in Concepción, not far from Talca-huano. I was glad to see that he had a new partner and seemed happier in his personal life than when Ricardo and I had got to know him during the months when he was painting the mural in the Town Hall in Chillán. I think this must have been before he heard that his mural there had been destroyed on the orders of the Junta. I did not see him again after that barbarous crime, which was what forced him into exile.

166

It was shocking to walk past the familiar shops in Chillán town centre and see in the shop windows fridges, washing machines, sheets and towels – all the things that had been unavailable for months before. Was it the proof of what we had suspected, that the organisations of the Right had deliberately encouraged shop-owners to hoard goods, with the aim of adding to the overall chaos they were hoping to achieve, and thus discourage the middle classes from supporting the Government? It was so sad to realise yet again that it was not only by force of arms that the Allende Government had been destroyed.

It is hard to transmit the sadness and desperation so many of us felt at this time. Sadness at dreams of a better life shattered, sadness at so much horrible news of arrests, torture and death. For me it was particularly difficult, since I was on my own, with no family and most friends keeping away, so as to save their own skins, since I was the partner of a political prisoner, and not only that, but of one of *los peces gordos*.

As I wrote in a letter to Ricardo:

> "Sometimes I wake in the morning and I have to make an effort to remember where I am, where you are... It's as if I cannot believe that this is happening in real life and not simply a nightmare. Often at night I dream of you, but they are dreams full of anxiety, searching, desperation, death... Today seems as if it will never end. It is 8.30 p.m. and the rest of the evening will seem never-ending. It is one of those interminable days."

University staff were told that all the "Marxists" among us would be classified into three groups: A - for those considered "political activists", and they were to be sacked; B - for those yet to be classified as A or C; and C - for those who, although "Marxists", had not "brought politics" into their classes – they would be allowed to keep their jobs. A commission from Santiago was due to arrive to help make this important, yet derisory, classification.

My moods went from optimism that Ricardo would soon be released and that this nightmare would at least in part be over, to black moods of despair when I thought of Ricardo being tortured or being sentenced to death or long years in prison. The not knowing was sometimes unbearable. At other times I made myself busy and would feel more confident. Someone who had been with our vet friend *Chepo* in the Regional Stadium of Concepción was suddenly released and phoned *Chepo*'s wife Gladys to tell her that her husband was all right. She was filled with hope that he would be released in time for their baby being born, which was due at the end of November. But I had no such news of Ricardo, except the occasional little notes he was allowed to send from the Quiriquina.

What was happening meanwhile with our Santiago friends? Poli Délano, our writer friend, left to join his parents abroad. His father had been President Allende's Ambassador in Sweden at the time of the coup, and therefore remained abroad, unable to return to Chile. English lecturer Pito Henríquez and his wife, María Angelica, an actress, left with their children for Canada, where Pito died soon after of leukaemia. Both Poli and Pito had sent Ricardo letters of solidarity when he was on Quiriquina Island. Luís Bocaz and his wife Nidia had fortunately been on study leave in Quebec when the coup happened, so they remained in exile, only returning many years later after the collapse of Pinochet's dictatorship. Ramón continued to work as a self-employed architect and in clandestine work for his party. Our other Santiago friends had not been political activists, so were not in immediate danger, and simply gritted their teeth and kept their heads down.

As for Ricardo's brothers, we knew nothing of what fate might have befallen Camilo, the oldest, who had been a Communist since his teenage years. We imagined he would have gone into hiding and continued the struggle clandestinely, which is what happened. He managed to evade arrest all the subsequent years, despite being a Party leader at local and regional level. The youngest brother, Jaime, who had been much attracted to the MIR during his early student years but who had subsequently joined the Communist youth, had moved shortly before the coup to his first academic post far away in the northern city of Antofagasta, so his political views were not well-known to his colleagues there. The other left-wing brother, Guillermo, had never joined any party, though he and his wife Eliana Cea, both long-standing journalists on the right-wing newspaper *El Mercurio*, had always supported the Popular Unity Government. Eliana had been elected national secretary of the journalists' trade union (*Colegio de Periodistas*) in March 1971, and as a result, shortly after her election triumph, had been invited to lunch with President Allende at the Moneda Palace. After the coup d'état she was promptly sacked by *El Mercurio*, but fortunately – as they had four children to feed – Guillermo, who was a much-respected journalist, managed to keep his job there.

As for the two policemen brothers, all we knew, from Ricardo's father, was that they had continued working as normal, which meant that they were now part of the new regime. We had no contact whatsoever with them until many years after the fall of the dictatorship. As in many families, fundamentally differing ideological or religious viewpoints can divide people and these rifts sometimes never heal.

Ricardo had asked me in one of his notes to send him a chess set, and our friend Roberto, who was a chess champion in Chile, sent him one of his. It was one of the ways the prisoners on the island managed to while away the time. One of the people Ricardo played against was Floridor Pérez, a teacher and poet from Los Angeles, a town to the south of Chillán, whom Ricardo and I had met a year or so earlier at a gathering of writers and poets organised by the University in Chillán. On that occasion he came with his partner and muse, a beautiful, quiet young woman called Natacha. A poem he wrote, dedicated to her, goes like this:

They've told her	Le han dicho
With that man you'll never even have a place to fall down dead in	con ese hombre no tendrán dónde caerse muertos
I've told her	Le he dicho
We'll have the whole world where we can stand up alive in.	Tendremos todo el mundo donde paramos vivos.

Floridor told his fellow-prisoners how he had been detained and brought to the Quiriquina; Ricardo later included it in his account of life at the concentration camp:

> "...(Floridor) had been lucky to get off lightly with an injured leg and bruises all over his body... They (the soldiers) had loaded a lorry with prisoners in a peculiarly fascist way: they covered the floor of the lorry with bodies and then they spread another layer of bodies on top until they completed seven layers. When the lorry was "suitably" loaded, a military squad of some thirty soldiers sat on top of the human pile. The surprising thing is that only some of the prisoners at the bottom were squashed to death, the rest only badly injured..."

Four prisoners died in this way during the 120 kilometre journey between Los Angeles and the Naval Base of Talcahuano.

While Ricardo was in the Quiriquina detention camp, our landlady gave me notice that she wanted us to leave. I had nowhere to go, of course, and I felt it was very unfair of her, since she lived with her mother in their own house, and I felt pretty sure that the only reason she was asking us to leave was for political reasons (we think she was a Christian Democrat supporter), or perhaps so that she could raise the rent to new tenants. I know she was also annoyed to see that the outside sink in the back garden had cracked, and it is true that I was to blame for that.

The night Ricardo was taken away by the military, I spent several hours looking for any incriminating documents I could find to destroy, and I used that outside sink in which to burn them. We had no inside fireplace, and I could not think of anywhere else that I could make a fire which would be contained and not leave much of a trace. It wasn't that we had anything much to hide, but in those days it was enough for the military to know that you were a member of any of the Popular Unity parties or the MIR for you to be arrested. So it had to be the outside sink. I burnt materials about Party meetings, motions and resolutions of Congresses and anything else I imagined could be turned against us as proof that we were dangerous enemies of the State. During the process, one of the concrete walls of the sink cracked.

The landlady was adamant that I had to leave. We had always paid the rent on time and had lived there for over four years, but it was not a good time to talk about tenants' rights. It was just one more problem to be confronted. I explained that Ricardo was not in a position to be able to do anything, and where would I go, I asked her. I had no relatives in Chile, and did not even know whether I was going to keep my job at the University. I was pretty sure that I would be sacked. Eventually *Señorita* Norma relented and said that I could move into the maid's quarters in the back garden, which could be reached independently through a high wooden gate between the wall of the house and the outer wall of the garden, next to the pavement.

So I started the job of packing up the books that the soldiers had not taken when they raided our house, and putting them in boxes and the trunk I had brought from Britain when I had first arrived in Chile. And I began arranging for the big items to be taken, some to Temuco to Ricardo's family – our lovely big desk, for instance, where we used to sit and work facing each other – and some to the little wooden cottage which had belonged to Ricardo's aunt Albertina in Quinchamalí. She had died some months before, so the house there was empty. I went to Quinchamalí and arranged for a relative of hers to come to Chillán with a horse and cart to collect our fridge, our double bed and the cane and wicker furniture that we had accumulated, as well as a lot of our books. If it had not been so sad for me to see our little home broken up in this way, it would have seemed funny: me riding in an old open cart, drawn by a horse, our household goods piled either side of me, swaying and jolting as the old horse trod its weary way the 30 or so kilometres to Quinchamalí.

The maid's room in the back garden, which had never been used as such by us, since we did not have a maid, was a longish wooden hut with a single bed, and at one end there was an electric hob with two rings. Just outside the hut, in the open air, there was a shower which emitted only cold water, and an outside toilet. It was primitive, and no doubt very cold in winter, but it sufficed. At least I had a roof over my head.

Actually it had been occupied for a few months that year by a couple of friends of ours, Manuel Miranda and Nora Eggers, who had slept in it for two nights during the week, when they travelled from their home in Santiago to teach classes at the University in Chillán. Their timetables were arranged in such a way that they were able to spend the middle of the week in Chillán, and the rest of the week in the capital. We used to eat together on those midweek days, and had a rule among the four of us that whoever returned home first at lunch-time would prepare lunch for all of us. Ricardo never got home first – often he did not make it home at all – so he never made lunch, but the rest of us took it in turns.

The four of us got on very well, and we enjoyed their weekly visits. Manuel was a writer and had already had two or three novels published. He had reddish-brown, curly hair and a pointed beard and looked for all the world like a *Don Quijote*. He taught Latin American literature, and Nora taught classical guitar. She was descended from Austrian immigrants and looked very European, with fair hair and green eyes. Manuel was a dedicated lecturer and his students loved him. He was passionate about spreading literature among the poor and uneducated people. When the Popular Unity Government set up a new publishing house called Quimantú (the word means *sun of knowledge* in the language of the Mapuche people, who live in the south of Chile and Argentina) which began to publish pocket paperbacks with the classics of Hispanic and world literature, Manuel became their champion, setting up stall on the pavement outside the University (the same place where I had been attacked by *Patria y Libertad* when they destroyed the Vietnam war exhibition Manuel and I had made) to sell the whole range of new paperbacks to all and sundry. He was a wonderful propagandist for all that was good about Popular Unity, and as a friend, he was kind, loyal, and unselfish in the extreme.

During the winter before the coup, Manuel and Nora had moved from the maid's room in the garden, which was too cold, and begun renting a small flat. This meant that they could spend more time in Chillán, something they increasingly wanted to do, as they became more and more integrated in the academic life of the city and in political activities like mounting exhibitions and Manuel's Quimantú book sales.

I suppose it was the fact that they were not well-known to the military authorities, since they had only been living in Chillán a year or so, that they escaped arrest after the September 1973 coup d'état. Soon after the coup and Ricardo's detention, I helped Manuel bury some of his most precious political books in the garden of their rented flat, since he feared their flat could be raided by the military. I don't know whether he managed to unearth them

171

before leaving for Santiago after his dismissal from the University – he was in the "A" classification. It was a worrying time for them, Manuel losing his job, and Nora heavily pregnant with her first child.

Manuel and Nora were very good to me during the first few weeks that Ricardo was held on the Quiriquina island. They would come round and help lift my spirits. Soon they would seek exile in Germany, where Manuel later worked for many years teaching Latin American literature at the University of Hamburg. In exile we continued our friendship, exchanging visits between Hamburg and London several times until Manuel's death in September 2000, in Hamburg.

Other friends whose company and solidarity were very important to me at this time were the poet, Sergio Hernández, whose anti-Junta anecdotes were bound to make me laugh, however low I felt; Oscar and Sylvia, who were from Angol and had only recently come to live in Chillán; Victor Reyes, a Socialist Party colleague and English lecturer at the University, who lived in Concepción; Gladys Bornand and Irene, our neighbour, and our friends from Antofagasta, Roberto and Edith. University theatre director Enrique Gajardo came to see me bearing tobacco to send to Ricardo. Other colleagues came once or twice to express their solidarity with me, like Fernando Guajardo and his wife, who once called with a bag of food for me. It was Fernando who had told Ricardo that it would be more likely that Ricardo would be arrested, not him – a prediction which turned out to be only too true. Fernando himself managed to keep his job at the University.

From Gladys's house I telephoned my parents once a week, reversing charges, on the insistence of my father. It was gratifying to hear his concern for Ricardo, since five years earlier he had been very much against my going to Chile to join Ricardo, who at that time, of course, was a married man with a family. It had been an extremely difficult time for me, and doubtless for him, during the months I lived at home from September 1968 to March 1969, working as a supply teacher to save up enough money for the fare to Chile, which in those days was very expensive. The atmosphere at home had been very awkward and hostile, relieved only by my dear mother's eternal understanding and sympathy for me. So now to hear my father on the phone saying "Love to Ricardo!" after five years of silence and animosity on his part, was music to my ears.

I learned from my father that he was going to London to see someone at the Foreign Office to demand they do something to help gain Ricardo's release. It was a great gesture on his part, I knew. I could imagine him travelling down from Derbyshire by train and arriving at the appointment at least half an hour beforehand, as was his wont. He would be smartly dressed, in Harris tweed suit and green or tan woollen tie, for all the world a country gentleman. For him a journey to London was not something undertaken frequently or lightly. I remember he did once come down to see me in 1967 after my appendix operation at the Elizabeth Garrett Anderson Hospital, which amazed me at the time since he so rarely travelled to London and, moreover, was not given to emotional gestures of any kind.

By 22 October 1973 all University staff had to go there every day to "sign in". I suppose the authorities wanted to see who was there and who had fled – something I so often wished we had done immediately after the coup. We had to give in all our class registers, lecture notes and marks for the year up to the September. I have always been a pretty methodical sort of person, so had no difficulty in producing these materials, but I knew there was no guarantee that they would help me to retain my job. I increasingly began to feel that our only hope as a couple would be to leave Chile and start a new life back in Britain. I knew, however, that Ricardo's love for his children would be a strong factor against leaving Chile, and that he would only be likely to agree – always supposing he were released, of course – if he saw no other way out.

I was in frequent contact with them, during the months of Ricardo's imprisonment. I wrote regularly to Ricky, who was 18 by this time, to let them know any snippets of news I had regarding their father. I heard from Ricky that he had not had any more encounters with the military since his initial detention, and that their mother had not had any problems at her school, information I was glad to pass on in my letters to Ricardo.

I knew, of course, that *I* was free to leave Chile and go back to Britain, and that I could even be given safe passage out of Chile by the United Nations Committee for Refugees, whose offices I had been to in Concepción. But I never entertained the idea of leaving without Ricardo - for me it was simply not an option. We had been so happy together for the last six years that I simply could not envisage life without him. I was also convinced that, together with my family in Britain, I could still do much to help get him released. Life was hard without Ricardo, as I wrote in a letter to him:

> "I miss you so much, my dear love. I think of you all day, I see in my mind's eye your shape, your face, your smile. Sometimes it seems so real in my imagination that I feel you by my side, I feel your physical presence. I see you coming in through the door, seated at our desk, lighting your pipe, having dinner at our table. So many moments of our daily life together come into my head during the day and at night."

I wondered what the prison chaplain, whose job it was to read prisoners' letters, thought as he was reading letters such as these? For him, the concentration camp's censor, I had to write in Spanish, otherwise Ricardo would not have been able to receive letters at all. Our friend *Chepo*, for instance, in Concepción's Regional Stadium, was not allowed to write or receive any letters: the only news his wife Gladys received for weeks on end was when someone who had been released from there phoned to give her long-awaited news of him.

One day I bought the local paper *La Discusión* – it must have been the 23 October 1973 – and saw with horror its front-page headline: four well-known Popular Unity leaders from the Concepción area had been shot dead after a "Council of War" (*Consejo de Guerra*). My heart sank. I still remember how I felt that morning, standing with the paper, my hands shaking, the news and its significance for Ricardo sinking in fast. If the Junta could sentence Concepción leaders to death in that way, would they not do the same to Chillán's leaders, the group they called the 'big fish'?

The four sentenced to death were Danilo González, who was a teacher trainer and Mayor of the mining area of Lota, just outside Concepción, and three miners' leaders from the region, Isidoro Castillo, Bernabé Cabrera and Vladimir Araneda. All had been detained on the day of the coup and were being held in the Quiriquina concentration camp. One day in mid-October the four of them, all leading Communists, were summoned by the Quiriquina loudspeaker: "To the doors, with all your belongings!" They were never to return.

They were charged with having explosives and being part of the much-vaunted "*Plan Z*" – the fictitious conspiracy cooked up by the Junta to justify all their arbitrary detentions, tortures and murders. The four miners' leaders were taken to the 4th *Comisaría* of *carabineros* in Concepción, interrogated and tortured. Apparently the military *fiscal* had asked for a 15-year sentence for the men, but, according to Alejandro Witker, our former colleague at the University of Ñuble[40], this had been overruled by the Junta, who demanded the death sentence.

There were many chess-players among the prisoners, and Danilo González was one of them. He had been in the middle of a game with Ricardo's friend Floridor Pérez, when he was summoned by the dreaded loudspeaker. Later Floridor, who is a poet, wrote this:

Quiriquina Island, October 1973

WHITE: Danilo González (*Mayor of Lota*)
BLACK: Floridor Pérez (*Rural teacher from Mortandad*)

---

[40] Alejandro Witker, a Socialist Party member, had been head of Extra-Mural work at our University, before transferring to a similar post at the University of Concepción. He was detained on the Quiriquina at the same time as Ricardo, and later wrote a book about his experiences there - "Prisión en Chile".

1	e4	c6
2	d4	d5
3	Nc3	dxe4
4	Nxe4	Bxf5
5	Ng3	Bg6
6	Nf3	Nd7
7	...	

Whilst he was deciding his seventh move, a corporal at the guard-post shouted his name.

I'm coming! he said,
handing me the little magnetic chess piece
As he didn't return within a sensible time
I jotted down, jokingly: *He resigns*

Only when the newspaper *El Sur*
printed next week in big letters
news of his death by firing squad
in the Regional Stadium of Concepción
did I understand the measure of his resigning

He had grown up in the coal mines
but was not the obscure Pawn he seemed
condemned to be, and no doubt died
with dignity, like a King in his castling.

Years later I tell this to a poet
All he says is:
– And if yours had been the Whites?

Two weeks later the Communist *Intendente* of Concepción, Fernando Alvarez, was dead. He, like Danilo González and the others, had been arrested immediately after the coup and was held on the Quiriquína. Alvarez was taken away from there on 5 November and died under torture three days later, at the age of 40. These were merely the most publicly well-known people of the region, but there were thousands of others, from all the parties of the Popular Unity and from the MIR, who were detained, tortured and killed in the same period.

It was all bad news. Every new death announced made my heart sink even further. But there was nothing I could do except wait, like everybody else, for news of war tribunals or anything that would indicate what fate awaited our loved ones. I only had the words of the Junta's Lt. Colonel Guedelhoefer to go on: he had told me that the charge against Ricardo related to his responsibility as Vice-rector of the University, nothing else. Yet in a letter Ricardo sent me to pass on to a friend, he talked of new charges against him relating to his being in the Party leadership. This, I feared, would be a much more serious charge.

We weren't allowed to write anything "political" in our letters. Anything that referred to news of what was happening was cut out of the letters. Towards the end of October I wrote to Ricardo suggesting that we should get married as soon as possible. In case he needed to be convinced, I said that the reasons were: 1) so that the British Embassy could take up his case; 2) so that if I were sacked from the University I would have the right to stay in Chile, by virtue of being married to a Chilean; 3) to make all the *tramites* (administrative procedures) easier – like being able to receive Ricardo's salary and deal with his affairs; 4) so that the military authorities would no longer be able to insult me for "living in sin". That day when I had been detained at *Investigaciones* this had been one of the accusations thrown at me.

At the end of October our neighbour Irene's baby died. Sickly at birth, he had not been expected to live long. Irene was as ever – practical, matter-of-fact, organised. I accompanied her on all the *tramites* to arrange the funeral for the following day. It was a sad affair. There were just a few friends accompanying poor Irene at the funeral ceremony. The following day Irene left for Santiago and soon she and her children left Chile to start a new life.

And a few days later, Gladys had her baby, whom she named Enrique, after his father, our friend *Chepo*, who was still imprisoned in Concepción's Regional Stadium. The baby was a little premature, but healthy, and it was a relief for Gladys that all had turned out well after quite a difficult pregnancy. "Doesn't he look just like his *papá*!" Gladys exclaimed. His little red face, topped by dark brown hair, looked creased, like a little old man's! I couldn't see the resemblance to either parent, but remember feeling quite envious of Gladys, to have a new little life to look after and the happy prospect of bringing him up.

On 10th November Ricardo and the rest of the group of the "*peces gordos*" were brought back to Chillán prison from Quiriquina Island. Somehow it seemed a relief, since I knew of some people who had recently been released from the prison. And so far in Chillán we had not heard of people being sent to face "*Consejos de Guerra*", war tribunals. It may have been a false sense of security, but I felt it was slightly encouraging that he was now in what had, formerly at least, been a civilian prison. We knew that the post of prison governor was a civilian one and that the prison guards were not military people.

We also knew that several of the guards were Popular Unity supporters, who had nothing against the hundreds of political prisoners they were now having to deal with. On the contrary, these guards did what they could to make life more bearable for the "*políticos*". They could not do anything, however, to prevent prisoners being taken from the jail to the Regiment where they were barbarously tortured before being returned to the prison. Our friend and colleague, Franklin Roach, history lecturer at our University, was one such prisoner. I had helped his wife, Mary, to take a mattress into the prison for him, since they did not have a car. She told me that he had been subjected to electric shock treatment at the Regiment, as well as being beaten up. It was routine procedure for all detainees taken there for interrogation. Most were never charged with anything, it was simply a means of terrorising the population into total submission.

If anyone had asked me, months before the 11 September coup d'état, whether Chilean people would ever stoop to torture or cruelty in any situation, I would most likely have said no. My entire experience of Chileans, not only our friends, but people one met in the course of living there, people in offices, policemen and soldiers, well-off people and poor people living in the poverty-stricken rural areas, had led me to think of the Chilean people as courteous, calm, hospitable, friendly but not intrusively so, patriotic, kind and extremely family-oriented.

It is true that I had seen the other face of Chileans, when *Patria y Libertad* had broken up our Vietnam exhibition outside the University and set fire to our train on our journey to Santiago the previous year. But I could never have envisaged that hundreds, if not thousands, of uniformed personnel in the different armed forces would turn into killers and torturers on the scale that actually happened. It proved to me that *any* nation could turn out people of the SS guard type, given a certain set of circumstances.

What were the circumstances in Chile's case? Destabilisation of the Government[41] by means of a deliberately-orchestrated scenario of chaos and economic disruption, the cutting off of bank loans and credits from the US, secret funding of extremist groups and the right-wing media bent on overthrowing the legitimate Government. The Christian Democrats' irresponsible behaviour in the months prior to the coup, as they unjustifiably and increasingly sided with the Right against Popular Unity without analysing what this would mean for the future of Chile. And within the armed forces, well-trained obedience to superiors throughout the ranks.

---

[41] According to Tanya Harmer in her book: *Allende's Chile & the Inter-American Cold War*, "US sources show conclusively that the Nixon administration's destabilization measures in Chile had begun *before* Allende even came to power and enacted his program."

For the first five weeks after their return, the Quiriquina 'big fish' group were held in solitary confinement and could not see anyone or write to anyone. They were joined in the *incomunicado* cells by Dr. Isidoro Tohá, who was a Socialist councillor on Chillán's municipal council and brother of José Tohá, Allende's Minister of the Interior, who was one of the top Popular Unity leaders being held on the infamous Dawson Island in the deep south of Chile. The Tohá brothers were very well-known, both very tall, slim and distinguished-looking.

Although they were *incomunicado*, the detainees each tried to occupy themselves in a variety of ways. The doors had a little grille, through which you could stretch out a finger. Ricardo told me later how he had managed to chip off some slivers of wood from the sweeping-brush he was given to clean his cell with, and how, when they were each taken out to the toilet, they would try to find anything on the ground that might come in useful, like a nail, or a shard of glass. They also kept the stones from the cherries and plums their families took them, and entertained themselves by making necklaces with these. Ricardo, who was not at all DIY-minded, made a pen out of a piece of wood he filed down and made smooth, and a little yacht with a tiny white sail, that he fashioned out of wood and a handkerchief. Though it took the *incomunicado* prisoners many hours to make such things, it was a way of killing time and keeping sane.

Occasionally, one of the guards who was sympathetic to the detainees, after checking first that no one was around, would let the men talk to each other through the grilles of their cell doors. It was on one such occasion that Isidoro Tohá was brought in to join the *incomunicado* group. As he was being accompanied to his cell he saw the other detainees showing each other, through the narrow grilles, what they had managed to make. On seeing the various objects of their handicraft, Tohá apparently exclaimed: "What? Is this a *Centro de Madres*[42], or what?!"

I was determined to get to see Ricardo, *incomunicado* or not. I could not accept that he was physically close, only four blocks away, yet I could neither see nor write to him. The other *presos políticos* (political prisoners) were being allowed twice-weekly visits. The only communication I could have was via the food I was allowed to take to the prison for Ricardo each day – at least that way Ricardo knew I was there and concerned about him – and by means of the tiny notes I hid in the top of the thermos flasks I took him, which the prison staff returned to me for washing.

---

42 *Centro de Madres*: Mothers' Centres – something like our Women's Institute groups, which taught women various handicrafts, etc. They were formed during the Christian Democratic Government of Eduardo Frei and were popular in the *poblaciones* and housing estates.

So I decided to go and see the top military commander for our province and demand the right to see Ricardo. I was granted an interview, there in the *Intendencia*, now called the *Comandancia*. I told him that my situation was intolerable, since I did not know whether I had a job, whether my visa would be renewed, and my "husband" was in prison yet no charge had been laid against him. I told him that I desperately needed to see Ricardo, to see for myself that he was all right, since I had heard nothing since his last letter sent from the Quiriquína Island concentration camp. I also told him that we intended to leave for my country as soon as we could. What I wanted, I told him, was a few minutes alone with Ricardo, as soon as possible.

Perhaps surprisingly, Colonel Guedelhoefer agreed. Perhaps he felt sorry for me, knowing I had no family here. I was a well-known figure around the jail, being the only Englishwoman in Chillán, young and auburn-haired. The military authorities had put a retired army captain, Eduardo Torrealba, in charge of the prison, above the existing civilian prison governor, obviously not trusting the latter to do the job they wanted. Torrealba was a self-professed devoutly religious man who pretended to be sympathetic to the prisoners and took the trouble to talk to the relatives sometimes as they waited outside, queuing to give in the food they had brought for their loved ones. Some of the relatives really thought that he would help get their loved ones released. I was sceptical, since it was obvious that he had been brought in by the military authorities to do a particular job, and I could not see how his pious Catholicism would make any difference. He always made a point, if he saw me at the jail, of coming over and asking how I was, how I was managing. I was disdainful of him: I have never been able to stand hypocrisy.

Lt. Colonel Guedelhoefer was true to his word. I was told to go to the prison the following day at 14.30, where I would be able to see Ricardo. I don't think I slept at all that night, so excited was I at the prospect of seeing Ricardo, however briefly, for the first time in ten or so weeks. My heart was thumping as I approached the prison the next day. I arrived at the appointed time and was shown into a small outdoor area, with white painted walls on all sides and an overhanging roof overhead. I was told to wait there.

After a little while, Ricardo was brought in by prison guards. He looked paler than usual, and had grown quite a beard, which was black, like his thick, black hair. As we looked at each other after embracing, each trying to reach the depths of each other's suffering, I noticed that he had a little bald patch on the left side of his moustache. During an interrogation, his torturers had pulled him by his moustache, tearing out the whiskers on that side. But apart from that, I was glad to see that he looked well and strong, and unbroken. He had on a blue windcheater with a zip, since it was already warm spring weather, and he was just as good-looking as I remembered him, his broad smile revealing his even white teeth and his kindly brown eyes as kindly as ever.

We knew we did not have much time. We both started to talk about the possibility of getting married. It turned out that Ricardo had been approached by the devout Catholic prison boss, Captain Torrealba, who had come to his prison cell and asked him if the girl he lived with was the English girl he had seen, who drove a little white Fiat car and had red hair? He had urged Ricardo to "make an honest woman of me" once he got out! And I, for my part, finally had the opportunity to ask Ricardo if he actually *wanted* to get married, since I had not been able to ask him that up till then, except in a letter when he was on Quiriquína Island.

We both agreed it was what we wanted to do, given the circumstances, and I was glad that he had been thinking along the same lines as me, without my knowing it. Ricardo told me what I would need to do to obtain the last remaining document of the Annulment procedure which our lawyer friend Eduardo, who had been working on the case, had never got round to issuing. I should go and see Eduardo's solicitor partner (since Eduardo was already in exile), to ask him to finalise whatever needed to be done. We talked of our plans for the future, uncertain though these were, but among which was the possibility of leaving Chile for Britain.

Soon the guards came up and said it was time to leave. We looked at each other and hugged each other tight, neither of us wanting to let go. Then he was led away back into his *incomunicado* cell and I was escorted out of the prison. I was elated and full of optimism now: nothing could spoil our future together.

The very next day I went to see Eduardo's legal partner, with whom he had shared an office in the town centre. He looked up Ricardo's file and saw that the annulment was practically complete. There was just one more procedure needed before the final legal document could be issued. He promised to do this very quickly and have it ready for the next day or the day after. Once I had that I would be able to go to the *Registro Civil* and arrange for a marriage ceremony, which could be held at the prison if Ricardo had still not been released by then.

The necessary annulment document was ready on time, as promised, and I went to the *Registro Civil*, where I was told what else I would need to be able to marry. My visa (soon to expire and still not renewed by the authorities), passports, certificates, application forms to be filled in – endless *tramites*. I had been told at the prison that Ricardo would soon be released, but there were always lots of rumours about people due to be set free which never materialised. I knew that we would not be able to marry while ever Ricardo was in solitary confinement.

Throughout the country, terrible things were still happening daily. We had heard of the notorious Caravan of Death in September and October, when Pinochet's generals, led by Brigadier-General Sergio Arellano Stark, flew by helicopter from the deep south to the far north of the country, stopping at each garrison and ordering the massacre of prisoners. Nearly 100 prisoners were summarily executed in this way. One of them, whom Ricardo knew from when they were both students in Santiago, was Jorge Peña, a music teacher and orchestral conductor who founded and ran a well-known children's orchestra in the northern city of La Serena. He had the misfortune to have taken the orchestra on a very successful and well-publicised trip to Cuba not long before the coup. That was enough to have him executed. Everything was arbitrary. Anybody could be shot dead on the whim of any officer. One day your heart was gladdened to hear of someone's release, the next you would again be in the depths of despair to hear of some prominent person's death after a so-called Council of War or shot "whilst trying to escape".

However, during the "Caravan of Death" a few army generals had apparently been unhappy about the savagery and arbitrariness of this process, and at the fact that orders had come down from the Junta, going over the heads of the local regimental commanders. So by November publicly-announced killings lessened somewhat. But raids on people's houses up and down the country were still resulting in men, women, and even entire families being taken out and shot on the say-so of some local officer or right-wing neighbour.

We heard of the terrible tortures inflicted on the Quiriquína prisoners, and the leading group from Chillán in particular. Santiago Bell, who had been one of the *intendentes* of the province of Ñuble, had been submerged in a barrel of water to the point of drowning, among other tortures. Most had suffered electric shock torture to the genitals, beatings on the soles of the feet, and being forced to swallow huge quantities of water. Pedro Hidalgo, who had been Allende's Minister of Agriculture, was treated to a mock firing squad, and later recalled thinking he must be dead when, with a pistol held to his head, he heard the shot go off close by.

And yet as I've said before, humour was always present among the prisoners, both those in the prison and among those who had been held on the Quiriquina Island. I suppose it is a way of defusing tensions and keeping spirits up in a situation which is terrifying and dire. One of the jokes which went about on the Quiriquina concerned Pedro Hidalgo, who had been President Allende's Minister of Agriculture, and ended up as one of the so-called "big fish" because he had been working in our region when he was captured.

The prisoners had to relieve themselves in outside latrines, which consisted of a wooden board, suspended over a pit, with four holes cut in the board side by side, thus accommodating four prisoners at a time. They were given three minutes, under armed guard, to use the latrines. The joke was that one prisoner, a rural leader in the region, found himself seated next to Pedro Hidalgo, and that, on recognising the former Minister of Agriculture, had joked: "Well, I'll be damned, all those months trying to get an interview with you about our locality's problems, and now here you are!"

I became friends with Pedro's wife, Elena, whilst our menfolk were held *incomunicado* together. Elena was from Santiago and had come down to Chillán so that she could be closer to her husband. She was deeply religious, and was staying at the local seminary, something her local priest in Santiago had organised for her. She was a quiet, kind woman, not very political, though extremely supportive of the Popular Unity Government and of her husband, who was a member of Allende's own party, the Socialists. Pedro was a highly qualified agronomist, and had been detained in Portezuelo, a rural area near Chillán, whilst working there.

We were not at all similar: Elena was rather upper middle-class and genteel, whereas I was outspoken, feisty and not averse to swearing at times. But we got on well together, and had already discovered that our menfolk had become friends inside. We used to meet at the prison, and I invited her back to my hut in the garden, so that she could prepare food to take to her husband, as I was doing for Ricardo. Once or twice I even accompanied her to mass in the rather beautiful San Francisco church, which was on the other side of the square from the prison. I say "even", because I am not at all religious, and had found it hard to comprehend that some detainees had apparently turned to religion whilst inside, and, according to some men who had been released, could be seen walking up and down reading the bible, during exercise-time in the prison yard.

This was hardly surprising, since the tortures were barbaric, and the fear and worry about families outside were too much for many to bear.

Elena once or twice invited me to dine with her at the Seminary. It was near the *feria* (folkloric market) and consisted of a long low building along all four sides of one block. We dined with two priests, and the meal was served by a woman *empleada* (maid). The dinners were excellent, and accompanied by fine wines. No wonder the priests looked well-fed, I thought to myself. It was somewhat surreal, Elena and I sitting there comfortably opposite two middle-aged priests, eating well-prepared and served food, talking of inconsequential matters, whilst the two men we loved were locked up and in solitary confinement, without formal charge or clear prospects.

The whole question of "charges" was preposterous. All the talk of "charges" was an invention of the military Junta to justify, in the eyes of the public, the horrific and unprecedented repression they had unleashed. It was to make it appear as if we, the supporters of the Popular Unity Government, were the guilty ones, not the Junta. And it was an attempt to wrap in a cloak of legality their "councils of war" and "tribunals" that had sentenced so many to death.

As more people came out of prison (to make room for others newly detained), we heard more and more about the barbarous tortures people were suffering. We heard that when the prison had a visit from the International Red Cross one prisoner had pulled down his trousers for all to see his body, beaten black and blue. I decided that one other person in high places that I could go and see, to put Ricardo's case, would be the Bishop of Chillán. Surely, as a man of God, he should do something to help those of his flock who were being tortured and beaten senseless? I found out from the Seminary priests where to find the Bishop, and called to ask for an audience.

I was told the Bishop would see me and given an appointment. I arrived on time, and was ushered into an ante-chamber, where I was asked to wait. I was then led into a large, rather grand, room, where the Bishop, a rather fleshy, portly man, was advancing towards me, his hand outstretched. I grasped his hand and shook it firmly, noticing the enormous ring which prodded my small hand as I did so, and was dismayed to feel his flabby, flaccid hand in mine – I felt no warmth, no vigour at all.

I told him of the prisoner who had shown the Red Cross the evidence of his beatings and that I feared for what would happen to Ricardo. I gave him as much information as I could about the tortures I had heard of, and the lack of any charges against detainees, who had been held for many weeks already, yet knew nothing of their fate. He listened in a perfunctory sort of way, making it clear that he had heard enough. I got the firm impression that he would not do much to help me, Ricardo, or any of the other prisoners.

It was only later, whilst telling my friends Roberto and Edith of my reaction to his flabby handshake, that they burst out laughing, explaining that the Bishop's proffered hand, with the big ring, was meant for the supplicant to kiss, not to take hold of and shake! You were supposed to kiss the Bishop's ring! I had no idea that that was part of the Catholic ritual. It literally did not even cross my mind, and the Bishop had said nothing either, only showing by his distasteful withdrawing of his hand that I was not to his liking – something I had assumed was because he almost certainly did not approve of my political views. It gave us a good laugh, anyway, every time we recalled my audience with the Bishop!

Most Chileans I met during my years there were believers, even if they did not go regularly to church. Weddings, funerals, baptisms, were all done in church. Ricardo and I once presenced practically the entire regional Party leadership taking part in a mass in Chillán on the occasion of the marriage of the daughter of one of them. The Party's General Secretary, Luís Corvalán, was once asked about the relationship between the Communist Party and Catholics; his answer was that there were thousands of card-holding Communists who were Catholics. However, for most people in the Popular Unity parties, religion did not play a very important part, and the hierarchy of the Catholic Church was felt to sympathise more with the opposition than with the Government.

I have always had respect for people who believe in God, though I have never understood this reliance on something utterly supernatural. My mother was brought up as a Methodist, and she always said that the ideals of socialism were not in conflict with the tenets of Christianity, rather that they were in fact very much the same, except that we believed in fighting for that better life here and now, on this earth. My mother had much respect for believers, and herself worked very closely with people from the Society of Friends (Quakers) when she and they set up, in Chesterfield, a Council for the Abolition of Nuclear Weapons, which later became part of the Campaign for Nuclear Disarmament when that was founded in 1958.

I have always loved Victor Jara's song "*Prayer to a Labourer*", which seems partly addressed to the labourer, and partly to God, in its plea for a better life here on earth:

Rise up and look at the mountain
Whence cometh the wind, sun and water
Thou who controls the course of the rivers
Thou who gather the harvest of thy soul.

Rise up and look at your hands
To grow, hold them out to your brother
Together we'll go forward, united by blood
Tomorrow's future can be now.

Free us from those who keep us in poverty,
Bring us thy kingdom of justice and equality.
Blow like the wind the flowers of the ravine,
Cleanse like fire the barrel of my gun.

Let thy will be done here on earth at last
Give us thy strength and thy valour to fight

Blow like the wind the flowers of the ravine,
Cleanse like fire the barrel of my gun.

Rise up and look at your hands
To grow, hold them out to your brother,
Together we'll go forward, united by blood,
Now and in the hour of our death, amen.
Amen, amen.

Before I went to Chile, I had read about Liberation theology and in particular the work of Hélder Câmara, a Brazilian priest, who famously said:

"When I give food to the poor, they call me a saint. When I ask why the poor have no food, they call me a Communist."

After seeing poverty and underdevelopment in Chile for myself, and talking about questions of poverty and socialism with my Spanish priest student of English, José Luís Ysern, I fully empathised with the liberation theologists, even though for myself, I continued to feel sure that change would only come about through political means.

After some five weeks, Ricardo and the others in the group of the so-called "big fish" were let out of solitary and joined the other hundreds of *politicos*. I immediately went to see the prison governor and his military superior, Captain Torrealba, and informed them of our wish to get married. Ricardo was let out of solitary on the Monday, and I got the civil registrar to agree to marry us in the prison two days later, on the following Wednesday. We needed two witnesses, and I asked our dentist friend Sylvia and the Spanish priest who had been a student of mine, José Luís Ysern, to do that for us.

We married in Chillán prison on Wednesday, 19 December 1973, three months after the bloodiest coup d'état in history, when the country was soaked in blood, and despair, anger, fear and sorrow were the prevailing emotions.

In a note I sent to Ricardo I wrote:

"I've made all the necessary arrangements, so prepare to be married at 15.00 hours tomorrow Wednesday (between 15.00-15.30) ...I suppose you've got your frock coat, tie etc. at the ready. Ha ha. I love you passionately, *Chiquitita*[43]."

I wore a slim-fitting lime-green linen dress which always looked nice when ironed, though it creased easily. Well, I would surely be standing up all the time, I thought. It was the nearest thing I had to a smart outfit apart from the rather formal suit I had worn to see the Junta's man in the *comandancia*. Sylvia, José Luís and I got to the prison just before three and were shown into

---

[43] *Chiquitita*: "Little one" – one of Ricardo's many pet names for me.

a small room inside the prison. The Registrar was already there, and smiled as we came in. Then they brought Ricardo in. It was the first time I had seen him in about three weeks, and I was glad to see from his broad smile that he was all right. He had on the same blue windcheater and looked tidy and clean.

We stood together, hand-in-hand. The Registrar recited the bit about pledging to look after one another, in sickness and in health, then the part which was still included in the Chilean marriage vows at that time, the promise the wife had to make to honour and obey! Ricardo squeezed my hand at that point, knowing that in normal life I would never agree to that, and gave me a knowing grin, as if to say, "Ah, I've got you now...!" Our witnesses signed what they had to sign, and suddenly it was all over. Ricardo was led back to his cell, and Sylvia, José Luís and I left.

Sylvia had to go back to work, so I thanked my witnesses and we all said good-bye. I went home to my lonely shack in the garden. I was happy that everything had gone successfully, but it was such an anti-climax when I got back, alone, knowing that Ricardo still had no idea if or when he would be released. Suddenly I felt very sorry for myself, seeing only a black future ahead.

I had not been in that frame of mind very long, when a knock came at the garden gate. It was a colleague of mine, an English teacher, Pedro Gajardo. He smiled broadly, said he had heard that we had married that day and so he and his wife wanted to invite me to a bit of a celebration at their house. It was such a surprise: I only knew Pedro professionally, not as a friend, and I had never met his wife.

They lived with their three small daughters in a bungalow at the other end of our street. We walked there and Cristina met me with open arms and kisses, congratulating me warmly on this special day. It was all I could do not to burst out crying. But their warmth and kindness were so genuine that I soon felt at home with them, and we had a lovely evening, even ceremoniously cutting the cake Cristina had made specially as a wedding cake for me, and for me to take later to Ricardo in prison.

Pedro had always kept himself aloof from politics at the University. He was a very conscientious lecturer, who always prepared his classes well and was polite and friendly to all, whilst keeping his distance. He gave the impression of being slightly shy, or at least reserved. But something happened after the 11 September coup to have a deep and lasting impact on him and Cristina.

It turned out, as we were to find out years later, that Cristina was a relative of Sonia Ojeda, wife of Chillán's Mayor, Ricardo Lagos. Ricardo and Sonia were murdered a few days after the coup together with Ricardo's son, Carlos, who was a student of mine. As relatives, Pedro and Cristina had to go to the morgue and identify Sonia's body. She was seven months pregnant. Years later, visiting us here in Britain, Pedro and Cristina told us what a shattering experience that had been for them and all Sonia's family.

That day, the Sunday after the coup on the previous Tuesday, Pedro had heard a military report on the radio that "shots had been fired from the upper floor of Ricardo Lagos's house and that the *carabineros* of Chillán Viejo had therefore had to "eliminate" the house's occupants." The Lagos house only had one floor, and moreover, Pedro and Cristina were sure that there could not have been weapons in the house since Sonia was in the advanced stages of pregnancy and was terrified of firearms. They went to the offices of the local newspaper to check whether the report was true.

Cristina's father managed to get permission for the bodies to be taken from the hospital morgue before the curfew which was at 18.00. Pedro and his father-in-law entered the morgue and saw the three bodies of Ricardo, Sonia and 20-year-old Carlos lying on a table, all with gunshot wounds. Such was the atmosphere of terror that reigned that they knew they had to get the bodies to the cemetery before curfew. They hurriedly put the bodies in the coffins they had brought and sped to the cemetery where the man in charge let them leave the coffins at the cemetery doors.

As Cristina wrote later: "We just had to leave the coffins there, on the ground inside the cemetery gates. We had to rush off to get home before the curfew, there was no time to weep or to take our leave of the dead, we just knew we had to save our lives. The following day Pedro returned and had the coffins put in the cemetery niche, but without any memorial stone or anything..."

It had been a terrible and terrifying episode for Pedro and Cristina, and they did not mention it to me the evening they gave the little wedding celebration for me three months later. Only years later did we find out about their connection with our friend Ricardo Lagos, when they were finally able to talk about it.

Now that I had our marriage certificate, I knew I would have more rights to demand Ricardo's release, and that the British authorities would be more willing to press Ricardo's case, since he was now married to a British citizen. In Chillán, the person I knew I had to see now was the military Fiscal, a man who before the coup had been a member of the fascist group *Patria y Libertad*, and who had been appointed by the Junta to prosecute the thousands of detainees in Chillán and surrounding rural areas. Mario Romero was a retired army captain, and was very soon known throughout the region as a sadistic brute of a man. In his hands lay the fate of all the prisoners, most of whom had had no charges brought against them and were simply languishing in prisons and police cells awaiting some sort of "trials", but nobody knew what shape these would take, since the rule of law had ceased to exist on 11 September 1973.

I went to see Romero the day after our marriage. He was in military uniform, busy among many other uniformed people scurrying about and besieged outside his office by long lines of relatives who had come to ask for information about their loved ones and plead their cases. I went up to him as he came out of his room, told him who I was and demanded that he set my husband free immediately, since no charges had been laid against him. He looked at me with a sardonic smile on his face and said: "Why, you are not married! Figueroa is not your husband! Don't try it on with me – I know your situation!"

"I am married," I replied firmly. "When did you get married?" Romero asked, sneering. "Yesterday!" I told him, "and I have the certificate here to prove it if you don't believe me!" At that, Romero's face dropped. He looked really shocked and dismayed. One of his "big fish" was about to escape his clutches, it seemed. It was obvious that he had never expected that the prison military governor would allow us to marry without asking his permission first. It was good that I had acted so fast, after Ricardo's release from solitary confinement.

Without saying another word the military Fiscal Romero turned on his heels and made to leave, but I caught his sleeve and repeated that I expected him to order Ricardo's release very soon, warning him that the British authorities were also now on Ricardo's case. I could sense that the prison's military governor, Captain Torrealba, was going to be in for it when Romero got hold of him. Torrealba had felt sorry for me, I was sure, and had wanted Ricardo "to make an honest woman of me" by marrying me, so had clearly gone ahead and authorised the marriage without perhaps even realising that the Fiscal would not agree to it. Or perhaps he did realise, but decided to follow his own heart and religion. I'll never know, but it certainly turned out to be our trump card.

After the adrenalin rush of the wedding and the meeting with the military Fiscal there was a very flat period, when nothing seemed to be moving. Ricardo was still in prison, among all the *políticos*, and I took him food and a thermos each day to the jail. I received a message that Ricardo wanted me to buy some leather from the local *feria* as the detainees were allowed to make things so that their dependents, many of whom were now without any income, could try to sell them. So I took him a piece of goatskin, and he busied himself there making shoulder-bags out of it. I still have the two lovely shoulder-bags he made, one for me, and one for my mother in England.

Visiting times were once a week, but could be cancelled at a moment's notice. I remember once, when I went to fetch Germán's wife, Ana, and her small children in our little Fiat, and she had got them all ready, in clean, fresh clothes, we were disappointed to find when we got to the prison that visiting had been cancelled for that day. No reason given, of course.

Now that Ricardo was no longer *incomunicado*, it was possible for his children to see him. His son and daughters travelled from Temuco to see him, and it was quite an emotional day for them. I think in a way it marked a turning-point for them in their growing acceptance of me, knowing that I had chosen to stay in Chile after the coup and that their father and I had now married. After all, I could simply have left at the earliest opportunity, as many foreigners without family or love ties to Chile had done. It was good to see Ricardo in the prison yard with his kids, hugging them, and listening to all their excited chatter about what had happened in Temuco and how they were doing at school.

I will always remember that afternoon, when we came away from the prison and they came back to my shack in the garden. They were horrified that I had been reduced to living in the maid's hut, and angry that we had been turned out of our house in that unceremonious way, when the house itself was not even being used by the owner – it was just empty. Suddenly we felt close to each other as we all realised, I think, that we were all suffering and all equally vulnerable. We knew one thing for sure, that we all loved Ricardo, which was at last something that united, rather than divided us. I took them to their bus back to Temuco, happy that they had been able to see their Dad and that we felt closer than we had ever felt before.

Ricardo's brother Guillermo and his wife Eliana, together with their close friend Violeta Munizaga, came to see Ricardo, travelling up from the capital. Guillermo had so far managed to keep his job as a journalist on the right-wing *El Mercurio*, but Eliana had already been sacked, as she was a union official and very well known as a Popular Unity supporter and activist. Violeta was a teacher of English whom Ricardo had known since their university days, and her husband Hernán Torres was one of his closest friends.

After they visited Ricardo in prison, which was quite an experience for them, I could see, I took them by car to Quinchamalí, to the wooden cottage where Ricardo's aunt Albertina had lived until her recent death, and we all spent the night there, since I obviously could not put them up in the shack where I was living. Violeta, who was always ready for a laugh, produced the potty that she had brought up on the train with her, since she was terrified of going out in the dark to the earth closet out there among the cherry trees some fifty metres from the cottage! We had a great evening, over a meal, recalling Ricardo and happier times and each of them telling funny stories from their past. It was a welcome relief from the tension of my normal days.

189

My time was occupied with packing our belongings, ready to send to England, trying to sell our typewriter, record-player and anything else of value, and running round trying to get the necessary papers for Ricardo to get a passport, as his old one had expired. As a detainee, Ricardo was certain to be sacked from his University post. We knew that our best option was to leave for the UK.

As a relief from packing boxes with our books (we have both always accumulated a lot of books) I sometimes went to play tennis with the friend of Ricardo Lagos's whom we had met soon after we had arrived in the city, who ran Chillán's tennis club. I found a couple of hours playing tennis with him was relaxing and good fun, as he was not too good a player, so we were more or less evenly matched.

I went down to Santiago to the British Embassy, to let them know that we had now married and urge that they take up Ricardo's case. I also went to see the United Nations Committee for Help to Foreigners in Chile, to let them know about Ricardo's case, and of our plans to travel to Britain once Ricardo had been released. They promised to help, noting down all the details of our case. They arranged for us to stay at a United Nations refuge just outside Santiago, called Padre Hurtado, once Ricardo was freed. On that trip, I went with my brother-in-law Guillermo to take the 11 boxes I had packed with our books and other treasured possessions to the port at San Antonio and left them there to be shipped to Britain.

Ricardo's parents travelled from their home in the far south, in Puerto Varas, to see Ricardo on their way to Santiago, but, as it happened, there were no visits that day. His mother (he always called her mother, though she was actually his stepmother) had made him some Chilean savoury pasties, *empanadas,* and as she handed me them she said, "Tell Armando (they had always called him by his second name) I made these for him, with all my love." For *Mamita* Santos, a deeply religious woman, it was a big gesture. For her, only criminals and delinquents belonged in prison, and she found it hard to accept that anyone connected with her could be imprisoned if he was innocent.

She said Ricardo should ask for forgiveness for what he had done, at which point I nearly exploded, but managed to keep down my anger, limiting myself to telling her that Ricardo had never done anything wrong or illegal. I knew it had been hard for her to accept that Ricardo had separated from his first wife, and she had only recently met me for the first time before this, so I guessed that the best policy was to keep my thoughts to myself on this one.

Ricardo's father was much more supportive of me and of Ricardo. Though not left-wing himself – he was more inclined towards the Christian Democrats (though not really a believer) – he knew that the Junta had turned the country into one big prison camp, and that not everybody could be "guilty", even in their terms. Ricardo also remembers when he was a child his father telling him, with some sympathy, about political exiles he had met years ago during the course of his police career. These people had been banished to far-off regions of the country in earlier times, during the Ibañez government at the end of the 1920s, when *Don* Ricardo was a policeman in Chiloé, an island in the south of the country. He saw that they read books and were educated people, not delinquents, and he marvelled at how thrifty they were, as they had little means of earning a living in those distant lands to which they had been exiled. So he developed a certain respect for them.

Ricardo was finally released at the end of February 1974. We slept the first night or two in the shack in the garden, very happy to be alive and together again. But we were acutely aware that we still had no security – Ricardo was forced to "sign on" at the regimental headquarters every week – so we could not leave Chillán until that order was lifted. And it seemed ominous that ever since Ricardo had been released, an armoured car would drive up after curfew and park opposite the house, its loud engine running for minutes on end. The second evening following Ricardo's release, we were in the shack in the garden when we heard loud knocking on the high wooden gate into the garden where our hut was. The knocking persisted. We were terrified, since we knew it could not be friends – it was long after the curfew. We froze still, quiet as mice, hoping against hope that they would go away. Fortunately, they did. Was it a warning? We knew that lots of people who had been killed had been released first and then seized again, only to be shot later "whilst trying to escape", or in "armed confrontation".

It was clearly not safe for us to stay in Chillán. But because Ricardo had to sign on every week at the regimental headquarters, we could not leave for Santiago either. We decided to go and sleep in Quinchamalí, at Ricardo's late aunt Albertina's cottage, which was empty and where I had taken some of our things for storage. We felt safer there, in the countryside, surrounded by the cherry orchard and an enormous fig tree.

It was while we were staying in that little wooden house in Quinchamalí, as we feared for our lives in Chillán, that by chance we met Iris, the young woman who was the maid at our first *pensión*, on a crowded rural bus. She felt keenly the tragedy that had befallen the country, and had heard that Ricardo had been thrown into prison. We could feel her solidarity, though little was spoken. We were able to leave shortly afterwards for the UK, but Iris, though not herself involved in the political struggle, would, we knew, like so many of her compatriots, suffer the economic privations, political clampdown and trampling of people's rights that went on under the infamous Pinochet dictatorship which was to last seventeen long years.

Ricardo had been released "to leave for Great Britain with his wife", according to the release papers, yet we could not leave because of the military Fiscal's imposition of signing on at the regiment. It was a Catch-22 situation.

The days and weeks went by and Ricardo was still forced to sign on. It seemed Captain Romero, the military Fiscal, was just not prepared to let Ricardo go. All the other members of the group of his so-called "big fish" were still in prison, and it seemed he just did not want this one to get away. One day a couple of men in plain clothes (we never knew who they were) went up to Ricardo in the street and gave him to understand that it would be better if he made himself scarce. After a week or so of travelling back and forward from the countryside, and no news of the signing imposition being lifted, we decided the only thing for it was to go and see the Junta's commander of the province, Colonel Cristián Guedelhoefer.

We went in together, and Ricardo explained what our problem was. Like the fascist Fiscal, Mario Romero, Guedelhoefer immediately contradicted Ricardo, saying that he was "not legally married" to me. We showed him the marriage certificate, and, unlike Romero, he accepted its veracity immediately, and said he would do what he could to get the signing-on imposition lifted, so that we could leave Chillán altogether for good. His word alone was no proof though, so Ricardo insisted he needed a signed letter to that effect. Fortunately Guedelhoefer acceded to Ricardo's request and provided him with a letter there and then.

So without more ado we decided to leave for Santiago. One afternoon we boarded a train bound for the capital (we had recently sold our Fiat 600), carrying our few remaining belongings. By the beginning of March we were safely in the Padre Hurtado refuge, under the auspices of the United Nations, with a big room all to ourselves, together with dozens of other ex-prisoners from different parts of Chile, all awaiting the necessary papers and arrangements to fly to a host of different countries under the UN refugee programme.

The sale of our car had been quite an experience. A couple of weeks earlier we had gone to Santiago for a few days between Ricardo's weekly signing-on ordeals at the Regiment in Chillán and had left our Fiat 600 with Ricardo's younger brother, Guillermo, who lived in Santiago, for him to put an ad in the paper offering it for sale. The money from the sale would be for Ricardo's children in Temuco, since we did not know when we would be able to start sending any money to them from Britain, our future there being totally unknown at that time. And even if Ricardo were to start trying to bring them over to Britain, once we were established there, we knew it would most likely be a lengthy process.

Guillermo heard from someone who was interested in buying the car, so one day during this trip to Santiago, we drove to the address he had been given, in the smart suburb of Providencia. *Avenida Pocuro* (Pocuro Avenue) was a tree-lined street of enormous houses. The house we sought was especially large, and half-hidden by trees and shrubs in the front garden. Ricardo rang the bell and we waited. After what seemed like a long time, we heard heavy footsteps approaching along what sounded like a hard flagstone floor. A youngish man opened the door and after ascertaining that we were the owners of the car for sale, invited us inside.

It was an incredible interior that met our eyes, a dark, wood-panelled hall like something from a Tudor mansion in England, with dozens of antique swords, guns, shotguns and rifles of all kinds hanging from the panelled walls. The heavy door had closed behind us and a bolt slid fast. I could feel Ricardo's hand grow clammy and both our hearts were beating fast. There was something very strange and unfamiliar, un-Chilean, about this house and we immediately began to fear that we had somehow been led into a trap of some kind.

The man, who was tall and somewhat swarthy, rang a bell and a young woman appeared. She had long blonde hair, and vacant expressionless eyes. We both got the impression she was under the influence of drugs. The man asked Ricardo how much he wanted for the car and whether he wanted payment by cheque or in cash. Ricardo consulted me, and we agreed cash would be better, since we knew that now we were living at the United Nations Padre Hurtado refuge, we could be flown out of Chile at very little notice.

The man, unsmiling and with a hard, almost unfriendly stare, told the girl to open a safe in an adjoining room. There was no small talk, none of the usual Chilean hospitality. The young woman appeared a while later with a bag full of new, unopened bundles of banknotes. Now the man passed over one bundle after another of the brand-new banknotes, for us to count. Our hands were shaking, I'm sure, as we counted these huge quantities, the like of which neither of us had ever seen in cash before or since. I could see that Ricardo was really terrified, and I must say the whole atmosphere in that house, with its dimly-lit interior and dark, heavy, wooden furniture and dark wood-panelled walls with their astonishing array of weaponry like that of some medieval English castle, was enough to make anyone scared, especially at that time, amid the killings and tortures of the Junta regime.

We did a pretty perfunctory count, as well as our trembling hands and inner fears would allow, and as soon as that was over, we stood up and made to go. The man called the girl, and told her to take us to wherever we indicated, and to drive the car we had just sold them back to that house. Even that was strange – the way he gave orders to her, as if she were an employee of some kind, and yet it was supposed to be a residential house. And the way she reacted, as if drugged, unsmiling, obedient, saying little.

But she *did* take us back to Guillermo's house, and the cash *was* genuine, so our fears turned out to be baseless. But both Ricardo and I are convinced to this day that that house was one of the many used for a variety of means by the Junta's new secret police, the infamous DINA[44], and that their job was probably to buy up all sorts of cars that could be used for rounding up suspects and delivering them to the new centres of torture like *Villa Grimaldi*, *Tejas Verdes* or *Tres Alamos*[45], since cars like our Fiat 600 would pass unnoticed among the population. Ricardo and I were just immensely relieved to have got out of that house alive, since we had both been fearing the worst: even when the girl drove us away we were still fearing that it might be a trap and that we could be being driven to some interrogation centre or other.

Padre Hurtado, the United Nations refuge where people awaiting deportation were housed, had been a Catholic monastery. It was a lovely old building, with a big refectory downstairs and long corridors of dormitories upstairs. Ricardo and I were given a big room with two single beds, a washbasin in one corner, and a window overlooking the extensive and beautiful gardens. Though the refuge was guarded night and day by armed conscripts put there by the Junta, and residents were only allowed out if they had legitimate business to do with getting papers in order and sorting out legal matters, we were happy to be there, and it was almost like a weird kind of holiday, except that our hearts were heavy with the knowledge of so many friends dead or in prison, and the tragic failure of our Popular Unity Government, which had striven so valiantly to succeed against such enormous odds.

We knew that thousands of people must already have been killed, both from what we heard on the Junta's radio and from local reports of those killed, though we did not know how many. Even today there is still no consensus on how many people died. Estimates have ranged from 3,500 (Junta's own figures) to 30,000. Thousands of these are people who were detained and subsequently simply "disappeared", leaving no paper trace.

The Padre Hurtado refuge had an outdoor swimming pool, which I loved. It was the end of the Chilean summer, and, since we had little else to do while we were waiting for news as to when we would be flown out, we had several swims a day, and spent our time walking round the gardens and vegetable plots of the former monastery, strolling in the warm evenings under the long pergola covered by vines, their ripe green grapes for the picking.

---

44 *Dirección de Inteligencia Nacional* (National Intelligence Department).

45 All infamous interrogation and detention centres in Santiago where detainees were savagely tortured, some to death, and from where many were simply "disappeared", their bodies thrown from helicopters into the ocean, or buried anonymously in unmarked pits. The British doctor Sheila Cassidy, who in 1975 had agreed to treat a wounded resistance-fighter, was tortured with electric shocks while held in *Villa Grimaldi*.

There were some eighty or so people at the refuge when we were there in March 1974, couples, families and single people who, like us, were waiting to leave Chile. Many of them had terrible tales to tell, having narrowly escaped death, most having suffered imprisonment and torture. We met there the brother of Franklin Carpenter, whom we had known in Chillán. Franklin had been in prison in Chillán some of the time Ricardo was there. I had seen Franklin once when I was outside the prison, waiting to take Ricardo his lunch *vianda*. He was among a group of prisoners, bloodied and mounting the prison steps with difficulty, brought back to the prison from having been interrogated under torture at the city's regimental headquarters. Franklin had been released from prison on the same day that Ricardo had been let out of solitary confinement, and they had said good-bye there in the prison yard, never suspecting that the next time they would see each other would be in Scotland, in exile.

The Carpenters were a well-known and unmistakable family of brothers in Chillán. As their name suggests, they had a Scottish ancestor and all five brothers were very tall and strong, with fair skin and blue eyes – features which were most uncommon among Chileans. Walterio, whom we first met now at Padre Hurtado refuge, was the oldest of the brothers, and was waiting to be flown out to Argentina. He had been detained and tortured, like most prisoners, but had unexpectedly been released, whereupon he fled to Santiago to seek refuge.

Walterio, like many Chileans, had a great sense of humour. It was he who related, in all seriousness and with a straight face how, after the coup, he had "looked up in his Party manual what to do in the case of a coup d'état" and hadn't found anything! As Ricardo observed wryly later, in that joke of Walterio's was encapsulated the tragedy of many Popular Unity supporters who, like us, had not escaped when we could have and in fact had no preparation of any kind as to what to do in the case of a coup.

That quip of Walterio's contained a veiled criticism of the political ideologies of Marxism and Leninism. The socialist and communist parties had not done enough to stimulate the ideological development of party members by relating theory to practice. What party members like Walterio felt was that we were good at obeying the political line as if it were a "manual". Ricardo appreciated the joke because he too felt the frustration of having been taken by surprise by the Junta's rule of terror and the ferocity and thoroughness of this terror, which had not only rapidly crushed all resistance, but had already started to have an effect on people's consciousness, in so doing subduing the entire people.

Were the party leaderships at fault in this? Personally I think the Communist Party's emphasis all the time on "No to Civil War" was totally misleading, since it gave the impression that part of the armed forces would definitely be on the side of the Government in any conflict, and I cannot believe that their intelligence would have led them to believe that. The Party had operated underground in the past, when it had been declared illegal, such as under the Gonzalez Videla dictatorship (1946-1952), so it had considerable experience and could therefore have done more to prepare activists better for what might lay in store.

However, I don't think any party of the left could have imagined a coup of such scale and ferocity as that unleashed on Chile in September 1973. And obviously all the efforts of the left-wing parties in the months preceding the coup were concentrated on bolstering the constitutional Government and doing all they could to combat the Right and fight for the right of the legitimate Government to carry out its programme.

Though we were safe whilst inside the refuge, we did not feel the same when we had to leave to go into the city to chase necessary documents to enable us to leave the country legally. For instance, Ricardo, as a former authority of the University of Chile, had to obtain a document from the University showing that there was no legal case against him as a public employee, that he did not owe the University any money, had not defrauded the University or been under investigation for any kind of financial misdemeanour. So we were taken into the city by a United Nations employee and told to get back to the refuge as soon as we had finished our business. The streets were dangerous places during those weeks – you could be picked up at any minute.

During that afternoon we met up with a friend, Fernando Ortiz, a leading Communist, who had been one of the main voices in the University Reform movement, along with Enrique París. Ricardo had known both of them since his early years in the Party, as they were all in the same Santiago branch at that time. Fernando had changed his appearance a little as he was by that time already working clandestinely. We had a chat with him on a street just round the corner from the Police headquarters of *Investigaciones*, where Ricardo had to go to obtain yet another document to enable him to leave the country legally. When he heard that we were going to be leaving for Britain, he told us to do our utmost to let the world know what was going on in Chile under the dictatorship, and ended with the words: "This nightmare will come to an end: I give it two to three years at most, and you'll be able to come back!"

I don't know whether his words were meant to give cheer to Ricardo as he faced leaving his country, or whether he really believed in what he was saying. It was false optimism which did not convince either of us, as we shook hands and kissed good-bye on the cheek. It was the last time we ever saw Fernando.

Fernando had been a long-standing political activist. He had even been General Secretary of the Communist Youth during the Gonzalez Videla government in the early fifties. But when I knew him, he was a history lecturer at the University of Chile, author of *El Movimiento Obrero en Chile* (The Workers' Movement in Chile) *1891-1919*, and one of the prime movers in the University Reform movement at the end of the sixties who had been elected member of the University's *Consejo Superior* (Supreme Council). We had had dinner with him and his wife several times over the years at friends' houses. He was great fun, someone who knew how to enjoy life as well as working hard.

Fernando Ortiz was a member of the Party's Central Committee at the time of the coup. In December 1976 he was snatched by the DINA and "disappeared", together with others in the clandestine leadership of that time. In March 2001, twenty-five years after his disappearance, Chile's *Instituto Médico Legal* was able to prove that some of the remains found in 1984 in the hills of the *Cuesta Barriga* between Santiago and the port of Valparaíso were those of Fernando.

Another leading light in the University Reform process was Enrique París, a psychiatrist by profession, whom Ricardo also knew quite well. He had come to our University to give the inaugural lecture one year and Ricardo had met him on subsequent occasions when on University business in Santiago. Enrique was President Allende's adviser on Higher Education and was in the Moneda Palace on 11 September 1973. At 10.30 that morning he telephoned his mother telling her where he was, that he knew that shortly the Palace was going to be bombed and asking her to look after his three children.

Enrique survived the bombing of the Moneda Palace – incidentally, by Hawker Hunter jets, sold to the Chilean Air Force by the British Government – but like most of the people in the presidential palace that day, was taken prisoner and driven to the Tacna Regiment twelve blocks away. He and some fifty other detainees were held there till the 13 September, forced into painful standing and crouching positions for all that time, trampled on by soldiers ordered to run over the prisoners, and tortured during interrogation by electric shock and other barbaric treatments. A witness saw the group of detainees which included Enrique lying, tied up, one on top of the other, in layers, in the back of a military truck which left the Tacna Regiment at about 2 p.m. on the day of the 13th. None of these were ever seen alive again.

It was learnt later, from a conscript who had been on duty on that day, that the detainees had been shot in groups of four at the edge of a pit dug at Peldehue military camp, just north of Santiago.

So many friends dead, so many in prison and tortured, so much terror and fear all around. We could not be happy, even if we were safe in Padre Hurtado

197

refuge. We both felt somehow guilty that we were there, out of imminent danger, when so many of our friends, and Ricardo's own children, could be at risk.

We were eventually flown out of Chile on 24 March 1974, and so began our new life in Great Britain. Ricardo was able to get his children and their mother out of Chile in the summer of 1976, which gave him a peace of mind he had badly needed. The long slog of solidarity with Chile began, taking up much of our time and energies over the next fifteen or so years.

AFTERWORD

Thoughts on the Popular Unity "Experiment"

Over the forty years since the tragic end of the Popular Unity Government of Salvador Allende I have obviously thought much about what happened, what was and what could have been, what was good and positive, and what was inadequate or harmful to its success. I am always wary of those who find it easy to draw "lessons" from any historical process, but at the same time, it is inevitable that I should have an opinion on the process, since I lived it from its inception right through to its tragic end. So here are a few conclusions I have come to over the years, after much discussion with comrades and friends of different political persuasions, Chilean, British and of other nationalities. The Popular Unity Government of Salvador Allende was a beacon for many people on the Left throughout the world, who saw the constitutional road chosen by Popular Unity as a feasible path for their own countries to achieve a fairer, more socially just, society. Many people who knew that revolution such as the Bolshevik one, or the Cuban one many years later, would be impossible in highly developed countries like Britain, France, Germany or the USA, felt sympathy for, and much interest in, this Chilean process established through elections and within the confines of an already existing constitution.

When trying to evaluate or assess a historical period such as the three years of Chile's Popular Unity Government, it is essential to situate it in the world as it existed at the time, not the world as it is now. The world situation in 1970-73 was very different from that of today. At that time the United States was extremely powerful, despite the drain on its resources from its war on Vietnam. Cuba was still a thorn in its side, having decisively routed the US-backed invasion of the island at the Bay of Pigs some ten years earlier. But the United States of America still regarded Latin America as its "own backyard" and was used to snuffing out any attempts by governments in that vast sub-continent to introduce economic changes to benefit the masses. The progressive Jacobo Arbenz government in Guatemala had been toppled by a CIA-masterminded coup in 1954, after United States interests in the United Fruit Company were deemed to be threatened by Arbenz's land reform programme. Many Latin American countries had dictatorships which pro-tected US economic interests in those countries – Brazil, Argentina, Paraguay, Uruguay, Nicaragua, Bolivia among them.

It is true that at the time the USSR and the so-called "socialist camp" were thought to be powerful too. The Soviet Union was supporting Cuba's economy by beneficial trade terms, but was reluctant to take on any further support to regimes which would entail a further drain on its resources, since the Soviet economy was burdened by the heavy expenditure of the arms race, and was already suffering from the stagnation and inefficiencies which would later be a contributory factor in the Soviet Union's collapse. The USSR may have been reluctant to endanger its hard-won policy of détente with the USA by giving succour to a government such as Allende's, whose future success and stability was still so uncertain. A report from the Latin American Institute of the Soviet Academy of Sciences described the situation in mid-1972 as "uncertain and unstable", as the Popular Unity only had partial political power, it said, and there was no clear strategy for achieving socialism in Chile (from *Allende's Chile & the Inter-American Cold War*, by Tanya Harmer, University of North Carolina Press, p.177).

So when Popular Unity came on to the world scene in 1970, Chile was the only Latin American country with a progressive government, apart from Cuba, ready to take on the might of US economic interests, i.e. the giants of the copper industry, Anaconda and Kennecott. In 1971, by agreement of all the main parties in Chile and after an unprecedented unanimous vote in Chile's Congress, President Allende had announced the confiscation of the enormous Chuquicamata mine from Anaconda, without paying any compensation, on the grounds that over decades excessive profits had been taken out of the country by Anaconda. The company estimated that it thereby lost two-thirds of its copper production. It is revealing that after the military coup, only two years later, a compensation of $250 million was paid to Anaconda by the Chilean military Junta.

The economic interests the United States had in Chile, together with the economic interests of Chile's own ruling circles, the owners of large companies and, of course, the big landowners – the *latifundistas* – were a major factor in the plot to unseat the new Chilean President, who from the very beginning declared "war" on those interests:

> "The revolutionary transformations which the country needs can only be carried out *if the Chilean people take power into their hands* and exercise it in a genuine and effective way.

> "The Chilean people, throughout a long process of struggle, have won certain democratic freedoms and guarantees, and they have to remain alert and fight unceasingly in order to preserve them. *But they do not possess the actual power.*

"The popular revolutionary forces have united not to fight for the mere replacement of one President of the Republic by another, nor to replace one party by others in the Government, but in order to carry out fundamental changes which the national situation demands, on the basis of *the transfer of power from the old ruling groups to the workers, peasantry and progressive sectors of the middle classes in the towns and the countryside.*" (From the Popular Unity Programme; my emphasis)

The question is, could Allende's Government have succeeded against the fierce opposition generated by the threat to such economic interests, both US-owned and Chilean-owned, given the prevailing regional and world situation? What could have been done differently? Were there factors within Popular Unity which worked against the success of the project?

One of the questions that has been analysed a great deal since 1973 is that of the divisions and disunity within the Popular Unity coalition. "Unity is strength" is an old truism. I have written earlier of the impressive level of unity that *was* achieved, in particular between the two biggest parties, the Socialist Party and the Communist Party. But there were considerable differences between parties on tactics, and even within the Socialist Party leadership, considerable differences between, say, Salvador Allende and Carlos Altamirano, the Socialist Party's General Secretary, in their public statements and actions, especially in the last year of the Government.

Other revolutionary processes have also begun with a number of parties and movements coming together around a common programme. In Cuba quite early on in the revolution, several parties merged to form one single party. More recently, in Venezuela, President Chávez saw the need to form one party out of the several trends that supported him, forming the United Socialist Party of Venezuela in 2007, although so far the Venezuelan Communist Party has preferred to remain outside. It seems self-evident that one single party is likely to be stronger and therefore have more chances of succeeding than if a process is led by a more disparate alliance.

In the case of Chile, however, I think the process was too new for any possibility of uniting the parties of Popular Unity into one single party. Neither of the main parties would have countenanced this so soon after being elected. It was not even on the agenda. And again, we have to understand that the whole concept of electing a government of the Popular Unity kind was something quite new, not only in Latin America, but in the world as a whole at that time. Such an alliance was not, however, unknown in Chile's own history, in that Pedro Aguirre Cerda's Popular Front government, which ran from 1938 to 1941, was also formed by an alliance of parties including the Communist and Socialist parties. In only three years, that Popular Front government had managed to introduce a number of progressive measures like the creation of CORFO[46] and the building of over 500 new schools, many in rural areas which had never had a school before[47].

Due to the fact that Popular Unity's presidential candidate, Dr Salvador Allende, was elected in September 1970 with a mere 36.6% of the vote, the subsequent fight had to be not only to win maximum unity within the Popular Unity alliance, but more importantly, to win over much of that section of the working class and peasantry that had *not* voted for Allende in September 1970. Objectively, it seems to me, this should have been possible. The vast majority of Christian Democratic voters were not big business people or landowners, but "ordinary" working people and members of the middle classes. There was nothing in the Popular Unity Programme that threatened any of their interests, quite the opposite.

Whilst the Popular Unity programme envisaged nationalisation of all the main natural resource industries – copper, nitrate, iodine, iron and coal – private insurance companies and banks, other monopolies, power, rail, air and maritime transport, communications, oil and gas, metallurgy, cement, petrochemicals, cellulose and paper, it stated quite clearly that there would be government protection for the private sector and the mixed sectors of the economy.

> "The State will provide the firms in (the private) sector with the necessary financial and technical assistance, so that they can fulfil the important function they have in the national economy, given the number of people who work in these firms and the volume of production entailed." (from the Popular Unity Programme)

Nowhere in the Popular Unity Programme was nationalisation of small and medium-sized companies envisaged. So there was really no *objective* reason why many Christian Democrat voters should not be won over for the Popular Unity movement. However, decades of anti-Communist and anti-Socialist bias in the media and in the Christian Democratic Party itself was not to be undone in a matter of months. As recently as the 1964 presidential elections, when Christian Democracy's candidate, Eduardo Frei, triumphed, anti-Communist propaganda had been exceptionally vitriolic and crude: the right-wing candidate warning of a bloodbath if the Left won, and that Russian soldiers would come knocking at people's doors to take away their children

---

[46] CORFO – Corporación de Fomento de la Producción (Production Development Corporation), which was set up to begin the industrialization of Chile. CORFO introduced several infrastructure projects which led to a better standard of living for the people.

[47] At the age of nine, Ricardo was at last – in 1939 – able to go to school for the first time, thanks to one such new school that had just been started in the far-off southern region where the family lived.

if Salvador Allende were to win the election. Among a population with a high rate of illiteracy at the time, this crude sort of propaganda doubtless had the desired effect, ensuring that Allende lost, in 1964, to the Christian Democrats.

With this history, it is not surprising that among the rank and file there was considerable antipathy within the main Popular Unity parties and within the MIR towards the Christian Democrats. Many militants failed to see the difference between the top leaders of the Christian Democrats, who had indeed sold out the people of Chile with their "chileanisation" of the copper industry and timid land reform, and the mass of ordinary Christian Democratic voters, whose interests were the same or very similar – objectively – to those of Popular Unity supporters. So, instead of a more intelligent strategy to split the Christian Democrats and wean away the party's more popular elements to the side of Popular Unity, what actually happened was that these more popular elements were increasingly pushed into an oppositional stance, which hardened more and more as the months went by.

In this sense it seems to me that the actions of the MIR were not only unhelpful, but actually played into the hands of the enemies of Popular Unity. The MIR's position right from the start was to remain outside Popular Unity, supporting the Government where it felt possible whilst retaining the freedom to criticise it when it felt it necessary. Whilst it is undeniable that the motives of the MIR and the majority of its members were well-intentioned, and they were certainly fighting for a socialist society in Chile, the MIR's actions in mounting unofficial takeovers of small or medium-sized firms, for instance, simply alienated the middle classes who either owned or worked in them. And since such takeovers were outside the remit of the Popular Unity Programme – yet the MIR supposedly supported the Government – they were unfortunately assumed by much of the population as having the tacit backing of the Government.

It is hard to write critically of the MIR when we know that many of its members were detained and savagely tortured after the military coup of September 1973. The courage and commitment of MIR members to the cause of socialism in Chile is undeniable. But with the benefit of hindsight, and after so many years have passed, all parties have had to carry out their own analysis of what went wrong, and I know that many MIR members have reflected long and hard on their role during those years. I am sure there are few people in any of the parties of the Popular Unity alliance who think that everything their party did during those years was blameless.

A major problem facing the new Allende Government was the fact that under the Chilean Constitution, the presidential, congress and municipal elections were all held at different times. So Allende was elected President in September 1970, but his Popular Unity alliance did not have a majority either in Congress or the Senate – the two houses in the Chilean parliament – and parliamentary elections were not due until March 1973, a whole two and a half years later.

This lack of synchronism in elections for the representatives of power was a distinct disadvantage for the Popular Unity Government, and would be, I think, for any government wanting to implement a radical programme on which platform a president has been elected. The obvious solution might seem to be for a newly-elected president to call a referendum on changing the constitution, so that presidential and parliamentary elections could be held simultaneously. But at that time in Chile, I do not think that President Allende could have called a referendum to do that without provoking a fierce reaction from the Christian Democrats and the National Party, whose votes, taken together, added up to more than Allende's percentage of the poll.

That this lack of synchronism in elections was seen as a problem even before Salvador Allende was elected is shown by the following paragraphs in the Popular Unity's Basic Programme:

> "A new political Constitution will institutionalise the massive incorporation of the people to state power.

> "A single State organisation, with national, regional and local levels, will be created, of which the People's Assembly will be the supreme organism of power.

> "All elections will be held together within the same period of time so as to establish the necessary harmony between the powers which emanate from the people's will and so that this can be expressed in a cohesive way."

Perhaps it was not viable to call such a referendum in 1970, but it might have been feasible the following year, after the April 1971 municipal elections, when Popular Unity increased its share of the vote to 50.86%, an increase of 14% in the six months since Allende's election. However, it is by no means certain that a referendum on changing the constitution, if held soon after the municipal elections, would have been successful, based on such electoral results.

More influential than any factors such as the lack of synchronism in elections, or the insufficient unity among the forces of the Left, or the actions of the ultra-left, was the single-minded strategy of the powers-that-be in the United States to destabilise and unseat this new, upstart government of Salvador Allende. I have told how in 1970 they tried to prevent Allende's election being ratified by the Chilean Congress. Even before his election, in July 1970, the United States International Telephone and Telegraph Company

(ITT), which had extensive holdings in Chile, offered $1 million to the CIA to prevent Allende's election that September. Later the CIA increasingly financed and gave support to groups, parties and organisations opposed to the Popular Unity Government. They sent finance to prop up right-wing newspapers, to help arm the ultra right-wing *Patria y Libertad* (Fatherland and Freedom), and to support the lorry-owners' boycott. The government of Richard Nixon and Henry Kissinger was simply not prepared to let another country, in addition to Cuba, "go communist".

I think that this outside interference aimed at destabilising the Popular Unity Government from the outset, and the prevailing international situation, where the rest of Latin America was ruled by pro-US juntas and governments, were the main factors in its demise – more important than any other internal factors.

I have mentioned elsewhere how the US financed the right-wing media in Chile, and the role the media played in Allende's downfall is one I have thought a great deal about over the years. As a foreign observer of the process, I felt that more could have been done, even under the law as it was at the time, to curb the excesses of the right-wing media.

We are very fond, in this country, of the term "free press". But to what extent is the press "free", in a society where one person, or a group of shareholders, can own a newspaper or a television channel? Can an editor be truly independent, when he/she is employed by that owner? "He who pays the piper calls the tune" is surely apposite, in this sense. It's true that, due to our parliamentary and constitutional traditions in Britain, most editors enjoy a good deal of independence, and do not have the owner breathing down their necks all the time. But if or when an editor goes "too far" in pursuing an independent agenda, he/she will pay the price for it. One can think of Piers Morgan, who as editor of the Daily Mirror took a consistent line opposing the Iraq war, and later lost his job after publishing some photos, which later turned out to be fake, of British troops abusing Iraqi prisoners. Who sent the Mirror these photographs, whether this was a stitch-up to discredit the Editor or not we shall no doubt never know, but the fact is that the editor of the only widely-read broadsheet that had opposed the Iraq war was fired.

Or take the case of Greg Dyke, who was ousted from his post of Director-General of the BBC, after the government's Hutton report had criticised the BBC for allowing its reporters, in particular, Andrew Gilligan, to broadcast stories casting doubt on the existence of Weapons of Mass Destruction (WMD) in Iraq before the US-led invasion in 2003, after talking with MoD weapons inspector Dr David Kelly, later found dead near his home in what some people feel were suspicious circumstances. Greg Dyke has always maintained that the Andrew Gilligan story *was* essentially true, that the government dossier (the so-called "dodgy dossier") *had* in fact been "sexed up" to make the justification for going to war more acceptable and that the government had then staged a "witch hunt" to deflect from the real issues surrounding the Iraq war[48].

I mention these cases simply to question to what extent editors are really "free" to question or challenge the status quo in society. When you have Rupert Murdoch owning a global media empire worth £30 billion, could anyone really envisage, in some hypothetical situation of the future, that he would allow his editors to support a new government anywhere in the world that would be likely to challenge the ruling elites, whether they be *latifundistas*, oligarchs or transnational companies and banks? I don't think so.

At the time of the Popular Unity Government in Chile, most of the press, TV and radio channels were privately-owned. In general they purported to support the constitutional road, but as President Allende tried to introduce his nationalisations and *latifundio* expropriations, they took on an increasingly anti-Government line. It seemed to me at the time that there were grounds to close down certain media outlets which periodically issued openly seditious calls on the population to act to bring the Government down. I was sure that neither such calls to bring down the Government nor the kind of character defamation there was against Allende would have been allowed under the law against a Prime Minister in Britain.

The freedom of the media is a sensitive subject, since we all like to think that in a free society we can say and do what we want, and the media too should be free to express the public's views. But the whole question as to how much the media "expresses" our views, and to what extent it "formulates" those views by means of its enormous influence over us, the public, is a moot point.

We all know that advertising works. The companies who pay for TV and newspaper ads would not do so if their ads didn't make people go out and buy their products. So why are so many of us convinced that we are not similarly influenced by the media we watch and read? If we are told by most of the media, day in and day out, over a period of weeks, that the Iraqi dictator's chemical weapons can be launched within 45 minutes and thus threaten us here in Britain, do not most of us simply believe that, without questioning the truth of it? It was clear from the reports of United Nations Chief Weapons Inspector, Hans Blix, who had hundreds of weapons inspectors working in Iraq, that Iraq did not in fact have such WMD. Neither, it turned out, did Iraq have anything to do with the destruction of the twin towers in New York on September 11th 2001 – the ostensible reason US

---

48 As told in *Inside Story*, by Greg Dyke, HarperCollins, 2004.

President George Bush gave for deciding to invade Iraq[49]. Yet many people throughout the world – in my opinion, swayed by the overwhelming media onslaught – thought the US invasion of Iraq was justified.

In recent years we have seen the media's demonization of Venezuelan President Hugo Chávez. He has often been called "dictator", yet over the last decade he won several elections no one denies were free and fair, and with big overall majorities. It is clearly ludicrous to call such a person a "dictator". All this means, it seems, is that when a leader pursues a line which is not to the taste of the ruling circles in the United States or the UK he has to be denigrated and vilified.

Unfortunately much of the news agenda is set by the big news services like UPI, AP, Reuters, and others, which feed the rest of the media with a constant supply of stories, and these invariably reflect the viewpoint of the USA on international affairs. The interesting thing in today's world is that other powerful news agencies, such as Al Jazeera in the Middle East, Telesur in Latin America, and Russia Today in Europe, which reflect different world views, are increasingly being seen by people thanks to the existence of digital television.

Just as I think the Popular Unity Government could have done more, even within the confines of Chile's Constitution, to curb the power of the private media, which became more and more vitriolic against the Government, so I am sure that Allende could and should have outlawed the sinister ultra right-wing organisation *Patria y Libertad*, whose aims, actions and financing certainly fell outside the law.

This paramilitary organisation was funded by the CIA during the first year of Allende's presidency, including via the Agency's Track II program[50]. According to Professors Michael Stohl and George A. Lopez, "After the failure to prevent Allende from taking office, efforts shifted to obtaining his removal. At least $7 million was authorized by the United States for CIA use in the destabilizing of Chilean society. This included financing and assisting opposition groups and right-wing paramilitary groups such as *Patria y Libertad* (Fatherland and Freedom).[51] One member of this group, and an agent

---

[49] "After the terrorist attacks of September 11, 2001, George W. Bush's administration felt a need to let the weight and wrath of the world's only superpower fall on more evil actors than just Afghanistan's Taliban regime. No target could have seemed more worthy of being crushed than Iraq's brutal dictator, Saddam Hussein. Sadly, however, the elimination of this tyrant was perhaps the only positive result of the war. The war aimed to eliminate weapons of mass destruction, but there weren't any. The war aimed to eliminate al Qaeda in Iraq, but the terrorist group didn't exist in the country until after the invasion." - Hans Blix, quoted by CNN on the 10th anniversary of the 2003 invasion of Iraq.

[50] "Covert Action in Chile 1963-1973" Staff Report of the Select Committee To Study Governmental Operations With Respect to Intelligence Activities, United States Senate, 18 Dec. 1975. U.S. Government Printing Office publ. 63-372

[51] "The State as Terrorist: The Dynamics of Governmental Violence and Repression" by Prof. Michael

207

of the DINA, General Pinochet's secret police, Michael Townley, was later convicted for the 1976 assassination in the United States of former Chilean minister Orlando Letelier, and was involved in the 1974 assassination of General Carlos Prats in Buenos Aires.

Patria y Libertad was mainly composed of upper- and middle-class young people from the wealthy suburbs of Santiago. They planted bombs, made Molotov cocktails and organised acts of sabotage of infrastructure, such as bridges and power installations. As I have mentioned earlier, I felt their hatred at first hand, when they destroyed the Vietnam exhibition I was looking after, and again when they set fire to the train on which Ricardo and I were travelling to Santiago. I was also left in no doubt of the visceral personal animosity the Junta's Prosecutor Fiscal in Chillán – who belonged to *Patria y Libertad* – clearly felt towards Ricardo when I went to see him about releasing Ricardo from prison.

As a paramilitary and mainly clandestine organisation, *Patria y Libertad's* activities were illegal and should have been clamped down on much more than they were. Even after the right-wing "trial" coup d'état, called the *tancazo*, on 29 June, 1973, in which *Patria y Libertad* leaders were implicated up to the hilt, insufficient action was taken against the organisation. The reason for this can only be surmised: it could have been because the Government did not feel that *Patria y Libertad* were big enough or important enough to warrant Government action to close them down, or, more likely, that Allende knew that *Patria y Libertad* had sympathisers and members among high-ranking military people, and was thus wary of doing anything that might offend the military or give the Right any grounds to accuse the Government of curbing liberties.

On that morning of the *tancazo*, 29 June 1973, President Allende had addressed the people by radio from his home on Tomás Moro Street. He declared his unequivocal resolution to defend the constitutional Government against any attempted coup d'état, and called on the workers of Santiago to occupy their factories and workplaces "and be ready in case it is necessary to fight alongside the soldiers of Chile", thus clearly indicating that he was sure that the army as a whole would continue to obey the Constitution and the elected Government.

The advice to occupy factories, workplaces, schools and universities in the event of an attempted coup was followed on the day of 11 September 1973. With hindsight, this was ill-advised. It enabled the military, obeying orders of the new Junta, to round up Government supporters in their hundreds, in well-planned and executed raids on major factories in Santiago, Valparaíso, Concepción and other big cities.

Stohl, and Prof. George A. Lopez; Greenwood Press, 1984. Page 51

Would it have made any difference if the advice of the parties of the Left had been to congregate in the centre in mass demonstrations of support for the Government? We have to remember that this was before the days of mass television, mobiles, computers and digital cameras. In the case of the 2002 attempted coup against Venezuelan President Hugo Chávez, huge masses of people took to the streets, surrounding all the governmental buildings and demanding the return of their President. This was seen by the world's media immediately, and this undoubtedly played a part in the eventual collapse of that coup attempt and the return of the legitimate president.

However, in that case, of undoubted importance was the attitude of the Venezuelan military, most of whom did not support a coup against Chávez. For one thing, the president was himself a military man and thus had much support among the military. It may also be that the Venezuelan military has less elitist training and traditions than the Chilean military. As D.L. Raby puts it in "Democracy and Revolution" (Pluto, 2006):

"...massive popular support and mobilisation might have contributed to changing the attitude of the military, but this is not to deny that the elitist recruitment, Prussian training and traditions of the Chilean armed forces made them a more difficult proposition for a progressive government to deal with than, for example, their Venezuelan counterparts."

After the June 1973 failed putsch, the parties of the Popular Unity made some attempts to procure weapons and distribute them, in a somewhat surreptitious way, to key supporters, in a last-ditch effort to have some means of defending the Government against any attempted coup. Again, this was either simply ill-advised, or too little too late, whichever way one looks at it. Raby calls it an "error":

"A further error in Chile (admittedly not one favoured by Allende until the very last moment) was the attempt by the UP (*Unidad Popular* – Popular Unity, Ed.) parties, along with the MIR, to create independent workers' militias and get sympathetic troops to distribute arms to civilians: again, this is like red flag to a bull to any military establishment, and while arming the workers is a traditional revolutionary ideal, it is suicidal (given the overwhelming superiority of the established armed forces) unless a large section of the military is already sympathetic." (Op.cit.)

If Chile had embarked on its transformations by means of the constitutional road, it is difficult to see how it could have changed to the road of armed struggle midway through the process.

Perhaps more could have been done by President Allende to promote more progressive officers within the military. But because of their traditions of strict obedience to the Constitution and therefore to the elected government of the day, no matter what its colour, it may well have been difficult for Allende to have known exactly who were the more progressive top brass. After all, in August 1973, General Augusto Pinochet himself was promoted to Commander-in-Chief of the armed forces by Allende, who obviously thought that he was loyal to the Government.

Taking into account all the above reasons or possible explanations for the failure of the Popular Unity experiment, one still comes back to the basic fact that the forces of the Left at that time in Chile did not constitute a clear majority. And unless there is strong popular majority support for revolutionary change, such change is not likely to succeed.

Popular Unity's valiant attempts to change Chile to benefit the poor, not the rich, failed. But the memory of that process, its aims and its achievements in only three years of government, live on in the collective memory of the people, not only of Chile, but of the rest of Latin America and the world.

The world situation and balance of forces is very different now, and this gives me reason to feel optimistic about the future possibilities for deep structural and economic change in Latin America, which the peoples of that sub-continent urgently need to combat their lifelong poverty, illiteracy and backwardness.

The United States is weaker now, at least economically, than at that time. It no longer dominates world affairs in the way it did. The US is far more isolated in the world than it was in the 1970s, and as I write these words, Latin America has other progressive governments in the shape of Venezuela, Bolivia, Ecuador, Argentina, Cuba and Brazil. Even the Organisation of American States (until recently totally dominated by the USA) recently voted to revoke the expulsion of Cuba from that organisation (though Cuba has declined to join).

Yet the reasons that gave rise to Popular Unity over forty years ago are still prevalent in much of the world today – poverty, disease, illiteracy. Whether it is Peru's indigenous people shutting down oil fields and gas pipelines and blocking roads, rivers, airports and other installations in protest at government decrees opening access to indigenous people's lands to facilitate oil, mining, logging and agricultural companies, or Brazil's landless peasants occupying unused land, where they have established cooperative farms, constructed houses, schools for children and adults and clinics, the causes of revolution are there for all to see. In Brazil, for instance, 1.6% of the landowners control roughly half (46.8%) of the land on which crops could be grown. Just 3% of the population owns two-thirds of all arable land.

Until such injustices are addressed, the reasons for revolution will continue to exist. Revolutions are not imported from other countries; they happen because the people cannot continue to live in the way they have been forced to live. They happen because most people everywhere want justice, fairness and a reasonable standard of living. They want access to education and healthcare and an equitable society where all can live peaceably and to their utmost potential. This is what the parties of Popular Unity wanted for Chile, and it is what most of the world's population still want today.

The End

Appendix 1

Salvador Allende's Last Words to the Nation

Shortly before his death, barricaded inside La Moneda, the presidential palace, President Allende recorded this speech on the morning of September 11, 1973, in the midst of the military coup d'etat against his democratically-elected Popular Unity Government.

"My friends,

Surely this will be the last opportunity for me to address you. The Air Force has bombed the towers of Radio Portales and Radio Corporación.

My words do not have bitterness but disappointment. May they be a moral punishment for those who have betrayed their oath: soldiers of Chile, titular commanders-in-chief, Admiral Merino, who has designated himself Commander of the Navy, and Mr. Mendoza, the despicable general who only yesterday pledged his fidelity and loyalty to the Government, and who has also appointed himself Chief of the *carabineros* (national police).

Given these facts, the only thing left for me is to say to the workers: I will not resign!

Placed in a historic transition, I will pay for loyalty to the people with my life. And I say to them that I am certain that the seed which we have planted in the good conscience of thousands and thousands of Chileans will not be shrivelled forever.

They have strength and will be able to dominate us, but social processes can be arrested neither by crime nor force. History is ours, and it is the people who make history.

Workers of my country: I want to thank you for the loyalty that you always had, the confidence that you deposited in a man who was only an interpreter of great yearnings for justice, who gave his word that he would respect the Constitution and the law and did just that. At this definitive moment, the last moment when I can address you, I wish you to take advantage of the lesson: foreign capital, imperialism, together with the reaction, created the climate in which the Armed Forces broke their tradition, the tradition taught by General Schneider and reaffirmed by Commander Araya, victims of the same social sector which will today be in their homes hoping, with foreign assistance, to retake power to continue defending their profits and their privileges.

I address, above all, the modest woman of our land, the *campesina* who believed in us, the worker who laboured more, the mother who knew our concern for children. I address the professionals of Chile, patriotic professionals, those who days ago continued working against the sedition sponsored by professional associations, class-based associations that also defended the advantages which a capitalist society grants to a few.

I address the youth, those who sang and gave us their joy and their spirit of struggle. I address the man of Chile, the worker, the farmer, the intellectual, those who will be persecuted, because in our country fascism has been already present for many hours -- in terrorist attacks, blowing up the bridges, cutting the railroad tracks, destroying the oil and gas pipelines, in the face of the silence of those who had the obligation to protect them. They were committed. History will judge them.

Surely Radio Magallanes will be silenced, and the calm metal instrument of my voice will no longer reach you. It does not matter. You will continue hearing it. I will always be next to you. At least my memory will be that of a man of dignity who was loyal to [inaudible] the workers.

The people must defend themselves, but they must not sacrifice themselves. The people must not let themselves be destroyed or riddled with bullets, but they cannot be humiliated either.

Workers of my country, I have faith in Chile and its destiny. Other men will overcome this dark and bitter moment when treason seeks to prevail. Go forward knowing that, sooner rather than later, the great avenues will open again where free men will walk to build a better society.

Long live Chile! Long live the people! Long live the workers!

These are my last words, and I am certain that my sacrifice will not be in vain, I am certain that, at the very least, it will be a moral lesson that will punish felony, cowardice, and treason."

Santiago de Chile, 11 September 1973